shopping

WHY WE LOVE IT
and how retailers
can create the
ULTIMATE
CUSTOMER
EXPERIENCE

PAMELA N. DANZIGER

KAPLAN PUBLISHING

This publication is designed to provide accurate and authoritative information in regard to the subject matter covered. It is sold with the understanding that the publisher is not engaged in rendering legal, accounting, or other professional service. If legal advice or other expert assistance is required, the services of a competent professional should be sought.

President, Kaplan Publishing: Roy Lipner
Vice President and Publisher: Maureen McMahon
Acquisitions Editor: Karen Murphy
Development Editor: Trey Thoelcke
Production Editor: Karen Goodfriend
Typesetter: Todd Bowman
Cover Designer: Jody Billert, Design Literate

© 2006 by Pamela N. Danziger

Published by Kaplan Publishing,
a division of Kaplan, Inc.

Printed in the United States of America

06 07 08 10 9 8 7 6 5 4 3 2 1

Library of Congress Cataloging-in-Publication Data

Danziger, Pamela N.
    Shopping / Pamela N. Danziger.
        p. cm.
    Includes index.
    ISBN-13: 978-1-4195-3636-6
    ISBN-10: 1-4195-3636-2
    1. Shopping. 2. Marketing. 3. Consumer behavior. I. Title.
    TX335.D345   2006
    381'.1—dc22

                                                                        2006020566

Kaplan Publishing books are available at special quantity discounts to use for sales promotions, employee premiums, or educational purposes. Please call our Special Sales Department to order or for more information at 800-621-9621, ext. 4444, e-mail kaplanpubsales@kaplan.com, or write to Kaplan Publishing, 30 South Wacker Drive, Suite 2500, Chicago, IL 60606-7481.

For all the retail Davids who each day must fight the growing legion of retail Goliaths.

Contents

Part Three

HOW TO CREATE A SHOP THAT POPS

Acknowledgments

Writing this book has been an absolute pleasure for me. I have had the chance to meet and learn from scores of people who love to shop. I have also visited scores of different types of stores scouting out shops that pop. But first and foremost has been the chance to learn more about the outstanding retailers that are profiled in this book. They represent the real "heroes" in my book. Special thanks for sharing so generously with their time and insights to:

- Marla Malcolm Beck, Bluemercury (*www.bluemercury.com*)
- Dan Bellman, Boxwoods Gardens & Gifts
- Kate Collier, Feast! (*www.feastvirginia.com*)
- Mary Carol Garrity, Nell Hill's (*www.nellhills.com*)
- Manny Gonzales, Tiger Lily (*www.tigerlilyflorist.com*)
- Kimberly Grabel, Saks Fifth Avenue (*www.saksfifthavenue.com*)
- Kimberley Grayson, formerly of Aerosoles (*www.aerosoles.com*), now with Forth & Towne
- Dennis Highby, Cabela's (*www.cabelas.com*)
- Sherry Keefe, Damsels in This Dress
- Tammy Kersey, Colonial Williamsburg Marketplace (*www.williamsburgmarketplace.com*)
- Ken Nisch, JGA (*www.jga.com*)
- Steve Riggio, Barnes & Noble (*www.barnesandnoble.com*)
- Doug Rose, QVC (*www.qvc.com*)
- Barry Rosenberg, Steiner & Associates (*www.steiner.com*)
- Michael Simon, formerly of Godiva (*www.godiva.com*), now with Pepperidge Farms snacks division
- Dan Tibby, Prairie Edge (*www.prairieedge.com*)
- Jim Tweten, Magnolia Audio Video (*www.magnoliaav.com*)

Introduction

Shopping Gives People Pleasure

*"We may affirm absolutely that nothing great in the world
has been accomplished without passion."*
GEORG WILHELM FRIEDRICH HEGEL

The hot new trend in the study of consumer preferences and behavior is neuromarketing. Neuromarketers study the physiology of the brain as it is stimulated by marketing and advertising messages and brand choices. Marketing companies all across the country are hanging up shingles to delve into brain physiology and translate findings from brain scans to branding strategies.

Nevertheless, you don't need to hook shoppers up to wires and electrodes or study them with a magnetic resonance imaging scanner to figure out that shopping activates powerful pleasure centers in the brain. All you have to do is talk to consumers, like these passionate shoppers:

- "I love everything about it. I love to buy stuff, but I sometimes feel guilty when I buy stuff that I really didn't need. But fortunately I can afford it. I love to shop."
- "I love to shop. It's therapeutic when I'm stressed out. I just go browse. I can go [shopping] for three hours and not buy anything, but I know where to buy the next thing the next time."
- "I love to spend money. I just love to shop and buy things."
- "I like Internet shopping, but I'm a very tactile person. I've got to feel it and touch it and see how that color looks, so I don't

think it will ever replace actually going shopping and having the experience."

■ "I love to go shopping with my shopping buddies. I love to socialize and spend time with my friends shopping. We often go to lunch at the mall and browse some of the stores. It is a fun little hobby."

■ "My husband is a shopaholic more than I am. He loves to shop. We're building our new house and he is busy picking out paint colors and furniture and carpet and stuff like that that guys normally hate to do, but he absolutely loves it."

While I am sure the fledgling science of neuromarketing, also called neuroeconomics, will provide valuable insights about consumers in the future, for now we still have plenty more to learn about shoppers just by using the traditional methodologies of psychology and behavioral studies.

What is missing in the neuromarketing approach to consumer research is how to translate learning from brain scans and MRI images into actionable marketing and retailing strategies. One of the pioneers in the new science, Read Montague of Baylor College of Medicine, conducted a study to test whether consumers prefer the taste of Pepsi or Coca-Cola and how their taste preferences translate into brand preferences. He found that people preferred the taste of Pepsi up until they learned that the one they didn't like as much was Coke, and then their brand preference changed to Coke. This research is interesting, but it doesn't provide any guidance to the Pepsi people about how to get people to buy more of their product. The good old-fashioned research approaches that probe people's motivations work better in giving insights marketers and retailers can use.

That is the objective of this book, *Shopping: Why We Love It and How Retailers Can Create the Ultimate Customer Experience*. Through consumer research we strive to understand what it is about shopping that people love. We also study stores where people love to shop. Through this multifaceted research approach we discover a set of unique identifying characteristics of these extraordinary stores that I call "shops that pop." Major national retailers like Nordstrom, The Apple Store, Saks Fifth Avenue, Aerosoles, QVC, Barnes & Noble, and Target evoke powerful consumer emotions, as do small independently owned stores, like Charleston's Tiger Lily Florist, Atlanta's Boxwoods Gardens & Gifts, Atchison, Kansas's Nell Hill's, and Rapid City's Prairie Edge. These stores share specific attributes, what I call the pop! equation, that make people love to shop in them and with them.

Throughout the pages of this book, you will learn more about the motivations, desires, and passions of shoppers; the characteristics of stores that evoke passion in their shoppers; and how to put these insights to work to transform your stores into a retail experience your shoppers will love.

People Love to Shop in Stores that Love Them Back

"He liked to like people, therefore people liked him."
MARK TWAIN

While many people enjoy shopping, get a thrill shopping for bargains or something really special, and shop for fun and recreation—I call these people the passionate shoppers—not all shoppers love shopping in all stores. What makes people love shopping in a particular store and makes them passionate about the experience in that store is that the store, in a very real sense, loves the shoppers back. By a store loving its shoppers back, I mean the store itself is passionate about delighting the customer. The staff shows a passion for the shoppers in the way they serve them and care for them. The design of the store shows passion for the shoppers' pleasure. The merchandise selection shows it. Everything in the store and in the experience of shopping in the store is designed to romance and entice the shopper. A shop that pops is one that puts the consumer first before anything else—it is passionate about the customer. This results in the customer being passionate about shopping there. The stores that offer extraordinary shopping experiences are also the ones that are truly consumer-centric in all aspects of their operation.

In turn, shoppers pay back these consumer-centric stores with a passion that is overwhelming. They love to shop there, so they shop more often and spend more time in the store, and as a result spend more money. They love to tell their friends about shopping there, so they become retail store evangelists sending out powerful word-of-mouth messages that entice more people to shop in the store. It is viral marketing of the retail variety.

Shoppers don't love a store simply because they love the merchandise they carry. They love a store because it touches them personally and emotionally.

What is really important to understand about shopping today is that shoppers focus on the total shopping experience. They don't love a store simply because they love the merchandise they carry. They love a store because it touches them personally and emotionally. Sure, they connect with the merchandise at some level, but what really evokes passion is the retailing experience. This shopper who loves shopping at Nordstrom says it best:

> *"I love Nordstrom, that's my favorite. The customer service is great. It's the best, because they're there if you need them, but they're not hovering. And I love the music. I love how they have the piano and the classical or the pop music playing. It's just a nice atmosphere. It's clean. It's well organized. They have space between the rows. You're not all jammed in there like at Macy's or somewhere where you can't turn around. It's just a pleasant atmosphere. It's a pleasant experience going in their store."*

Note that she doesn't say a word about the merchandise or the brands, she only comments about the display of the merchandise.

This shift toward the shopping experience marks the biggest change to occur in the retailing landscape over the past century.

This shift toward the shopping experience marks the biggest change to occur in the retailing landscape over the past century. A shift away from retailing as a business of selling more merchandise—a products-based business—into a business that creates shopping experiences for the consumer—a people-based business—with the objective of selling stuff purely as a consequence or end result of that experience. Retailers, large and small, who operate on a national scale or out of one store front, and those who sell over the Internet, through catalogs or host party plans, must embrace this experiential shift.

Everything About Shopping Has Changed

"The best way to predict the future is to create it"
PETER DRUCKER

Throughout most of the 20th century, the business of retail at its root did not fundamentally change. A retailer, for most of the last hundred years, would look for a good location, hang up a sign, go out and buy a bunch of products at wholesale that they could sell at retail, and then arrange all the products they bought in the store for the customers to come and buy. Shoppers largely bought into this model and expected retailers to scour the world to find the products they needed and make them available at a reasonable price. While many individual retailers have come and gone, the fundamental principles of the retailing business have remained pretty much the same as for those early retailing pioneers like Misters Gimbel, Fields, Wanamaker, Sears, and Woolworth.

However, dramatic changes have been afoot in the retailing landscape over the past thirty years or so that are rendering that old retailing business model obsolete. At its root is a shift in the role and expectations of the shopper. No longer content to simply accept what the retailer thinks they want to buy, shoppers today are demanding more from the retailer than simply a wider selection of more stuff. Today the shopper wants more—lots more—when he goes shopping.

Way back when, people needed to buy material goods and they didn't have a lot of choices about where they could buy them. Therefore, the few retailers that were out there made a valuable contribution to the commercial landscape and American consumers' quality of life. In the last three (or more) decades of the 20th century, however, the number, selection, and diversity of retailers has exploded.

People have more places to shop and so they can be more discerning about where they want to spend their valuable time.

So much stuff fills most people's homes that shopping increasingly is less about what they really need and much more about what they want and desire.

Along with the rapid expansion of places to shop, retailers have fewer and fewer truly unique things to offer the consumer because Americans' standard of living has risen to such heights. So much stuff fills most people's homes that shopping increasingly is less about what they really need and much more about what they want and desire.

I Don't Need Another One Of Those, But I Sure Do Want It!

Because it is largely want and desire, not need anymore, that drives American consumers in the marketplace, retailers have to appeal to shoppers' emotions. They must focus on new and original ways to entice the shoppers to spend more money on more stuff that they really don't need. Unfortunately, to the detriment of the balance sheets of entirely too many retailers, they have "dumbed down" the ways that they entice shoppers to one simple factor: cheap price. They have followed the lead of Wal-Mart by playing that one note over and over again. While shoppers get a kick out of finding good stuff for less, that isn't their only source of joy when shopping. As a result, many shoppers get fatigued with so much emphasis on discount shopping and turn toward a desire for more luxury in their shopping experience.

Increasingly, success at retail is less about what the retailer has to sell and more about how they sell it. This is the new experiential paradigm shift in shopping.

It is because of this experiential shift toward shopping for wants based upon emotions and away from needs that the retailers' job has gotten so much harder. It isn't enough anymore to find great products and price them right, because now it is more than products that stimulate shoppers to buy. With shoppers' desire taking the lead, the shopping experience turns toward the psychological realm, an area where executives trained for traditional retailing have little expertise. Retailers must learn how to appeal to the shoppers' psychology throughout the entire selling process. This will become even more critical in the future as success at retail will continue to shift toward how well retailers play to the emotions, psychology, and feelings of the shopper. Increasingly, success at retail is less about what the retailer has to sell and more about how they sell it. This is the new experiential paradigm shift in shopping.

The "Pop! Equation" Means Success for Retailers to Enhance the Shopping Experience

Due to the experiential shift, making a retail concept work today is far less about the tangibles or objective aspects of the business—product, location, price—and all about the intangibles that color and flavor the shopper's experience in the store. In retail the bar has been raised. In order to be successful a retailer must offer an enhanced, truly memorable, and distinctive shopping experience to its customers.

THE PAST—THE PRESENT—THE FUTURE OF RETAIL

- 1980s The Decade of the Mall—This was the time when mall developers littered the retailing landscape with big, bulky enclosed malls. The novelty attracted shoppers and they passionately patronized these behemoths of retail.

- 1990s The Decade of the Discounters—During this decade the concept of mass-merchant discounting took hold with the explosion of Wal-Mart, Costco, the dollar stores, and all the rest of the off-price retailers on the national scene. As recently as 1995, Wal-Mart was just a regional department store chain.

- 2000s The Decade of Luxury—In this first decade of the 21st century, fickle shoppers got tired of "how low can you go" pricing and instead turned to stores that offered greater and greater luxury value at a reasonable, though not necessarily cheapest, price. Thus the boom in luxury retailing got into full swing, with retailers like Target, TJ Maxx, and Kohl's offering luxury for the masses; Nordstrom and Neiman Marcus presenting luxury for the classes; and retailers Coach, Ralph Lauren Polo, and Estee Lauder offering luxury for everyone in between through their range of branded full-priced stores, department store boutiques, and discount outlet stores.

- 2010s The Decade of Experience—What's next for retail is shoppers' new emphasis on the experience found in the store and the shopping environment itself. With the explosion of shopping choices over the past thirty years, shoppers have virtually anything and everything they could want literally at their fingertips through the Internet. In the next decade of retailing, the *experience*

The Pop! Equation: Field Guide to Shops that Pop

In the future retail will continue to transform toward an emphasis on entirely new kinds of shopping experiences. Shoppers are rejecting the old concept of "hunting and gathering" shopping in favor of a more involving, interesting, dynamic retail experience. The profiles of shops that pop in this book are stores on the cutting edge of the new experiential retailing paradigm. The distinctive features they share, called the pop! equation, include:

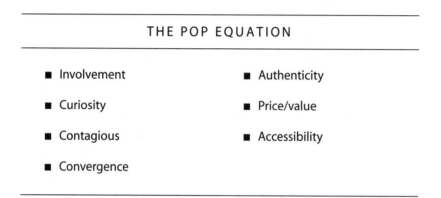

THE POP EQUATION

- Involvement
- Curiosity
- Contagious
- Convergence

- Authenticity
- Price/value
- Accessibility

- High levels of customer involvement and interaction—Shoppers do not just want to browse the aisles. Shops that pop encourage customers to touch, feel, taste, try on, and participate in the store in a more involving way, like Charlotteville's Feast! gourmet food store, Washington, DC's Blue Mercury beauty apothecary, and Atchinson, Kansas' Nell Hill's home store.
- Evocation of shopper curiosity—Shops that pop excite consumer curiosity to explore and experience, from the shop windows and entrance through the different displays. Atlanta's Boxwoods Gardens & Gifts lures shoppers through a maze of wonderful displays that promise a new treasure around every corner.
- A contagious, electric quality—A shop that pops exudes energy and excitement. They are so kinetic that even shoppers not all that into the category feel there is something in the store for

them, like Magnolia Audio Video stores, Cabela's, the chain
for outdoor enthusiasts, or Charleston, South Carolina's Tiger
Lily award-winning flower shop.

- Convergence between atmosphere, store design, and merchandise—A shop that pops presents a comprehensive vision
that captures all the tangible and intangible elements. Colonial Williamsburg Gift Shops and Stores are true to their colonial 18th-century roots throughout, while The Apple Stores
propel us into the future.

- An authentic concept—A shop that pops is more than just a store
selling stuff. It is conceptually driven and reflects a visionary's
values. It transcends being just a store into a new realm of experience, like Rapid City's Prairie Edge where the shopper can
touch, feel, and participate in Native American culture through
art, crafts, fashion, jewelry, books, and home furnishings.

- Right price/value proposition—A shop that pops must offer
superior value at a reasonable cost. They aim to get the price/
value proposition "right," and price their goods neither too
high nor too low for the value. Pricing is a powerful communicator to consumers of value, and a price that is too outrageously low sends a signal that maybe, after all, the item isn't
worth it. Shoppers value both Target and Nordstrom because
they offer an outstanding price/value proposition that pops.

- Accessibility, no exclusivity, and freedom from pretensions—
Shops that pop have all the preceding qualities, plus another
essential feature—they are immediately accessible to everyone,
free from pretensions of exclusivity or snobbishness. The new
lifestyle shopping centers, like Columbus, Ohio's Easton Town
Center, get rave reviews from shoppers because they are so
much more accessible than the old-fashioned enclosed mall.
Saks Fifth Avenue carefully selects the best-of-the-best luxury
and warmly welcomes both shoppers and browsers into the
store to experience the best.

All the stores profiled in the pages to come embody each of these
pop attributes to a greater or lesser extent. To show how the pop
equation works, let's look first at The Apple Store, a retailer that is so
electric it exerts a magnetic pull that draws shoppers into the store.

The Apple Store

■ Once You Take a Bite of This Apple, You Can Never Go Back to the Ordinary Computer Store, or Computer, Again

You might think the Apple Store is a new retailing concept by the buzz of activity swarming around every single storefront, but the first store opened in Tyson's Corner Center, Virginia, a DC suburb, in May 2001. Since then over 100 stores have launched, including flagship stores in New York, Los Angeles, Chicago, and San Francisco, distinguished by their larger size and Internet Café from the regular Apple Store models. They have recently gone international with a five-story store in the center of Tokyo's Ginza shopping district and a new double-decker model on London's Regent Street. A stunning glass staircase in the center of each multilevel store invites shoppers up to the next level.

Speaking at a *Success for Design* conference, Ron Johnson, the former head of merchandising at Target who was tapped to head up Apple's fledgling retail business in 2000, claimed the company's grounding in design as the springboard for their success, "I think it is all about Apple's grounding in design, applied to a different business from products—to a retail strategy." Johnson describes the feeling the store's design aims to deliver as high touch shopping that creates an ownership experience for the customer. It's not just about selling the customer another computer, iPod, or other gadget; it is about building a lifelong relationship with the customer that transcends the time spent in the store making the purchase. Johnson explains, "We didn't think about the experience in the store. We said, 'let's design this store around their life experience.'"

"We didn't think about the experience in the store. We said, 'let's design this store around their life experience,'" said Ron Johnson, senior vice president of retail, Apple.

Key to the Apple store shopping experience is the store layout, clearly revolutionary in today's increasingly cluttered retailing environments. With a minimum of product on display, a sparkling contemporary design workspace showcases each computer and piece of peripheral equipment. Shoppers are welcome to get hands-on with the equipment (with the exception of the hot new nano-iPods, which are in a Plexiglass display case to keep these super-mini gadgets out of undeserving shoppers' pockets), check their e-mail, and give each computer model a test drive. Johnson explains that the unique layout of the store is intended to "guide the intellectual and emotional experience of the customer through the store." In design, The Apple Store is more like a public library than a typical computer store, with its distinct sections devoted to specialized tasks, like the Apple kiddie table with iMacs displayed on kindergarten-sized tables and chairs. So the front of the store is devoted to products, with a section further back for music and photos, and accessories and software are grouped around the checkout counter on the far back wall where no cash registers are visible, thus reinforcing the feeling that you are not in an ordinary retail store anymore.

However, the centerpiece of every Apple Store—and what really sets it apart from all the rest—is its Genius Bar, where the real magic of The Apple Store experience is conjured. The Genius Bar is where you go for help and someone who wears a badge saying Apple Genius (so you know you are in capable hands no matter what the technical challenge) services you face-to-face. Today with most computer technical support delivered only by telephone, Apple lets you bring your troublesome machine right into the bar where you get your very own genius to tackle all the mechanical details. The Genius Bar is the heart and soul of The Apple Store and where you can usually find a flock of people of all ages gathered around discussing this and that and tweaking the innards of some machine or another.

In a recent shopping trip to our local Apple Store in King of Prussia Mall, outside of Philadelphia, I got my first personal taste of The Apple Store experience. My teenage son, who owns an iBook laptop—required college freshman equipment these days—insisted that I trade in my old-fashioned Microsoft Windows-based machine for a super-cool, easy-to-use, and virtually virus-immune Apple computer. Guess it's been a while since I went computer shopping, but Apple doesn't have those big bulky boxes where you plug in all your disks and wires anymore, unless you are a super-computer nerd and want that extra baggage. The sleek new iMac model I looked at came with only an 18-inch flat screen on a stand, a keyboard, and a mouse. The brains of the machine were all inside the screen; no box and no more digging around under my desk when something goes wrong. Moreover, the speed with which the computer could open and run layers of different programs demonstrated it didn't lose any horsepower by its compact size.

If I ever get into trouble, I can pick up the lightweight screen and lug it on over to the Genius Bar. They offer classes that I can schedule on the store's Web site even before I leave home so they will be ready for my lesson when I get to the store. Best of all, I can use some kind of backup program to make my home Apple machine a virtual Web site somewhere out there in cyberspace. That means when I am in my office on my Windows machine I can tap into any home Apple file with the Web browser. So, I signed myself up for this new Apple computer that I expect will revolutionize my ability to use the computer. Even though the new computer system, software, yearly support, and all will cost around $2,000 or so (about double the price of the last Windows computer I bought), I feel the value is there and thus justifies the price premium. The key value for me is the personalized support. Frankly, my problem isn't *knowing* what a computer can do, but figuring out how to make it do what I want. In my backward Windows world, there isn't a soul around to help with the details, but I will now have a computer genius at my beck and call to show me how to do it, hands on, face-to-face.

It's magic and the results for the Apple Company prove they have a shop that pops. The company claims they average about 85,000 store visitors each day. Before launching their stores, Johnson reports, the company's only direct contact with ordinary customers/users was the Annual MacWorld trade shows, which at its peak drew 80,000 visitors to a single show. Now Apple has personal contact with that many customers each day. The viral-spread of the Apple computing revolution is really starting to pick up steam as it moves from the early-adopter nerd fringes to the mainstream and definitely nontechno-freaks like me. The company has already reached a milestone in the retailing "Guinness Book of World

Records"—fastest retailer to ever reach $1 billion in revenues. Prior
to that, The Gap held the honor.

Commenting on The Apple Store's success, Johnson said, "fundamentally, we think what makes our stores successful is the design
decision to put the customer at the center, but not the buying experience—the life experience." That is where the real retailing magic
begins, enhancing the customer's life experience before, during, and
after the in-store shopping experience occurs. Johnson recognizes
that The Apple Store is at the forefront of that revolution, not just for
the Apple Company, but for retailing in the 21st century, when he
explains that the right concept can change not only a company like
Apple, "but can start to influence retailing all over."

[Johnson quotes extracted from article at *www.ifoapplestore.com/
stores/risd_johnson.html*]

Previewing What's to Come

*Shopping: Why We Love It and How Retailers Can Create the Ultimate
Customer Experience* is organized into three parts. Part 1 is devoted to
understanding the passion of shoppers, what they value in their shopping experiences, and how they view today's retailing environment
and retailers. Their perspective is gathered from a series of focus
groups held with affluent (household incomes of $100,000 and
above) women who "love to shop" and a detailed quantitative survey
among 1,250 middle-income to upper-income consumers (household incomes of $50,000 and above). Interspersed throughout this
section are other consumer-specific findings from my company Unity
Marketing's research studies, including our quarterly Luxury Tracking study, which measures consumer behavior and purchases in the
luxury sector, and our Gift Tracker study, the only research source
available of consumers' gift-giving behavior. Adding color to Part 1
are selected profiles of shops that pop for consumers, including
Target and Nordstrom, retailers that the shoppers we interviewed
love and feel passionate about.

Retailers big and small face the same basic challenges now; shoppers are demanding more than just a selection of merchandise at a reasonable price from the stores that they frequent.

Part 2 focuses on exploring retailers in more depth, and understanding how they work the various aspects of the pop equation to generate shopper passion. Through interviews with these retailers, this part of the book explores how shops can achieve each of the pop factors. Retailer profiles, studying in detail those aspects of their stores that really make their stores pop for the shoppers, fill this section.

Part 3 takes all the information about the previously studied shoppers and retailers, and lays out principles for your retailing success in the future as the shoppers continue to go more experiential. It tells how to create a shop that pops, whether you are a small independent retailer, a medium-sized multilocation chain, or a retailer with national—even international—scope. Retailers big and small face the same basic challenges now; shoppers are demanding more than just a selection of merchandise at a reasonable price from the stores that they frequent. They want their shopping experiences and the stores that they frequent to really pop with special features that involve the customer, build their curiosity, give off a contagious energy that converges into a store design, atmosphere, and merchandise that present an authentic concept offering goods at the right price with added value, and that are accessible and free from pretension. That, in a nutshell, is what this book, *Shopping: Why We Love It and How Retailers Can Create the Ultimate Customer Experience,* is all about.

Part One

WHY WE LOVE SHOPPING

Understanding the Passionate Shopper

CHAPTER ONE

Understanding the Mind of the Shopper

THE NEW QUANTUM THEORY OF SHOPPING

*"Know where to find the information and how to use it—
that's the secret of success."*

ALBERT EINSTEIN

This is a book about shopping, or more specifically the new experiential trend in shopping and how retailers must transform their way of doing business for success in the future. I approach this study of shopping as a professional market researcher, having spent the better part of the last dozen years focused on understanding the mindset of the consumer.

In addition, I come to this book with one other qualification that really makes the difference—I love to shop. In effect, I am both researcher and research subject, which gives me a unique perspective on this study of the new experiential shopping trend. Therefore, while I try to wear my objective researcher's hat, I can never escape the fact that I have a personal passion for shopping. Moreover, truth be told, you as readers—most likely from the retailing profession—also have this same split between your profession as a retailer and your personal experience as a shopper. Together let's bring these two perspectives—our objective professional understanding and our personal shopping experiences—into this study of shopping.

As a researcher, I believe passionately in the power of intuition. True understanding comes when you make the leap between objective, observable facts and intuition. That was what happened during a recent shopping trip for a pair of shoes when I discovered what I call the "quantum theory of shopping." In a flash of inspiration I found the four essential values that factor into shoppers' decision to buy and how these factors work together to explain why people buy. It amounts to a mathematical formula that is the essence of shopping. My apologies in advance to the mathematically challenged and to those for whom the mere vision of the formula that follows causes panic. It really is a simple little formula that encompasses everything you need to know about shopping, so please stick with me as I explain the quantum theory of shopping.

$$P = (N + F + A) \times E^2$$

In English, P, the propensity for a shopper to buy, is found by adding Need and product Features and Affordability, and multiplying that sum by Emotion squared. Let me explain.

The Search for the Red Velvet Shoes

Everybody has their consumer soft spot, that special thing that irresistibly attracts them and that they can't say no to when they shop. For my husband it is some obscure 40s-vintage DVD release; for my sister it is something for her grandson; for my youngest son, the musician, it is just about anything related to music; for me it is fashion, in particular, shoes.

Back in the spring I was browsing through Scoop, a NYC shop that pops for fashionistas, when I happened upon a to-die-for pair of green velvet pumps—over 3 inches high heel, a discreet bow, and the latest round toes. The shoes also came in a rich burgundy red, which I gave some consideration to, but because I recently had bought a hot new Diane Von Furstenberg green dress and a green Coach bag to match I needed to complete the outfit with the green velvet shoes. The price, about $450, as I recall, and the fact that I was shopping with my husband, who, as understanding as he is, would have seen buying two pairs of the same shoe as excessive, deterred me from buying both the red and green shoes together. Also, I naively figured it would be much easier to find another pair of red shoes than green ones.

After that I started a valiant search for a similar pair of red shoes, velvet would be nice, but I would have settled for an attractive pair in a deep burgundy color. I had no luck at the usual shopping suspects like Nordstrom, Neiman Marcus, Bloomingdales, Macy's, and countless other specialty shops that I browsed. DKNY had something close to what I wanted, but I fell instead for a pair of burgundy boots. I finally decided that burgundy red was just not the color this season for shoes and I would have to wait until next season.

Months later, and the red shoe search long forgotten, I had an overnight stay at the Regent Beverly Wilshire Hotel to give a speech for a conference on luxury marketing. That hotel just happens to be at the corner of one of the greatest luxury shopping districts in the country, Rodeo Drive in Beverly Hills. After dinner there was nothing else I wanted to do but window shop along that street. And what do you think I found on my stroll but the perfect pair of red velvet shoes? The store was closed so I had to delay my shopping gratification until after I gave my speech the next day.

As soon as the speech was over and courtesy allowed, I made a beeline to the store, the Sergio Rossi boutique, to see the price, try them on, and buy them if they met my criteria. This is where the *eureka!* moment occurred—when the formula that explained the quantum theory of shopping popped into my head.

$$P = (N + F + A) \times E^2$$

Here is how the formula explains my propensity to buy those lovely velvet shoes. My Need for those shoes, i.e., do I really *need* another pair of red shoes, was nil. Of course, I don't have another pair of deep burgundy red velvet shoes, but I do have other red shoes and other shoes in velvet, so strictly from an objective standpoint my need for those shoes was very slight. However, the product Features of those particular red shoes in the Sergio Rossi window were the real draw to me. They were a lovely, deep rich red color. They had a high heel, but somewhat stacked, not stiletto, which gives better balance when you walk. The toe box was rounded, a feature I like since I have tired of pointy-toed shoes. Moreover, they were velvet, a super luxurious, special, and different material for a pair of shoes. So my need was fairly low, but product features that attracted me and drew me emotionally were very high.

Key to the purchase decision was Affordability, given that I was looking at a pair of shoes on Rodeo Drive and in a store I wasn't personally familiar with. In my mental calculation I figured the shoes wouldn't cost more than $800 and probably not less than $400, but who knows, when you can walk into the Hermes store and pick up a fairly unremarkable bag for a mere $18,000. I decided if the shoes were over $800 I wouldn't buy them, because it just seemed silly to me to pay that much for a pair of shoes, no matter what. If they were around $400, I would pick them up in a heartbeat. If they were between $400–$800, then I would need to try them on and see how they felt and looked.

Ultimately, the critical factor, the one that dominated the entire purchase formula, was Emotion. It was how I felt in those shoes that could push me over my superimposed maximum price of $800. The Emotion could drive up the need if when I tried them on they really were different from any other shoes in my closet. The Emotion could play off the product features to make the red color even more spectacular, the design even more sophisticated, and the look even more perfect when I had them on. Emotion might well have sent me right back out the door if the salespeople in the store were snooty and didn't want to help me in obtaining my prized red velvet shoes. All my rational, left-brained assumptions I brought into the shopping formula were simply a minor factor when it came to the dominant E-factor—the emotion.

Happily, I bought the shoes. I was astonished that they only cost $350—so there really wasn't any question at all. In fact, you could go so far as to say I saved $450 on the purchase because I had been willing to spend $800 for them. Now I've got a stunning pair of deep red burgundy shoes that give me a thrill every time I wear them.

Quantum Theory of Shopping Explains It All

Taking myself out of the picture, what we need to understand is that emotion drives the consumer and while it is an intangible, highly individualistic thing, it controls the consumer when they shop. Tangible factors play a role in the shopping decision, but they rarely dominate. The tangibles, i.e. need, features, affordability, are additive, $1 + 1 + 1 = 3$, whereas emotion works exponentially, $(1 + 1 + 1)$ $5^2 = 75$. Emotions magnify need, they play off features, and they make a desired item more or less affordable, thus sending the shopper to the cash register with whatever it is they hunger for.

Emotions magnify need, they play off features, and they make a desired item more or less affordable, thus sending the shopper to the cash register with whatever it is they hunger for.

As marketers and retailers we can control to some extent the tangibles, but not a whole lot. For example, consumer need is a very personal thing and no marketer or retailer can create the need for a particular item. Either you need a new pair of red shoes, a cookie sheet, a bathroom scale, a set of sheets, a cashmere sweater, a scented candle—all, incidentally, recent purchases I made—or you don't. No amount of advertising, marketing promotion, in-store advertising, or window displays can impact the need. Need often drives consumers to the stores to shop, sets them on a mission, and moves them to action but there really isn't a thing that marketers or retailers can do about building need. On the other hand, they can create desire, which is a purely emotional response. So the Need part of the formula is strictly personal and individual for the shopper and not a factor that an outside entity can impact.

By comparison to Need, the marketer and retailer have much more control over the Features part of the formula. They can stack up all kinds of added-value benefits in the products and the merchandise they stock, so that the shopper can discern key quality differences about particular items. Features are what make one item more attractive than another. It distinguishes better quality, better style, better design, longer life, greater functionality, and better "better." Features are a hot button that pushes the shopper's buy response. Features operate independent of need, for if there is no specific need, all the wonderful product features in the world won't cause a shopper to buy. For example, in my recent cookie sheet purchase, I bought the luxury cookie sheet, the nonstick Calphalon model, but

I never would have even thought about this purchase if my old cookie sheet hadn't been totaled by baked-on pumpkin pie filling this past Thanksgiving.

Affordability is one of those tangible factors that is at once both highly personal and easily manipulated by marketers and retailers. On a personal level everyone has a certain amount of money that they can spend on specific things; so sheer dollar volume is a limiting factor. However, most people have a range within which they can spend—they can borrow from Peter to pay Paul. We all do this. Therefore, we buy the generic store brand of soda, but splurge on imported wine; or buy ordinary American cheese for sandwiches, but buy the expensive artisanal Brie for snacking; or eat out at Panera's instead of a better restaurant in order to save money for a week's vacation in Cancun. Everybody stretches their budget for certain things that they really care about and pulls back in other areas that aren't as important. Some people just have more room to stretch than others.

For example, I could have stretched to pay more than $800 for the red velvet shoes. How much more I am not sure about, but I assure you I am not in the league to pay $18,000 for an Hermes handbag. Another person, like many of the shoppers I met in the course of this research, wouldn't think of paying $400 for a pair of shoes. It simply would have been out of the question for them, but they would spend $400 on new steam cleaning vacuum in a heartbeat, a budget expense I would never bother with. So how much you spend and where you spend it is very much a personal, individual factor just like need.

Nevertheless, marketers and retailers have a much greater influence on consumers' buying decisions when it comes to affordability than they do in relation to need. An item found for a cheap price, even if the need is fairly low, can push the shopper to buy. Janet, a 37-year-old woman who likes to shop, explains it this way: "My husband likes to say that we go broke saving money. That's what we do, because I always come home with things I find on sale. It doesn't matter if we need it or not, but I always find this great thing that I just have to have . . . It's not that I go specifically to find something, but if I find that deal or that great thing that we might need ten years from now, then I go ahead and buy it, because it's such a good deal."

> *"My husband likes to say that we go broke saving money. I always come home with things I find on sale. It doesn't matter if we need it or not," says a bargain-hunting shopper.*

Over and over again in the focus groups, shoppers express how an item found on sale stimulates them to buy even when need is very low. Chapter 4 explores this factor of affordability and retailers' manipulation of it because it is an important issue in shopping that we must mine for deeper insights.

$$P = (N + F + A) \times E^2$$

But of far more importance than the tangibles in the shopping formula—Need, Features, and Affordability—is Emotion, which touches off and interacts with each of the tangible features. High emotion, such as a passion for a particular type of item, can spark need, thus the example of my perceived need for those lovely red shoes. High emotion can enhance the perception of product features, whether it is a favorite brand one feels emotional about, or a favorite color, designer, specific feature, style, material of composition, size, and so on. Perception of product features can be personal; for example, somebody might really dislike the color red for shoes, but frankly good design and product quality are pretty objective and removed from one's personal taste. Marketers can create and retailers can stock goods that embody a specific set of core product features that define superior quality in that category. Thus they stand a far better chance to stimulate a shopper's emotional hot buttons to buy.

Affordability is very much influenced by emotion. What we really, really want, we are willing to pay a lot of money for. Where the need is fairly low and the product features are not all that spectacular, a super price touches the emotional hot button—getting a steal—and makes us buy. Today's marketers and retailers tend to push this hot button more often and more aggressively than any other, oftentimes to the determent of their long-term profitability and success. After all, today's shopper is trained to expect discounts and sales, so shoppers are ultimately discouraged from ever paying full list price.

> *The key factor in the quantum theory of shopping that marketers and retailers have the most power over, the most influence over, and that they can use to manipulate the shopper to buy is Emotion.*

To recap before we look at a specific example: marketers and retailers can't create need. They can stock great products and price them well, but ultimately product qualities and affordability are interpreted personally by the shopper. The key factor in the quantum theory of shopping that marketers and retailers have the most power over, the most influence over, and that they can use to manipulate the shopper to buy is Emotion. This is both the good news and the bad news for consumer businesses today, for emotion is totally removed from reason. It doesn't operate predictably or follow known rules, and it is not easily controlled. Left-brain-dominant business executives are at a distinct disadvantage in the emotional realm, yet that is where they need to learn to play because emotion rules in the future of shopping.

Nell Hill's

■ A Store in the Middle of Nowhere That has Built a Thriving Business Serving Customers Who Drive 100+ Miles to Get There

Challenging the conventional wisdom that the success of a retail store is location-location-location is Mary Carol Garrity's Nell Hill's home furnishings store located in Atchison, Kansas, of all places. (*www.nellhills.com*) Garrity has done what few retailers can ever hope to do: built a highly successful retail business that has grown to three storefronts in a location where 97 percent of her customers have to drive from one hour and fifteen minutes to three hours to get to the store. Nell Hill's sits roughly 50 miles from Kansas City, Missouri.

Nell Hill's as a store where people love to shop came up in a focus group in Chicago where one of the respondents shared her favorite place to shop: "It's a day thing, and we go to this store that is designed like an old house. Everywhere you go there is something new. She [Garrity] is so innovative and so fun. People come from all over to this little tiny town in Atchison, Kansas to go shopping at Nell Hill's."

When I asked Garrity why a shopper who lives in Chicago, more than 500 miles away, and who can quite easily shop on Michigan Avenue's Magnificent Mile, some of the best shopping in the country, likes her store best, she, in her very understated, no-nonsense way said it was all because of the prices. "Our price is perfect. We have the best prices because it is such a value. It's beautifully displayed, it's wonderful quality, and the value points are there because people are always saying, 'I can't believe these prices.'"

Frankly I didn't buy that price is the primary reason why Nell Hill's has been so successful. At today's gas prices nobody drives 500 miles to save a few dollars on home furnishings. So I pushed and finally got Garrity to admit that having attractive prices only contributed to making her store pop, but it wasn't the key. It was that her store is wonderfully entertaining shopping. "Price is a lot of it, but our stores have beautiful displays. We give great service and have three delivery trucks. And it is fun to come here. It is entertaining. Someone described it as an eight-hour cocktail party without the alcohol."

What happens in the store is magical. People who don't know each other start talking and comparing notes. Because Garrity offers such attractive prices and draws such passionate shoppers through her doors, the merchandise shifts in and out quickly. There is always something new to see and explore in Nell Hill's store. "People will travel a good hour and a half to come visit every couple of weeks, because our merchandise changes so dramatically. There is a lot of energy going on here. People say, 'I can't believe how much everything has changed since the last time.'" She concludes, "People who shop here know that if they see it and want it, they better buy it. It won't be here the next time they come."

The source of Nell Hill's dynamism is Mary Carol Garrity herself. The author of three books on home decorating with a fourth set for publication in September 2006, Garrity provides the vital spark that keeps the stores constantly evolving. "I don't do it for the money. I do it because I love it. For my staff and myself, we are very high energy and very passionate about it. That passion is contagious to my staff and it's contagious to my customers."

"People who shop here know that if they see it and want it, they better buy it. It won't be here the next time they come," says Mary Carol Garrity, Nell Hill's.

One of the secrets of Garrity's success is she is totally dedicated to the customer, delivering the kinds of products and shopping experiences that thrill and delight. In order to stay in tune with the customer, Garrity refuses to have an office but spends her time on the sales floor constantly rubbing shoulders with shoppers. "My manager has an office but I still don't have one. I love being out on the floor. I love working with my customer. I love listening to what they are asking for and what they are saying. I learn from my customer."

And because the shopper is always changing, so are Garrity's business plans. "One of the keys to our success is that I'm constantly changing the direction we are going in. Nell Hill's has been great because we haven't locked ourselves into any certain thing. We have been flexible and changeable." It is this versatility that keeps Nell Hill's drawing more and more customers into the store to find out what's new.

Interestingly, Garrity started her business running a cheese and gourmet foods store. She added gift items as a natural outgrowth of the gourmet food focus and that led to where she is today: owner of Nell Hill's, the flagship "home emporium" specializing in home accessories and furnishings; G. Diebolts, a linens and bedding specialty shop housed in an old bank building; and Garrity's, located in a turn-of-the-century Masonic lodge and dedicated to furniture and antiques.

The shift from gourmet foods to home furnishings was more evolutionary than revolutionary. She says, "I first added kitchen gadgets. Then I got into Crabtree and Evelyn bath items. The way it worked out was every time I'd go to market, I'd add a new category, like artwork or lamps, and I just kept adding them. Pretty soon I found out it was easier to sell a lamp than a half pound of coffee and grind it, and it was more profitable. So that is how it gradually happened."

But Garrity doesn't just sell great home decor, she lives and breathes it. Her merchandising strategy is simplicity itself. "We just buy stuff we love. Ninety percent of the things we have in our three stores, I would gladly have in my own home in a heartbeat." Her deeply personal touch doesn't go unnoticed by the enthusiastic customers, like the focus group respondent who drives 500 miles to shop, and who describes the feeling in the store: "It's an amazing store. It's got a cozy feel, like you're shopping in a home. And as people are in there by the hundreds, and they're taking stuff out, people working in the store are redoing everything so it doesn't look like something is gone."

One of the traditions Garrity established for her store around the time her first book, *Nell Hill's Style at Home,* came out was an annual open house and garden tour. "I have an old 130-year-old home so I opened up my home for a house and garden tour. This became something we did three times a year for the last six or seven years. We put up a huge tent next to the house and offered hors d'oeuvres. We sell books out there too along with merchandise we don't even have at any of the stores. I hire a bus to go around the circle all day long [bringing people from the downtown stores]. It's a huge ordeal and I have promised my family we won't do it again. But we have thousands of people come through and it's been wonderful."

While Garrity is pulling back from her personal open house, hosting special events to boost the store's presence is part of her overall business strategy. They do charity events, school functions, and special holiday events. She explains the effort directed to promotions, "The more things that you do outside of your store the better. It gets people talking. You just can't have great merchandise, and open up your doors and twiddle your thumbs. You've got to get people into the door."

In her very understated, self-effacing way, Garrity concludes, "It is wonderful. I'm the luckiest shopkeeper I know. Things just fall into my lap." Luck, I think, doesn't have much to do with it. However, what she does do that is truly special is she turns whatever "falls" into her lap into a success through hard work, clear vision, and knowing and caring enough to truly delight her customers.

CHAPTER TWO

Need

TRANSFORMING DESIRE INTO NEED

"We are driven by five genetic needs:
survival, love and belonging, power, freedom, and fun."
PSYCHIATRIST DR. WILLIAM GLASSER

Propensity to buy = (Need + Features + Affordability) × Emotion^2

Shoppers' need is one of the most misunderstood concepts in marketing today, and it is frequently used interchangeably with shoppers' desire. But I assure you: Need and desire are two entirely different things. Need is true necessity within one's cultural framework. It is something that is required for a person to function in society. Need inevitably must be referenced to one's culture, because need for people in a less developed culture is far different from need in our own. One reason need is so hard to clearly define is that it is a fluctuating thing. But if we stay grounded within our cultural framework, we can begin to distinguish needs from wants or desires. So for most Americans a place to live, a telephone, indoor plumbing, a refrigerator and stove, some form of heat and some form of air cooling (fans or air-conditioning depending upon location), electricity, basic furnishings, clothing, personal care products (shampoo, soap, etc.), medicines, and food are necessities.

But as our cultural standard of living rises over time, we get used to that higher standard of living and are extremely hesitant to give up comforts that are really satisfied wants and desires, rather than strictly needs. I clearly remember my "starving graduate student days" when t-shirts and blue jeans made up my wardrobe, my furniture was hand-me-downs, and my makeup came in blister packs from the drugstore. I survived, even thrived, during those days, but clearly I don't want to give up the comforts, pleasures, and luxuries that my lifestyle affords me today. I try not to confuse my real needs with my desires, but as marketers and retailers we should err on the side of caution and recognize most of what we sell and market is meant to satisfy desires. Outside of the realm of food and pharmaceuticals, very little of shopping and buying today in 21st-century America is directed toward need.

Need Stimulates Lots of Shopping, While Desire Drives Purchases

Need most often sends us out to the store, while desire plays a dominant role in getting us to make purchases. Given our busy hectic lives, it is often hard to find the time to go shopping. Few of us enjoy lives of leisure that aren't filled to the brim balancing family and work responsibilities. Time spent socializing, being entertained, or in recreational pursuits are luxuries we permit ourselves after we take care of the chores, obligations, and responsibilities of life. One of the responsibilities that every American must make time for today is shopping. Like death and taxes, shopping is inevitable.

Most people view shopping as both a chore and a recreational pastime. In our latest Unity Marketing survey among shoppers (survey methodology is described in Appendix A), nearly three-fourths of shoppers say that "shopping is something that has to be done." Only 60 percent say that "shopping is fun." Their frequency of shopping bears out this distinction—that shopping is more often a duty than a pleasure. The typical shopper goes shopping nearly nine times (8.9 times) per month for necessities, i.e. basic personal, family, and household necessities such as food, drugs and prescriptions, basic clothing and necessities, home cleaning and care supplies, home equipment, and so on, as compared to 4.4 times for fun or recreation. That amounts to two shopping trips driven by the need for necessities for every one shopping trip undertaken for fun or as recreation.

SHOPPING FACTOIDS

Typical shopper per month:

Necessities shopping 8.9 times	Spends on average $710
Recreational shopping 4.4 times	Spends on average $374
Total shopping trips 13.3 times	Spends on average $1,804

Source: Unity Marketing, Recreational Shopping Report 2006

But as we have discussed, need, either real or perceived, is the driver for most shopping trips. It is in the course of shopping for necessities that retailers can serendipitously attract shoppers for things they might not strictly need but desire. In my recent shopping trip stimulated by a need to replace a burnt cookie sheet, I shopped at Bed, Bath & Beyond. As a shopper, I am only "warm" in the home category, and would much rather spend my limited shopping time in clothing and fashion stores. When I finally went shopping for a new cookie sheet, I bought more of a cookie sheet than I needed. (If you can even say I needed it at all because I bake rarely. But the idea of not having a cookie sheet when I got the inspiration to bake cookies was unsettling, so I went shopping in anticipation of a real need.) I got the cookie sheet with extra nonstick features and a superior brand name compared to the sheet I was replacing.

The need sent me to the store, but the added value features directed my purchase—and I also picked up some extra sheets and pillowcases while I was in the store, a purely opportunistic purchase. Another shopper who is "hot" in the baking, cookware, and home categories might have come away from that shopping trip spending several hundred dollars, as compared to my $75 or so. Who in the world really needs an electric ice cream maker—but a shopper planning a holiday party might well find an attractive additional purchase when shopping for a tablecloth for her upcoming party.

One Person's Desire Is Somebody Else's Need

In focus groups among shoppers, distinguishing between need and desire was a question that stimulated lively discussion. Kimberly, a married mother of two school-aged children, said, "Necessities are things like toothpaste or clothing. There are some things that aren't necessarily necessary, but they're important, like educational things. Like buying your child a violin—that's not really a necessity, but it doesn't really come under the category of something you go and splurge on for yourself. It isn't a luxury." In other words, given one's financial status, value system, and place in life, the definition of what is necessary and what is not varies. This parent puts the development of her children before herself; thus a purchase like a violin is highly justified.

On the other hand, Diane, a baby-boomer empty-nester, sees her real "needs" as very minor indeed: "Some people would say they have to go out and get a dress for this event on Saturday night, and they really believe that they have to go shopping for it. They believe there is no way they can wear the same formal dress they've worn in the past. They have to get one. But for me, I think I need nothing right now in my life. Probably I could live with nothing for the rest of my life, so most things fall into nonessentials, but I think some people think otherwise."

"But for me, I think I need nothing right now in my life. Probably I could live with nothing for the rest of my life, so most things fall into nonessentials, but I think some people think otherwise."

This comment was part of a broader discussion about needing to buy a dress for an upcoming special event. As an observer of this interchange, I found it interesting how people can truly believe that shopping for a new party dress is actually a necessity. Personally every woman I know has a basic black dress or pair of pants in her closet that can be dressed up for any formal, dressy occasion that crops up. I also know that when I am picking out an outfit to wear, I almost never remember exactly what I wore before or when I wore it. And if

I can't remember what I wore on a previous occasion, surely nobody who was there is likely to remember either. But those are the very reasons why people view shopping for a new party dress as a need, not a want. Meg, a 30-something stay-at-home mom, explains, "Sometimes buying a formal can be a necessity, because we go to formal events with a lot of the same people. You can wear the same dress maybe a couple of years later, but you might have a picture of it. So it does matter. My husband asks why I don't wear his favorite dress that I have only worn once to an event. He just doesn't understand why I can't wear this dress again. People notice and they make comments."

Sherry, a grandmother of two, sees shopping for a gown as a necessity too, "Sometimes I shop for a necessity like an outfit for a party. I don't want to go and buy it, but I have to because I have to go somewhere. So I need to spend today at the mall to buy something appropriate. So it's a necessity for me to have a new outfit."

Borrowing from Shakespeare, "The lady doth protest too much, methinks." These women are deadly serious and profoundly confused. That is because they actually believe their own justifications or excuses for making specific desire-based purchases. Thus we see the power of justifiers in transforming need into desire in the buying formula.

Justifiers Turn Desires Into Needs and Give Shoppers Permission to Buy

At their most basic, justifiers are what transform a desire into a need in the consumers' mind. Justifiers are the reason, the rationale, and the excuse that gives the shopper permission to buy. It is the reason why Meg, whose husband really likes her in one dress, can reject his preference and go out and buy another dress. As a clotheshorse of the first magnitude, I have often fallen back upon this excuse to buy another outfit. An upcoming speech or television appearance always works for me as a reason to go shopping. And with the purchase of that new outfit, I have justification to buy a new handbag, shoes and jewelry to match. But being both researcher and subject at the same time, I never confuse my desire (i.e., I want to add something new to my closet) with my need (i.e., nobody I will be speaking to has seen me in any outfit that is in my closet and nobody seeing me on

TV will ever remember). Nevertheless, the majority of women in the focus groups really buy into their justification and believe that their desire is actually a real need. Thus, the enormous marketing power of justifiers in getting people to buy.

Justifiers are the reason, the rationale, and the excuse that gives the shopper permission to buy.

Other powerful justifiers that turn desire into need include making oneself or one's home more beautiful. Karen, a working mother, is always on the lookout for decorative things for her home. This gives her life more meaning and reinforces her role as a homemaker when she makes her home more attractive and pleasant. "I like to shop for the house, more than I like to shop for myself . . . I love the stuff at Pottery Barn. I like to change the house, especially in the fall. It's not expensive and they always have new stuff. I find it [shopping] relaxing and enjoyable."

Besides beauty, people justify purchases as being about pure pleasure. New body lotions, flowers, books, clothes, wine, and gourmet food all offer a pleasurable experience for the consumer, thus the pleasure justifier transforms the desire for an item into a need because of pleasure the item will deliver. In other words, the shopper says, "I need a little excitement, stimulation, indulgence, and pleasure in my life right now, so I will buy this [whatever at the moment strikes one as promising to deliver that pleasure]."

Giving your children, or yourself, a boost in the school and career department or simply learning something new to enhance your life is another powerful justifier people use that turns a desire into a need. Kimberly who bought a violin for her daughter saw this purchase as a need, not a want, as it would improve her daughter's life. This is a favorite justifier to buy a new home computer and all the essential peripherals.

Buying an item to provide relaxation or stress relief is an increasingly important justifier in today's hectic world. We are all so stressed out with overflowing schedules and increasing responsibilities that getting stress relief is becoming a need, not a want. Unfortunately, few of us focus on alleviating the root cause of our stress, like moving closer to our jobs to reduce commute time or simply limiting the kids to one after-school activity per week. Rather, we prop ourselves up with tools and techniques that make the rising level of stress handle-able. All kinds of consumer goods offer the promise of relaxation and stress relief, from little luxuries like candles or massage oils to big luxuries like hot tubs, premium priced inflatable air mattresses, and stylish recliner chairs that are so well designed they look attractive, not tacky.

Buying something to be entertained is another primary justifier. In fact, the category of entertainment and recreational goods is the most favored category for purchases by people who love to shop. So we shop for fun and to be entertained and we buy for fun and to be entertained. Emily, a 40-something mother of older children, can't quite figure out whether her book purchases are necessities, non-necessities, or luxuries, but given her value system, she is definitely leaning toward them being a need, rather than a want. "I'm a big book person, and I was sitting here trying to figure out are they necessity, non-necessity, luxury. I'll spend full price on a book when I won't spend full price on clothes. Go figure that one out, but I love books. They're necessities to me, but they're not really. They are too important in my life. To not have a book to read would be really tough for me. So it could even be a luxury, because it is so important to me. It is something I really treasure." Her desire to be entertained or find escape in a good story is translated into a need for a new book, so she will pay $25 for the latest book by Dan Brown of *The DaVinci Code* fame, but resist spending that much on a new t-shirt. Or even more practically, she could go to the library to borrow the book, but instead she buys.

Replacing a worn-out item justifies buying something you really don't need. Like my recent cookie sheet purchase, I bought it in anticipation of a future desire to make cookies or another pie that must be baked on a cookie sheet. Clearly not a need, because I can go the rest of my life without ever baking or even eating another cookie, but that is hardly something I desire to do. So in order to be able to give myself an emotional boost by baking a batch of chocolate chip cookies and to reduce stress by not having the appropriate sheet to bake them on, I bought myself a new and improved Calphalon cookie sheet just in case.

The search for emotional satisfaction is another reason why people buy things they don't need. They need an emotional lift, which that new dress, new vase, or new perfume promises to deliver. Other justifiers that turn desires into need include a hobby, gift for oneself or for others, status, and a purely impulse purchase.

JUSTIFIERS TRANSFORM DESIRES INTO NEEDS

- **Special occasion**—Gift occasion or a special event can send shoppers to the store to buy. Marketers and retailers can play up the special occasion appeal of specific goods.

- **Beautify self or home**—Things to make oneself or one's home beautiful give an emotional boost. Marketers and retailers need to display goods to maximize beauty impact and send beautifying promises to consumers.

- **Pleasure**—Shoppers derive pleasure in the having, owning, and using, as well as in the buying. Anticipating a new purchase and searching out something wonderful can be part of the pleasure of shopping. Retailers and marketers need to maximize the pleasure in the shopping experience itself.

- **Education**—Being better educated, more learned, and gaining new understanding and skills is an important motivator for the purchase of many categories of goods, notably home computers and peripherals, books, DVDs, and music and musical instruments. Improving one's education is a key way Americans achieve a higher standard of living.

- **Relaxation and stress relief**—Finding solace, relief from everyday stress, and achieving inner peace and harmony are favored motivators for buying many types of goods that offer an experiential value, like candles, aromatherapy, bath and body lotions, whirlpools, hot tubs, and others. Stress relief is delivered by the specific products, as well as the shopping experience itself. "Retail therapy" is real.

- **Entertainment**—People crave entertainment to relieve boredom, and stimulate the imagination and the mind. Entertainment also brings people together to share fun. This is a key justifier stimulating the purchase of many recreational and entertainment products. Shopping too can be an entertaining adventure.

- **Replacing a worn item**—Most shopping trips are motivated by a practical purpose, so many shoppers are in the store specifically to replace an existing item. This can also be a powerful motivator to move upscale to a more differentiated product or brand and to buy add-on items necessitated by a specific purpose. So a shopper replacing a worn-out chair also buys a new rug and curtains to match.

- **Emotional satisfaction**—Many shoppers get pleasure from browsing, while others need to make the purchase to maximize their emotional satisfaction. About half (48 percent) of passionate shoppers agree with the statement "I am more of a buyer when I shop than a browser," so the other half gets emotional satisfaction simply from looking when they shop. Emotional satisfaction comes from feelings of satisfaction such as finding that special something or getting a really good deal. Retailers and marketers must play to the emotions of the shopper.

Ultimate Justifier— Enriching One's Quality of Life

While a wide range of justifiers are used by consumers to give themselves permission to make purchases they otherwise don't need, the ultimate justifier that transforms want into need is how a particular purchase will ultimately enrich the quality of one's life. Enriching the quality of one's life can be measured objectively, like the greater comfort you get from 400-thread count Egyptian cotton sheets or the better sleep quality delivered by a new luxury pillow-top mattress, but most often is subjectively measured, i.e., how the consumer feels. This is the drive that motivates consumers to improve their standard of living. It drives them to buy bigger houses, more expensive cars, more fashionable clothes, more up-to-date appliances, better furniture, and all the rest. It is why we don't just stay where we are, but pursue aggressively the means to improve the quality of our lives.

Marketers and retailers need to position their products, merchandise their stores, and design their overall shopping environment to enhance people's quality of life.

Marketers and retailers need to position their products, merchandise their stores, and design their overall shopping environment to enhance people's quality of life. We want to buy the best item with the highest levels of quality and the most superior features that we can afford. Anyone who uses an OXO kitchen tool can immediately recognize its superior usability over the ordinary generic model. It is also why consumer product companies regularly and routinely reconfigure their products to the "new and improved" version. New and improved promises to enhance the quality of the consumer's life in some meaningful and measurable way. In other words, we don't need a new OXO kitchen gadget or a new and improved version of Tide; what we really need is to enrich the quality of our life. So we buy the OXO instead of the generic model or the new and improved Tide instead of the generic store brand because we believe—or more correctly, hope—that it will add that special something that will make our life better. Enhancing or enriching the consumers' life works throughout many different dimensions of our existence. Certain products play into enhancing the quality of life in one aspect or dimension than another, such as:

- Intellectual—At the intellectual level, education and special knowledge are widely recognized as a means for individuals to improve the quality of their lives. Education makes it possible for a person to find a better job with greater opportunity for advancement. More education also helps people deal more effectively and productively with the day-to-day demands of 21st-century life, so we older folks have to struggle to learn how to use computers and other electronic appliances, while our children who have used technology all their lives just get it intuitively. Many products target this need, such as books, DVDs, and computers, and shopping environments can be positioned to stimulate curiosity and provide new insights and understanding. Learning about new products and new brands is an important motivator for 75 percent of people who love to shop, not far behind browsing and seeing what is new (important to 88 percent of passionate shoppers).

- Physical—Robust health, freedom from pain and disease, and a strong body that can meet the day-to-day demands we place on it are key aspects of quality of life. The physical dimension of quality of life also includes stamina, energy, comfort and safety, and freedom from physical threats. Meeting one's physical needs drives many necessity-based purchases, but more and more as the consumer population ages, it is a motivator for discretionary shopping for health supplements, purified water, sporting and exercise equipment, and household gadgets and appliances that hold the promise of better health or greater ease of use.

- Spiritual—The spiritual dimension of life has increasingly become recognized as a key contributor to an enhanced quality of life. People's relationship with God, whether one recognized by a major religion or a personal spiritual presence, is a major source of comfort and security. Through the spiritual relationship, people have a means to deal more effectively with the unknown, with personal loss and suffering, and with their own impending death. While having a formal religious affiliation is not necessary, the major religions all offer traditions, rituals, and ceremonies that provide structure and solace to people when they face situations that are emotionally confusing and humanly inexplicable. Even in our increasingly secular society, most polls find that 90 percent or more of Americans believe in God.

- Emotion—Emotional health and harmony are critical to one's quality of life. As we explore the emotional dimension in the shopping formula, we find that things in and of themselves don't provide happiness, but each of us has a powerful drive toward happiness and emotional fulfillment. That is the need that we want our purchase of things to fulfill. The emotional component includes the pleasures of love and happiness in the home, freedom from stress, and a home environment that relaxes and provides emotional fulfillment. Shopping, too, delivers emotional rewards. Some 45 percent of people who love to shop agree that shopping is therapeutic and 44 percent agree it is relaxing.

■ Social—Our social connections and network of family, friends, and associates greatly enhance the quality of our lives. Our social network confirms that we are not alone, that we belong. Success in the social milieu yields enhanced quality of life through feelings of competence and accomplishment. Let's face it, getting together with our friends is just a joy. Products we buy can enhance the social aspects of our lives, things like party decorations, tableware, and other things to entertain or gifts bought to build on one's social relationships. Perhaps more important, though, is that shopping itself is a social occasion that encourages people to buy. Half of passionate shoppers (51 percent) say that for them "shopping is social/ something to do with family and friends."

Shoppers Want to Improve the Quality of Their Lives

The buying and getting of material goods today is directed most toward improving the quality of the shopper's life. True physical need—food, clothing, shelter—most often sends us to the store, but higher-level needs—improving the quality of life—directs most spending. Psychologist Abraham Maslow, who originally discovered the hierarchy of needs, provides more insight into how desires are transformed into needs.

Because of the enormous wealth present in our culture, most 21st-century Americans have satisfied the lower-level physical and safety needs, as defined by Maslow. Shopping today, though it can be linked in certain categories and under specific circumstances as a means to satisfy the love, affection, and belongingness need and the

MASLOW'S HIERARCHY OF NEEDS

- **Physiological Needs:** Biological needs, such as needs for oxygen, food, water, and a relatively constant body temperature.

- **Safety Needs:** Safety needs have to do with establishing stability and consistency in a chaotic world. These needs are mostly psychological in nature. We need the security of a home and family, freedom from physical violence, crime, and so on.

- **Needs of Love, Affection, and Belongingness:** Love and belongingness are the next need. Through the expression of these needs, people overcome feelings of loneliness and alienation.

- **Needs for Esteem:** There are two types of esteem needs. First is self-esteem which results from competence or mastery of a task. Second is the attention and recognition that comes from others. This is similar to the belongingness level. However, wanting admiration has to do with the need for power. Desire for status and the aspiration for status symbols, like expensive cars, are an expression of this need for esteem.

- **Needs for Self-Actualization:** The ultimate need that is expressed only after the foregoing needs are satisfied. The need for self-actualization is "the desire to become more and more what one is, to become everything that one is capable of becoming." People who have everything can maximize their potential. They can seek knowledge, peace, esthetic experiences, self-fulfillment, oneness with God, and so on.

Derived from Abraham Maslow, *Toward a Psychology of Being,* third edition (New York, John Wiley, 1998)

need for esteem, is primarily a drive toward self-actualization. As we look to the future of shopping and study the experiential change in it, it is self-actualization that will become the dominant motivator for consumers. Shoppers will buy goods and services that in some way offer the prospect of personal transformation and help to create a

new, more idealized self. This need is described by Maslow as "the desire to become more and more what one is, to become everything
that one is capable of becoming." It explains the pursuit of self-fulfillment through spiritual enlightenment, greater knowledge, peace, appreciation of beauty, culture, art, and aesthetics. It motivates
consumers in hobbies, pastimes, exercise, and sporting activities that
will lead to personal growth and development.

---

*The desire to enhance one's quality of life is one way people express
that drive toward self-actualization, and our culture is fascinated by
the concept of self-actualization and personal transformation.*

The desire to enhance one's quality of life is one way people express that drive toward self-actualization, and our culture is fascinated
by the concept of self-actualization and personal transformation. The
new reality show craze, including television shows like *Survivor, Trading Spaces, What Not to Wear, The Swan, Plastic Surgery: Before and After,
Project Runway* and all the rest, reflect this passionate interest to watch
and vicariously participate in personal transformation. While all
these shows focus on transformation on the outside, (i.e., a newly designed room or a new wardrobe, new hairstyle, or makeup), in actu-
ality the real transformation is taking place on the inside with the
participants stretching themselves, challenging their old assumptions
about themselves, trying on new identities, and learning new skills. By
watching these shows, the viewer is reassured about trying out their
own personal transformation in order to test how far they can fulfill
a newly idealized personal identity.

So the next time you visit a mall, watch shoppers as they window
shop down New York's Fifth Avenue, or stop at Target for bathroom
cleaner, you need to think of all the people you see not just as shoppers, but people in search of self-actualization and personal transformation. It opens up an entirely new way to look at the world of
shoppers—not just as a bunch of people looking for more stuff to
buy, but people in search of a new, more self-actualized self.

> *It opens up an entirely new way to look at the world of shoppers—not just as a bunch of people looking for more stuff to buy, but people in search of a new, more self-actualized self.*

For those in the business of selling goods, this will lead inevitably to your own personal transformation. It will transform the way you look at the products you create, not as another new thing, but as a means for consumers' personal transformation. This transformative quality applies to the merchandise you stock in your store; the way you display your goods; the way you design your store; the way you staff your store; the way you light your store; the music you play; the way the parking lot is laid out; and a myriad of other details that ultimately touch the shopper. Help them transform themselves and you will build a loyal shopper who will return to your store again and again, because personal transformation is not a once-and-done thing, it is a perpetual, never-ending process.

Target

■ Where You Can Get Anything You Need, and a Lot That You Want

Shoppers have an enormous affection for Target stores. In a word, they love shopping there. In Unity Marketing's new survey on shopping, Target is tied with Best Buy as passionate shoppers' favorite shopping destination for fun. Target is second only to Wal-Mart in places where they shop for necessities. But Target has it all over Wal-Mart in shopper sentiment. In focus groups I frequently hear gripes about shopping at Wal-Mart, like the lines are too long, parking is bad, the store is not clean, and so on, but I never hear things like that said about Target.

Target, for many shoppers, is in another class entirely, as this shopper explains: "They are definitely different. They've got better quality. They are a little more high-end. Target is more contemporary." She goes on, "There are two different types of people, Target people and Wal-Mart people. I go to both, but there is stuff I buy at

Target I wouldn't think of buying at Wal-Mart. Like clothes—I buy clothes at Target, but I wouldn't buy them at Wal-Mart."

The reason why Target is best in class among the discounters and stands above the rest is their emphasis on enhancing the shopping experience, as this shopper says: "Target is more aesthetically appealing . . . . Like when you walk in, it's got shiny floors. It has a premium store feel. It is not as cluttered."

Target is a shop that pops because they have a values-driven concept that guides everything they do, from the merchandise they stock to the store environment. Their motto—Expect More. Pay Less—says it all. Target stores were founded in 1962 by Dayton Company. Their Web site explains their "department-store roots evolved into discount-store savvy."

Today, Target operates more than 1,300 stores in 47 states, including over 140 SuperTarget stores that include groceries, in-store bakery, deli, meat, and produce sections. With revenues of $46.8 billion in 2004, Target has been in high growth mode since 2002 with sales growing 25 percent in the past two years.

At the core of the Target experience is a commitment to design in both merchandise and environment of the store. They are famously credited with being the leading retailer of luxury for the masses—they aren't called "Tar-zhay" for nothing—by teaming with first-rate designers like Michael Graves, Mossimo Giannulli, Isaac Mizrahi, and Cynthia Rowley for cutting-edge styles in home and fashion.

Shoppers like the stuff they get at Target and they also like the low prices they are asked to pay, but what really sets Target apart from the other discounters is simply the environment of the store. They pay special attention to having their stores neat and clean, well-organized, and logically laid out. Their "racetrack" design encourages shoppers to cruise the whole store, not just go to one specific section. And they locate related merchandise departments right next to each other, again encouraging customers to visit the next aisle over just so they don't miss something wonderful.

When shoppers compare Target to Wal-Mart and Kmart, they notice the aesthetics first, as this shopper explains: "There is more of a warehouse feel at Kmart or Wal-Mart, and then the racks there just look tired. The price tags look tired. Everything at Target just looks fresh and new, and they don't have huge racks and racks of extra bottled water sitting up on top. It doesn't look cluttered. It just looks neat."

Nonetheless, Target is not about to rest on its laurels. Target continues to evolve in order to make its already competitively superior shopping experience even better. The company is now rolling out a new P2004 store prototype that features expanded food departments and new departmental adjacencies to encourage cross-shopping. So far some 100 stores have been redone and more than 200 others have had selected improvements. For example, under the new plan, sporting goods and toys are grouped with home electronics and media into one Entertainment Central department. The new prototype also collocates baby consumables, such as diapers, formula and wipes with baby products, including furniture and car seats, in the Baby World department. The goal of these new efforts is to increase the typical Target store customers' average 12 visits per year, according to Bill Dreher, senior research analyst with Deutsche Bank, as well as drive up average spending per visit.

The new feature I am waiting for at my local Target store is the "Guest Call Buttons" where the guest—Target doesn't call us shoppers, but guests, which may be why they treat the customer differently—can put out an emergency SOS to find someone to help fast. That way, instead of having to search around for help, all I have to do is push a button and somebody comes to my aid. The goal is to answer a guest's SOS in 60 seconds, and Target reports they are meeting that goal 90 percent of the time. Call buttons are a clever idea and super responsive customer service is a shopper's dream come true. That is just what I, and many other shoppers, have come to expect from our Target store.

CHAPTER THREE

Features

ADDED-VALUE FEATURES TOUCH
EMOTIONAL HOT BUTTONS AND
COMPEL SHOPPERS TO BUY

*"The aim of marketing is to know and understand the customer
so well the product or service fits him and sells itself."*
PETER F. DRUCKER

The second variable in the quantum theory of shopping is product Features, those distinctive attributes, values, and qualities of products that make the shopper chose one item over another. It is what makes the shopper say, "I'll take this."

Propensity to buy = (Need + Features + Affordability) × Emotion^2

As we plan for the transformation of shopping brought about by the experiential paradigm shift, it is a mistake to think that product doesn't matter. On the other hand, product manufacturers and marketers tend to overemphasize the importance of product in the buying formula and think that product, above all else, is the reason why people buy. The shopping formula above illustrates the role of product and product features—like need, product features are primarily important insofar as they play off emotion.

The emphasis of product shifts, not to the product features themselves, but to how the shopper interacts and interprets features emotionally, and internalizes them for a personal response that says "buy." So it is not the product so much as the way the shopper experiences the prospects and possibilities of the item that is of utmost importance in the shopping formula. In this context, then, we need to understand how the product itself delivers an experience to the consumer.

The emphasis of product shifts, not to the product features themselves, but to how the shopper interacts and interprets features emotionally and internalizes them for a personal response that says "buy."

Products Deliver Emotional Experiences— That Is Why People Buy Them

In the new experiential world of shopping, the role of the product is to stimulate shoppers' emotion and get them to pick up the item, put it in their basket, and take it to the register to buy. It is not the thing itself that people buy, but the promise of how that thing will perform emotionally and experientially for them. We overlook the concept of product performance, which comes so naturally to us when we think about things that have gears and switches like cars, watches, television sets, and a whole host of other mechanical things, when it comes to things that primarily deliver or perform emotionally. Yet it is through this concept of product performance that a material good is translated into an experience.

Products perform in many different ways, not just in the physical or mechanical realm, like cars, watches and electronic devices, but we also expect them to perform on the emotional and experiential level. Fashion brands perform by making the wearer look and feel good. Stylish fashion communicates that one is smart and up-to-date. That kind of emotional performance is as equally valid to the shopper as how well a new dishwasher cleans dishes or how fast a car accelerates. In the experiential shopping world, all products must "do" (i.e., active verb), rather than simply "be" (i.e., passive noun).

What those products promise to do or deliver is very important to the shopper. In Unity Marketing's latest research among passionate shoppers, that is, high-income consumers who love to shop, merchandise-related features were ranked the most important factor overall in drawing the shopper to a particular store to shop, as opposed to store values related to pricing, customer service, or other store attractions. Out of a total of 20 different store attributes, a majority of shoppers (58 percent) rated those related to merchandise as far and away the most important in their decision about where to shop. In particular they value a store that offers, in order:

1. Wide selection of merchandise (named by 23 percent of passionate shoppers)
2. High-quality merchandise (12 percent)
3. Other items they can shop for (7 percent)
4. Unique merchandise (7 percent)
5. Always something new, different, interesting to look at (4 percent)
6. Stock of the latest, hottest new items (3 percent)
7. One's favorite brands (2 percent)

Shoppers' emphasis on stores that offer a wide selection of merchandise reflects in their favorite types of stores in which to shop for fun. They are in order:

1. Discount department stores (18 percent), such as Wal-Mart, Kmart, and Target; Target, by the way, is tied for shoppers' favorite store for all recreational shopping
2. Electronics and appliance stores (13 percent), such as Circuit City and Best Buy; Best Buy is tied with Target for their absolute favorite destination for shopping fun
3. Clothing and clothing accessories stores (11 percent), such as Talbots, Ann Taylor, The Gap, and Old Navy; Old Navy ranks among the top 10 places to recreationally shop
4. Traditional department stores (8 percent), with Macy's among the top ten
5. Nonstore retailers (7 percent), including Web sites like amazon.com, another top ten favorite for shopping, and eBay, but also catalogs, television shopping channels, and other retailers that bring their storefronts into the shoppers' home

FIGURE 3.1 Most Important Factors in Store for Recreational Shopping

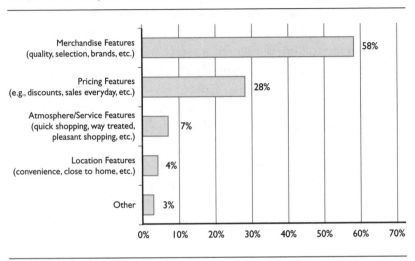

Quality Features Are Strictly in the Eye of the Beholder

Ranked second as the most important merchandise-related feature that influences shoppers in their choice of stores for recreational shopping is one that offers high-quality merchandise. What makes for a good quality product is highly category-specific. Features that distinguish a good quality man's dress suit are very different from those that characterize a good quality upholstered sofa or television set or computer. But perhaps even more differentiated than quality across product categories is how the individual shopper discerns the elements that comprise quality for him- or herself. Just like one person prefers tweed and another favors worsted wool or one likes two-button and another three, what is a quality suit for one shopper may well be very different from a quality suit for another. Quality is one of those words, like customer service, that can mean anything and everything and because of that, inevitably it means nothing at all.

For certain mechanical things, like automobiles and appliances and other products whose composition can be measured and quantified and tied directly to preferred attributes, like vitamins, food products and other consumables, quality features are more or less

---

SHOPPING FACTOIDS

Recreational shoppers' favorite stores for:

Necessities Shopping	Recreational Shopping
1—Wal-Mart	1—Best Buy
2—Target	Target
3—Kroger	2—Wal-Mart
4—Albertson's	3—Barnes & Noble
Safeway	Costco
5—Costco	Kohls
ShopRite	Macy's
Publix	4—Michael's
Meijer	Amazon
6—Stop & Shop	Borders
Giant	Home Depot
CVS	Lowe's
Giant Eagle	Old Navy
	Dollar Tree

Source: Unity Marketing, Recreational Shopping Report 2006

commonly understood. That is why the Consumers Union can make a business out of product testing, ranking, and reporting. But even in these categories where quality features are more widely recognized, there is a matter of individual taste and need. In a car, one driver might prefer an automobile that offers the quality of fast acceleration and speed, while another wants the quality of high gas mileage.

For shoppers, the perception that a store carries quality merchandise often is linked to the brands the store carries and nowhere is brand more important than in the realm of luxury shopping. Luxury marketers invest heavily in imbuing their brands with meaning. A luxury label transmits quality and style messages to the shopper, along with other key luxury values. A Chanel handbag costs more, but for many it is worth it because it is a classic bag design that will be appropriate this season, as well as next season. In fact, a Chanel bag promises to never go out of style, so it is made to last with high quality leathers and detailing. Coming from the house of Chanel, it also carries a message of impeccable good taste in the tradition of Coco Chanel. Is a $2,000 Chanel bag ten times better than a $200 Coach bag? That all depends on how one defines better quality. Objectively, there may be little difference in handbag performance; in other words they are the same sized bags so they can haul around the same amount of stuff. On the other hand, from a fashion perspective, it would be hard to argue that a Coach bag is of the same quality as one from Chanel.

A luxury label transmits quality and style messages to the shopper, along with other key luxury values.

Quality is highly subjective and that is why marketers and retailers have to understand the range of quality dimensions about which their shoppers make judgments and buying decisions. Then they need to make sure that they continue to enhance the quality, adding more and more value where the shopper believes that quality resides. A recent study conducted by my company Unity Marketing for American Express, the American Express Platinum Luxury Survey, investigated the quality dimensions of the fine dining experience among luxury consumers. Going into the research, we naturally assumed that quality luxury fine dining was largely about the food. What a surprise to discover that in luxury fine dining, consumers simply expected great food—that was largely taken for granted. Where they really discern a high-quality, luxury dining experience is not in the food that comes out from the kitchen so much as in the experience they have in the dining room. It is how the maitre d' welcomes them; how the coat check person cares for their coat; how the waitstaff serves their needs; the suggestions and services provided by the wine steward; how the table is set; and the music and lighting in the dining room. All the little nuances that happen in the dining room set a standard of quality and define luxury in the fine-dining experience. In other words, fine-quality dining is largely determined by what happens in the dining room, not what happens in the kitchen.

The learning for restaurateurs then is clear: they need to attend more closely to where luxury and quality reside for the consumer and that is in what is happening in the dining room and the experience of the patron rather than what is happening in the kitchen. But people get into the restaurant business largely because they are into food. Therefore, if a restaurant owner spends 80 percent of his or her time

focusing on the kitchen, he may well be misusing his time and resources, because quality for the customers happens primarily
through the dining room experience. That means the bulk of their
management time and resource needs to be directed toward the dining room and service experience where the customer really discerns
quality.

Find Out Where Quality is for the Shopper, then Deliver More and More of It

When it comes to the product features' variable in the shopper
formula, marketers and retailers need to investigate the many different dimensions of quality that characterize their product categories
and how the shopper ultimately perceives them. Many times the
shopper is nowhere near as attuned to the quality dimensions in the
products they buy as the product manufacturers or retailers. People
in the business know a whole lot more about product quality attributes than the shopper can ever be expected to because they live
and breathe the product day-in, day-out. However, they often take for
granted that the consumers are on their wavelength. They mistakenly
think the shopper intuitively understands the better quality that their
product brands promise to deliver. This is a very dangerous mistake
for a marketer or retailer to make. For example, shoppers today overwhelmingly believe that higher thread-count sheets naturally make
for better quality sheets. Therefore, a set of 600-thread count cotton
sheets are de facto better than 350-thread count sheets. That is not
necessarily the case. Paul Hooker, president of SFERRA Fine Linens,
a company with European roots that provides premium Italian sheeting and luxury linens to Neiman Marcus and Saks Fifth Avenue
among others, explains, "It's not thread count. That has become a
misnomer. Thread count is nowhere near the whole story. I recently
felt 1,000-thread count sheets from China that the salesman said, 'It's
1,000-thread count. It must be good.' But the quality of the yarn just
wasn't there. Quality is far more than just thread count."

Paul goes on to stress the role of the retailer in delivering the
highest quality to the shopper, thus reinforcing the role of the shop
in selecting higher quality brands for their shopper. "The luxury

---

SHOPPING FACTOID

Shopping for recreational items (DVDs, books, CDs, toys, entertainment equipment such as televisions, computers, iPods, etc.) is the top choice of passionate shoppers.

Items Shopped for Recreationally, Regularly/Occasionally

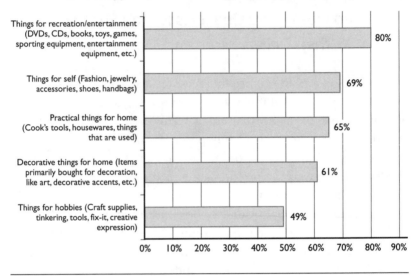

sheeting business from our perspective comes down to the reputation of the store that's selling it. That is number one. The customer comes in and knows if they are buying from that store, it is going to be quality . . . it is going to be good. The education has to come from the salesperson selling it."

There is an interconnection between an individual store and the quality and brands of the products they choose to carry. The quality of the products reflects back on how the shoppers perceive the quality of the store, as do the store's brand and the merchandising selections they make reflect on the brand names that are carried in the store. For example, when you shop at Neiman Marcus you have an expectation of finding superior quality luxury brands in that store. If you are in Neiman Marcus and happen upon a brand that you are not personally familiar with, you feel quite confident that Neiman Marcus' merchandisers selected that brand because of its outstanding quality. So the perception of quality merchandise reflects both on the perceived quality of the store and the quality of the brands that the store chooses to carry.

Bling Makes an Item Pop!— Add Value in Order to Attract the Shopper

When it comes to selecting one item over another, the one that pops, that has those unique product features that make the item distinctive, unique, individual, worthy of notice, and remarkable in some special way is the one that will be bought. The fact is, a product in a store has but a split second of time to attract attention and reel in the shopper to take a closer look. The bling factor, that special something that makes an impression, is how an individual product can be made to stand out.

> *The bling factor is what transforms the ordinary into the extraordinary and justifies the consumer paying significantly more for that extra special version.*

The product itself can incorporate bling through color, style, design, added features, and so on, or it can be crafted through in-store displays and attention-grabbing presentations. The bling factor is what transforms the ordinary into the extraordinary and justifies the consumer paying significantly more for that extra special version. Everybody everywhere craves more bling, which may range from a cashmere sweater accented with Swarovski crystals, a pair of jeans made extraordinary with embellishments that take the price from $30 to $300, or a sleek, super-sophisticated Vaio FJ series laptop which the Sony Web site describes as a "fashion statement—productivity tool."

Fashion and design can and should be applied to ordinary, everyday objects, like the elegant Purist Hatbox Toilet from Kohler, the 2005 *BusinessWeek* annual design award gold winner in consumer goods. This high-design toilet eliminates the tank so designers and decorators can "place the Purist where toilets have never been placed before," as *BusinessWeek* describes it. Shoppers are increasingly sophisticated about design and style because they are exposed to more upscale, sophisticated products through the shopping magazines they read, like Conde Nast's *Lucky* for women's fashion and *Domino* for home; the television shows they watch, HGTV, Style Network, Discovery Home and more; and the Internet, shoppers' most important shopping aid now and in the future. As a result, product marketers are going to have to work extra hard to add bling to their ordinary, everyday products. Shoppers will demand it because they won't pay attention to anything else.

Fashion needs to come to all categories of consumer goods which reflect the unique, distinctive eye of a designer. Uniqueness is one of the prime qualities that shoppers desire in the products they buy. Offering up unique items is a powerful influencer on places where people like to shop, as well as an important attractor for purchasing individual items. Carol, a trailing-edge baby boomer, says that finding unique things for her home and herself are one of her shopping hot buttons. She says, "I like looking for bargains and different things that no one else has. So I'll go to different stores and find something that is unique, for the house particularly—decorative type things or jewelry for myself. It's not necessarily trendy, but something that I really like." Another shopper describes a similar sentiment when discussing shopping at the Chicago-area Walter E. Smithe furniture store: "They have very unique things. They customize your couches and their vignettes are neat. They are a little higher priced, but you are not going to see yourself coming and going if you shop there."

For many national retailers who design and source their own products (think The Gap, Banana Republic, Ann Taylor and Ann Taylor Loft, Talbots, Brooks Brothers, and on and on) the lack of unique product may well prove to be one of their fundamental strategic flaws in the future—their Achilles heel. Maybe for a very basic pair of black slacks or a simple A-line skirt, buying off the rack at one of these stores will never become passé, but purchasing any kind of distinctive piece, say a print blouse, a dress, distinctive style jacket or outer garment, you run the risk of looking like dozens of other people who pick up the same outfit.

For holiday 2005 season J. Crew tried to address the ubiquitous overexposure of their styles with limited editions. From a limited edition jeweled silk camisole in papaya for $400 to a "Luxurious Italian radzimir silk faille gown" for a whopping $2,995, J. Crew made no claims about the number of items in their edition, but they controlled distribution through their catalog and Web site only. Their pricing strategy for the limited edition line, however, looked a little out of whack. Their ordinary camisoles weighed in around $100 or so. Offering a limited edition, even with embellishment bling, four times that price seems a little steep. Likewise with their $2,995 limited-edition gown, because a perfectly acceptable substitute gown with that "look for less" style is available from J. Crew for only $325.

For those who don't get Style Network, *The Look for Less* show is one of my personal favorites. Participants are given a $150 budget and the guidance of a celebrity stylist to reproduce a runway fashion look including shoes and accessories in a one-hour shopping spree. When it comes to fashion, anybody with lots of cash can drop $3,000 and get a great look. But it takes real skill and shopping savvy to stretch $150 and make it look like you spent over a thousand. Today it is really tacky to talk about how much you spent on an outfit when you dropped a bundle for it, but you get bragging rights when you put together a very special runway-worthy look for a song.

The Product Must Touch the Shopper's Hot Buttons

The product dimension of the shopping formula boils down to how much the product touches specific personal hot buttons for the shopper. People don't buy an item simply because it is good quality, made by this or that designer, and has bling or any other specific feature. They buy the product for the specific performance attributes it promises to deliver, whether those attributes are mechanical or emotional. The value inherent in quality is meaningful when translated into the way quality improves performance. The way the thing performs for the consumer, how it does what it is supposed to do, is measurable and meaningful from a consumer perspective, whereas quality is simply an attribute the thing possesses.

For example, I buy a $500 Dana Buchman jacket not because it is better quality than a similar $250 Liz Claiborne suitcoat, its corporate sister brand. Both brands may be made in the same factory, on the same machines, by the same operators. They will wear equally as long and whether I am wearing the Buchman or Claiborne jacket, I won't look like a rube. However, the Dana Buchman label, in many instances, offers a higher fashion performance as defined by better fabrics, finer details, crisper prints, and more fashion-forward styling. The challenge for marketers is to focus on the performance, how the thing does what it is supposed to do for the consumer, and not the thing itself.

The way the thing performs for the consumer, how it does what it is supposed to do, is measurable and meaningful from a consumer perspective, whereas quality is simply an attribute the thing possesses.

The key is getting those performance measures right for the product category and the target market. You can't come at this exercise with preconceived notions. Rather, you need to have a healthy dose of skepticism and challenge the basic assumptions and the conventional wisdom that operates in your company and within your industry. Just like consultants Marcus Buckingham and Curt Coffman did in their book about management thinking *First, Break All the Rules: What the World's Greatest Managers Do Differently,* product marketers need to be revolutionary in how they view their brands and how those brands connect with the consumers. They need to do something different from everyone else. They can't follow the market leader, rather, they need to find a sphere where their performance aligns with consumers' expectations and exceeds other brands in the same category.

All Chocolate May Taste Good, But Not All Deliver a Really Special Experience

Let's look at how this concept of enhanced performance plays out in the real world market for chocolate candy, a category most of us are familiar with. All chocolate candy brands perform similarly in several areas. All chocolate candy tastes good; some might be more appealing to one person's taste versus another, but they all have great taste. They all melt at body temperature, which translates into the unique mouth feeling you get only from chocolate candy. Furthermore, virtually 99 percent of all chocolate brands are affordable for everyone across all income categories. Maybe you have to buy smaller sizes in some brands, but most people can afford a taste of just about any chocolate brand. So in these three performance attributes (taste, mouth feeling, and affordability) most chocolate brands are pretty comparable.

And all chocolate is a treat, an indulgence, a special, personal luxury. Joan Steuer, the founding editor of *Chocolatier* magazine and president of Chocolate Marketing, a consultancy specializing in chocolate tasting, marketing and forecasting, explains that all chocolate delivers a luxury experience, "Chocolate is a luxury that can be a pick-me-up, a calm-me-down, a reward, an escape, an indulgence, a treat. Everybody has that special experience they love to indulge in, whether it's a bubble bath or a candle or that 'I'll just close my eyes and enjoy savoring the mouth-feel and the slow-melt of my favorite chocolate.'" Nevertheless, this indulgence quality is a performance value that certain brands deliver much better than other brands. A super-sized candy bar, even a regular-sized candy bar offered by Hershey's, Mars, and other mass brands, does not deliver that special feeling of indulgence and treat. There is something kind of gross about eating an entire chocolate bar alone. It doesn't leave you eager for another similar experience; rather, you feel guilty and ashamed of being so gluttonous. This is where chocolate brands that really play up the indulgence value enhance their product performance. Godiva chocolates are not sold in bulk, but in bite-sized pieces. Each piece offers a unique and different taste and mouth-feel sensations. The way the brand is packaged, sold, and offered hardly lends itself to gluttonous feasting, but instead to careful tasting and ultimate personal enjoyment.

Another performance value that adds bling to a product is its presentation and packaging. Chocolate candy is a special treat and is a favored gift item where the presentation experience matters. Gifting is all about the emotional connection between people and an important part of expressing emotions is a wonderful gift presentation. Likewise, Godiva performs significantly better as a gift than do other mass chocolate brands.

Performance in the world of chocolate brands is all about taking the ordinary and making it extraordinary by enhancing specific values that express and represent luxury to the consumer. In terms of crafting chocolate into delectable bite-sized pieces, less becomes more as the luxury indulgence value is enhanced. Packaging and superior presentation improves the performance of chocolate as a gift for either someone else or even for you.

Godiva

■ Delivering an Enhanced Luxury Chocolate Shopping Experience

Campbell Soup Company's Godiva brand has been described as the Starbucks of the chocolate world—the first national brand of luxury chocolate. Distinguishing the brand through its roots some 80 years ago in Brussels, Belgium, Godiva Chocolatier was introduced to the American market in 1966, and is noted for "the use of ingredients that are not only superior, but dramatically different in flavor and texture," the company claims.

While the company pays careful attention to maintaining the superior quality of its product, they also carefully manage retail distribution to deliver a luxury retailing experience. Michael Simon, formerly vice president of marketing and merchandising at Godiva, and now vice president/general manager of Pepperidge Farms snacks division, explains the critical role of delivering a full wraparound, 360° luxury experience to the customer: "While Godiva is in the business of selling the chocolate product, it really is selling an experience of pleasure. All the cues and touchpoints that we provide the consumer have to reinforce that notion."

"So we are very strategic in the way we communicate to them, including advertising, direct-mail pieces, point-of-sale, the kind of programming and promotions we execute. And our packaging, our product, our store environment is crucial too," Simon explains. Godiva Chocolatier operates more than 270 specialty boutiques in upscale malls and shopping locations, as well as distributing through finer department stores and specialty retailers. A mail-order catalog targeting gift occasions and a company Web site, *www.godiva.com,* extends their reach into multiple retailing channels.

"Within the Godiva store environment, we are very deliberate and disciplined around delivering a luxury experience—things like music, uniform, aroma, all of the sensual cues that consumers take in when they experience the brand," says Michael Simon, Pepperidge Farms.

The Godiva Chocolatier stores best express the total brand experience. Simon explains, "Within the Godiva store environment, we are very deliberate and disciplined around delivering a luxury experience—things like music, uniform, aroma, all of the sensual cues that consumers take in when they experience the brand."

Despite Godiva's premium price, in the $35–$50 per pound range, their creative packaging and presentation in boxes of two to four pieces on up make Godiva chocolates an affordable luxury. With a foothold as a marketer of luxury for the masses, Godiva is reinventing itself to express luxury in a more modern contemporary context. Simon explains, "We define our transformation as the difference between aspiration and inspiration. We want to continue to be aspirational to our moderate customers, yet we want to be inspirational for our 'class' customer as well."

Inspiration for the future of the Godiva brand comes with the recent launch of an ultra-premium line called the G Collection. Priced at about $100 per pound, the G Collection is far more than just an ultra-expensive Godiva chocolate. The brand is highly differentiated and positioned to appeal specifically to the prestige customer and includes 15 pieces designed by pastry chef Norman Love, formerly of the Ritz Carlton hotels. Handcrafted and hand-decorated, Love describes each piece as "an edible work of art." Even though the chocolate brand is priced in the stratosphere, through clever packaging, a nine-piece box retails for $25, the "sweet spot" for gifting.

Key to G Collection's prestige appeal is very limited availability due to its short shelf life and focused distribution in a select few retailers who can store and present the line properly. Adding to its luster, the line is only available from December 1 to February 14.

"That results in a real craving and desire from customers who demand the best and a truly special experience," Simon says.

Godiva has followed the success of the ultra-premium G Collection with a new Platinum Collection which the company describes as the "next generation of Godiva chocolates," priced between the company's flagship line and the G Collection.

By maintaining aspiration for the core Godiva line and innovating through the inspiration of the G Collection and Platinum Collection prestige lines, Godiva Chocolatier is reinventing itself as a more modern and contemporary luxury retailer. "We've even defined this line [G Collection] as the fusion of art and chocolate, a clear nod to our artisanal heritage expressed with a more contemporary sensibility. Our heritage reaches back 80 years ago when we were a one-shop chocolatier in Brussels and delivered our product in a very authentic, handcrafted way. That is something that distinguishes this line from our core Godiva line," Simon concludes.

CHAPTER FOUR

Affordability

BOTH AN ABSOLUTE AND A RELATIVE VALUE

"I don't own any of my own paintings because a Picasso original costs several thousand dollars—It's a luxury I can't afford."
PABLO PICASSO

The third variable in the quantum theory of shopping relates to Affordability, whether or not the price of the object is within the absolute or relative means of the buyer.

Propensity to buy = (Need + Features + Affordability) × Emotion^2

Absolute affordability is simply a measure of whether one's budget or bank account can stretch to meet the purchase. Relative affordability is the challenge that shoppers face more often. Relative affordability is the measure of how much a particular item is worth to me. Every one of us understands the concept of absolute affordability and virtually 99.9 percent of all Americans live under some constraints of absolute affordability—whether or not one can swing the payments for a personal jet and its monthly upkeep, or the monthly time-share fee for the "virtual" ownership of a personal jet, or simply the cost of a round-trip ticket on Jet Blue from New York to Los Angeles—the concept of absolute affordability is clear.

Where things become hazy is in the realm of relative affordability—how much is that purchase worth to me? What am I willing to trade off to make that purchase, for example, am I willing to cut back on my daily double lattes and brown-bag lunch to work every day for the next month in order to save for a week's Caribbean cruise?

To Encourage Buying, Retailers Push the Affordability Button Hardest

In examining the first three of the key attributes that influence the shopper's propensity to buy—Need, Features, and Affordability— the affordability hot button is the one that retailers and marketers push most aggressively and most consistently in order to stimulate shoppers to make purchases. As we have seen, retailers and marketers are largely powerless in the realm of need. They can't make anyone need their products, though they have some ability to make them desired. They also can pump up the product features to make an item highly desirable and better than all the rest, but in most instances people don't buy an item in the store simply because of its features. They need more than that and that is where the variable of affordability plays into the formula. Strictly depending upon the price, an item can be transformed from something you simply overlook and walk right by on the way to what you came shopping for into an item to die for and that has to be bought immediately.

Nearly two-thirds of passionate shoppers (61 percent) agreed with the statement, "I often buy things I see on sale that I don't strictly need, but are at such a good price that I can't pass them up." (Unity Marketing's Recreational Shopping Report 2006.) It is the price, and oftentimes the price alone, that moves the shopper to buy.

Even for Those Who Can Absolutely Afford It, They Don't Want to Pay Full Price

There is no question that the U.S. population as a whole is getting more affluent. The average household income in 2004 reached $60,528, up 40 percent from the mean of $43,133 in 1994, according to Census Department statistics. While over 55 percent of U.S. house-

FIGURE 4.1 Households by Income Range, 2004

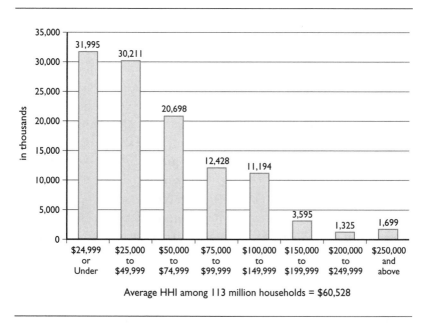

Average HHI among 113 million households = $60,528

holds have incomes under $50,000, more than one-fourth (27 percent) have household incomes of $75,000 and above.

Only 2 percent of U.S. households can reasonably claim to be "rich"—the 1.7 million that make $250,000 or more—and that segment's whole average income is $438,338. Because these households at the top of the income pyramid are bringing in nearly half a million a year on average, just about any kind of consumer purchase imaginable is easily within their grasp.

Nonetheless, in survey after survey that Unity Marketing conducted among the next rung down in terms of affluences (i.e., consumers in the top 25 percent of U.S. households with household incomes of $75,000 to $249,999), consistently we have found that the majority of luxury consumers made their last luxury purchase on sale or at a discount off the list price in each of the 14 luxury consumer product categories tracked but one. The sole exception is luxury cosmetics and beauty products, the most affordable luxury product category and the one where a single dominant competitor, Estee Lauder, long ago established the rules of cosmetics retailing. In luxury cosmetics, products are rarely discounted, but shoppers regularly enjoy promotional offers where they get goodie bags of sample-sized cosmetics with their regular purchase of $20 or so. The word from reliable sources in the Estee Lauder Companies is that a fairly high percentage of the company's revenues are directly attributed to sales during their promotional events. Thus even luxury cosmetics purchasers are taking advantage of discounts of the promotional variety.

In the elite world of the luxury consumers, discount prices are a big draw. People who can afford to pay full price simply don't have to. They know where to find the discounts and take advantage of them freely when shopping. When we think about pricing in the luxury goods realm, the focus isn't on the price, but the meaning. The affluent can pay more and are willing to pay more when the value (i.e., the meaning) is really there. Most often, however, they opt for paying less because they can easily find whatever they want for less.

Finding and getting a bargain yields tremendous emotional benefits to the shopper and that increasingly is the hinge on which the purchase decision rests.

In luxury shopping, price is far less about the absolute dollars charged and more about the meaning or the experience the item promises to deliver. When the value isn't there, then the meaning or the experience that drives the shopper becomes the thrill of getting a bargain. Finding and getting a bargain yields tremendous emotional benefits to the shopper and that increasingly is the hinge on which the purchase decision rests. The question for the shopper then isn't what the price is, but is it worth that price to me? Saving money, getting something for less is hardly the need, but it factors big in the realm of desire.

"We can afford all that we need;
but we cannot afford all that we want."
FRANKLIN D. ROOSEVELT

Discount Retailing Is the New Kid on the Block

Call it the Wal-Mart revolution in retailing, but shoppers have experienced a shift in how they look at discount shopping—a change from an occasional occurrence to something they expect to find everyday. When I was growing up through the 60s and into the 70s, most shopping was done in downtown department stores and a shopping trip downtown was usually a full-day affair. There were shopping centers with discount or value stores, think Woolworths and Kresges, dotted across the suburbs, but most people didn't shop in those stores unless they had to; translation: they couldn't afford to shop anywhere else.

In the old world of department stores, big sales happened a couple times per year—remember the January White Sales at the end of the season to make way for the new merchandise? There are still vestiges of this old way of bi-annual sales shopping remaining with some of my favorite luxury retailers—Neiman Marcus, Nordstrom, Saks Fifth Avenue—but more and more, these twice-a-year sales events are becoming anachronisms in the face of everyday low prices and steady, regular, routine discounting of select merchandise. This strategy is clearly paying off in the world of 21st-century retailing. While sales in traditional department stores languish, declining marginally from $215.657 billion in 2004 to $214.658 billion in 2005, the warehouse club and superstore retailing sector is booming, up 11.6 percent from $242.423 billion in 2004 to $270.771 billion in 2005, according to the U.S. Department of Census.

I grew up on the west side of Reading, Pennsylvania, just a stone's throw away from the granddaddy of all factory outlet stores, Vanity Fair. The Vanity Fair Factory Outlet officially opened in 1970 in a small corner of their main factory building and sold surplus hosiery, lingerie, and sleepwear. They expanded in 1974 by offering shopping space to other manufacturers who wanted to get rid of their overstocks, thus pioneering the multitenant outlet mall industry. Today the outlet center, now called VF Outlet Village, has grown to 450,000 square feet of space and houses outlet stores for designer brands like Dooney & Bourke, Coach, Geoffrey Beene, Tommy Hilfiger, Liz Claiborne, Jones New York, and a whole host of others, besides VF Brands such as Wrangler, Lee Jeans, and Vanity Fair.

The factory outlet industry as a whole is represented by its own association, The International Council of Shopping Centers, which includes some 225 outlet mall shopping centers made up of some 16,000 individual stores. The big draw of the outlet malls is virtually the same as at the very beginning of the trend: deep discounts. The VF Outlet Stores offer a straight 50 percent off list price discount on their first-quality Wrangler and Lee Jeans, along with all the other apparel and lingerie they sell in their stores. Other outlet stores have their own pricing policies, but the message is clear. Outlet shopping gives you more of your favorite brands for less. I still live close to the VF Outlet Village, plus the competing Tanger Outlet Center in Lancaster, Pennsylvania, that is anchored by the Polo Ralph Lauren outlet and 60 other stores including a Brooks Brothers outlet. As a result, I have a real disincentive to pay full list price for some of my favorite brands, like Coach, Dooney & Bourke, Polo, or Brooks Brothers, because their outlets are so accessible.

Shopping Is a Competitive Sport— She Who Scores the Most Stuff for the Least Amount of Money Wins

Today, rather than being something to hide, discount shopping is cool and what cool people do. In Unity Marketing's survey of passionate shoppers, over 80 percent of people who liked to shop agreed with the statement, "I like the satisfaction I get from getting a bargain." Three-fourths agreed with "Finding a bargain or a really good deal is what I enjoy most when shopping."

Shoppers are powerfully motivated to buy stuff on sale and they use cheap price as a justifier to buy something they don't need. They get a real thrill from scoring a great price. A young mother who loves to shop describes it this way: "It's like a game. I have a Ralph Lauren bedroom ensemble so I love going to TJ Maxx and Marshalls just to see if my sheets happen to be there. It's like a find. I wouldn't go shopping to buy those sheets at full price. That's part of the game . . . the entertainment."

As the French proverb says, "Appetite comes with eating; the more one has, the more one would have." Shoppers respond to sales so retailers offer more sales and deeper discounts thus increasing the expectation for shoppers to save even more, and on it goes.

This passion for discounts is so prominent in the market today that it was a major point of investigation in group discussions with shoppers. If we want to understand shoppers better, then we really need to understand this powerful drive to find it for less. It is important to mention that in my research the shoppers don't shop discount because they have to. Quite the contrary; the shoppers in Unity's recreational survey have an average income of $111,800, hardly shoppers forced to save money at Wal-Mart. The dominance of this passionate search for cheap demands a careful investigation of the many dimensions found in shoppers who aggressively pursue discount shopping. One of the most important and profound dimensions of the passion to get something for less is that shoppers don't need to do it.

Bargain Shoppers Need Lots of Extra Money to Buy All the Stuff They See On Sale

One of the greater ironies in this passion for cheap is how much extra money people actually spend to save money. They buy based upon price, not need; thus they spend on things they wouldn't otherwise purchase. This 50-something affluent shopper explains her most recent recreational shopping trip and what she scored on sale that she wouldn't have bought otherwise: "I went to Bloomingdale's because a friend of mine had a purse that I liked that she said she got there. So I went and found a great purse on sale. They were giving 15 percent off so I also found a skirt. So I got a skirt and a purse for about $250 which I wouldn't have bought if they hadn't been on sale." Even if what she bought was worth $300, $400 or $500, she still spent $250 extra making a purchase she wouldn't have made if it wasn't on sale.

Betty, another middle-aged discount shopper, explains the mental calculus that justifies her frequent sales purchases. "I am not one of these people who can go shopping just to look. It's no fun to just go look. I can't go somewhere and not come home with anything. I need to go out and find a deal for something that I'm going to need down the road." Not only does this shopper need lots of extra cash to pay for her sale purchases, but she also needs lots of extra room to store the stuff she buys until it is needed.

As the author of a book with the provocative title *Why People Buy Things They Don't Need*, I am frequently asked about the rising debt burden in America and other doom and gloom scenarios arising from our profligate spending habits. The fact is, people with means, like the passionate shoppers surveyed with average incomes over $110,000, have so much extra that they can buy stuff they have little use for now or ever just because it is on sale. This is reminiscent of the nutritional contrarians, like Walter Willett, chairman of the department of nutrition at the Harvard School of Public Health, who argue very convincingly that the obesity problem in America today has been exacerbated by, if not caused by, the advice to limit fat in our diets, along with the giant food marketers who exploit the "fat is bad" mantra with low-fat and diet foods. In other words, as low-fat foods are making us fat, buying stuff on sale is making us poor. But that is an argument that I will leave to people like Juliet Schor, author of *The Overspent American: Why We Want What We Don't Need,* and financial guru Suze Orman, of whom I am a fan. For my readers who are in business and are interested in getting their share of shoppers' spending, whether it is wasteful or not, I think it intriguing that it takes a whole lot of extra cash for people to take advantage of sales and buy all the stuff that they see for less.

Discount Shoppers' Satisfaction Comes from Beating the System

Shoppers get a kick out of finding things for less and part of the thrill is beating the system. Of course, they ignore the fact that for many stores, offering up deep discounts is actually part of the system, but no matter, one of the main joys of discount shopping is scoring a win against the retail giants. Holly, a full-time homemaker with college-aged children, says, "I like the satisfaction of getting a bargain. I never—well, I shouldn't say never—rarely pay full price for anything. I like to walk out of the store knowing I have done something really well in terms of getting a good deal." She continues, "I get a big bang for my buck. I enjoy getting value. That's part of the fun. It's a challenge."

Sharon, the 30-something mother of two boys, tells about her feelings of elation at finding matching $99 comforters on sale for $12 each in the clearance bin at JC Penney's. "That was as big a high as I could get. It really is almost a sickness. I got into my car [with the purchase of two deeply discounted comforters] and thought how I found something great. It really is a high to get a great deal." She expresses a tremendous feeling of accomplishment in making that purchase and she continues to derive satisfaction well after she made her score.

This shopper is hardly abnormal, but is fairly typical among the recreational shoppers in the discussion groups. Most shoppers get a real thrill from finding stuff on sale. Another shopper brags, "I'm definitely a bargain shopper. I hardly ever buy anything that is not on sale. My three favorite words in the English language are 'take an additional' . . ."

It Takes Real Skill, Talent, Persistence, and a Little Luck to Score a Deal

Bragging rights come from saving, not spending money. This is a real turnaround from the conspicuous consumption days of the 90s. Because people don't need to save the money and have plenty of extra to spend, the true challenge comes from finding it for less, as we see on the Style Network's *The Look for Less* show where designer runway outfits are recreated on the cheap in an hour's shopping spree.

This shopper perfectly expresses this new twist on the old conspicuous consumption lifestyle. "Some people brag about how much they spent on something, like this was $2,000. But I like to say, 'I got this for $30.' I'll brag about that because I feel fulfilled and proud about saving money. It isn't about spending a lot of money even if I can afford it."

Effective Discount Shopping Today Takes Experience and Knowledge

Shoppers today have an incipient professionalism about shopping that can't be ignored. The profound sense of accomplishment expressed by Sharon after finding the $99 comforters for $12 is akin to the feelings of professional achievement I get after giving a presentation to an audience where I feel we really connected. We all have a need for attainment and recognition for our accomplishments and many of these shoppers get it directly from the shopping experience itself—in how much money they saved. Shopping then becomes more than something they have to do for their families. They become quasi-professional shoppers investing time and energy to master the intricacies and the special skills required to be a successful discount shopper.

There is no question that with the explosion of shopping choices, the most effective bargain shoppers have to devote considerable attention to the endeavor. First of all, they have to have an incredible mental database of brands, stores, items, and comparable prices in order to take the true measure of the discount price offered. Second, they have to know of different retailers' markdown drills. They learn by trial and error how long something is likely to remain on display before it goes on sale and how many intermediate markdowns a store might take. They also have to know where coupons for extra discounts are published and other details that will lead to success in the search for cheap. Third, they have to be regularly scouting the stores seeking out those desired discounted items before somebody else gets them first. Success in discount shopping is not for the faint of heart or slow starters. It is a competitive sport and they need to keep up a constant training regime for ongoing success.

Success in discount shopping is not for the faint of heart or slow starters. It is a competitive sport and they need to keep up a constant training regime for ongoing success.

This shopper explains her strategy for finding things on the cheap: "I might wait a while, but in certain stores I know better. If you don't get it when you see it, you're never going to get it. Generally I will wait a bit, but there are things I won't wait for."

These quasi-professional discount shoppers have actually been trained by the stores themselves in how to work the system. Listen to this Parisian shopper: "I love to go to Parisian and Parisian has great sales. So for me to go to Parisian and pay full price for something is silly when I know it will shortly be marked down or I will find a coupon in the paper. I can't see myself paying full price. And they have great quality clothes. They've got all the top designers in my world at Parisian. But why pay full price when it will eventually go on sale?" Another shares a similar point of view: "I will never pay full price for something at Parisian or Dillard's or Macy's. Everything goes on sale. It just makes no sense to pay full price."

Nature or Nurture—Is Bargain Shopping Passed Down in the Genes?

I am not a bargain shopper, though I will visit factory outlets on occasion and certainly browse the sale racks in my favorite boutiques, but saving money is personally not a strong motivator for me. A minority of shoppers in the recreational shopping focus groups share my persuasion. Like me they feel that hunting down bargains is simply too much work and the rewards too few. This shopper shares my perspective: "If I like it, I'll buy it. I don't wait on a coupon or sale, because when you come back to the store, it is often gone. I don't have time to run back and forth to get a bigger discount. For me my time is more valuable."

Except for clothes and shoes, and I always "need" these things, I am one of the 23-percent minority of shoppers that don't agree with this statement, "If I see something at a really good price, I will buy it even if I don't need it right away." In this way I am very much like my mother. In her day she was an inveterate clotheshorse. She knew how to shop till she dropped and rarely went in for discount shopping. Rather than flocking to the sales, she stayed away from stores when sales were in progress in order to avoid the crowds. While she didn't have a career, my father's executive position required her to dress up for various corporate events and she took every opportunity presented as an excuse to go shopping. My father, on the other hand, was far more frugal—he had to be in order to support my mother's shopping habit. I clearly inherited my mother's shopping "genes" and was carefully trained in her style of shopping ever since I was a little girl. Like mitochondrial DNA, the shopping gene must be passed along from mother to child, because I missed out completely on my father's frugality.

In the focus groups we found that familial habits and patterns in shopping were clearly passed down through the generations. A grandmother in one of the groups told of her first shopping excursion with her granddaughter in her stroller. "There is a certain indoctrination that goes on in your family with sisters and daughters about shopping. When my granddaughter was only a few weeks old, we took her out to the mall. As we came into the vestibule area, I started to take off her blanket and outer clothing and just said to her, like you do with a baby, 'Honey, this is the mall and you're with Grandma. We're going shopping and if you want anything, you just let me know.' I was just soothing her and I had no idea there was a man standing behind me. He says, 'So that is how you women teach them to shop . . . when they are in diapers.' He was convinced that we program their minds. And even though I was just teasing, I really am teaching her to shop."

Another shopper tells how her daughter has been so fully indoctrinated into the discount shopping mindset that on a recent shopping trip the daughter wanted to make a really special shopping day by not starting first in the sale section. "Not long ago my daughter said to me, 'Can we make this a special day?' I asked her what she meant by special, and she said, 'Can we look at the rack that doesn't have the green Sale sign over it?' That was the first time I realized that my kids know that I go straight to the green sign every time."

Discount Shoppers Always on the Lookout

You've got to take advantage of every opportunity to be successful in discount shopping. Shoppers are always on the hunt for sale prices and spend time during most shopping trips doing the scout, which involves browsing around looking for anything priced low that strikes their fancy. It is through these impromptu scouting trips that discount shoppers get the lay of the land and learn the range of prices for specific product categories. Susan, a 40-ish mother of three under 12 years old, explains her strategy: "I don't have a lot of free time, so when I go shopping, it's usually because I need something, but I always go on scouting trips on the side. If I am shopping for shoes, I will always look around the store just to see, looking at the styles, what is new in decorating colors. This is my therapy. I like to spend money, but I feel especially great when I come home with a bargain and I sometimes come home with things I didn't plan on because they were such a bargain."

Successful bargain shopping demands an opportunistic approach in order to take advantage of the great finds you happen upon, as this shopper explains: "I shop all year for Christmas and for clothing. If you see something on sale, even if you are shopping for something else, you have to take the time to try it on. If you are out looking for a baby outfit for a shower, but find a $100 gown on sale, you've got to take it to the dressing room because it is usually priced at $200. You have to do that on the spur of the moment because you will never find it when you really need it. You have to be watchful to find those sales."

Another shares how effective this opportunistic shopping strategy is for her: "I look at shopping as a hobby. I don't shop for anything specific. I need to go out and find a deal for something that I am going to need down the road. Some people say I have to go out and find a black dress, but I've never done that in my life. I always have a dress just because I've bought it when I found a deal."

Being a Successful Bargain Shopper Takes Dedication and Commitment

It is pretty clear from this discussion that the concept of bargain shopping transcends the simple need to save money. These shoppers have a passion for finding a $200 jacket on the sale rack for $100 that is akin to winning the lottery. Saving $100 by spending an extra $100 for a jacket on sale gives a thrill where squirreling away $100 into a bank account couldn't begin to give that kind of emotional thrill.

These shoppers have a passion for finding a $200 jacket on the sale rack for $100 that is akin to winning the lottery. Saving $100 by spending an extra $100 for a jacket on sale gives a thrill where squirreling away $100 into a bank account couldn't begin to give that kind of emotional thrill.

This phenomenon when viewed through the lens of the retailer is both a blessing and a curse. The simple fact is that the majority of shoppers responds and responds very strongly to the sales lure, but as they learn more and more about the markdown tactics of retailers (and it takes experience to learn the drill), they come to expect deeper and deeper discounts. Where 10 or 20 percent off might have given them a thrill before, today they want 50 or even 60 percent off.

With retailers' racks so overstuffed to begin with, any reasonable shopper has learned that an awful lot of what is packed in there has got to be marked down to move it out soon. Shoppers have been trained to expect just that, and so they are discouraged to pay full price except in very rare circumstances. If you don't need it to begin with and you are going to be back in the store in a week or so anyway, why wouldn't the savvy discount shopper check back in just to see if the price has dropped?

One shopper in focus groups explained her view of the markdown drill: "If I see a shirt for $75 last week, but it is on sale for $37.50 this week, then I know it was overpriced by $37.50 before." Given the rampant rate of discounting, shoppers simply don't believe the list price is really the price any longer. They hold out to see what the real price is going to be once those initial and intermediary markdowns are taken.

Retailers need to explore other ways to stimulate the shopper beyond the dumbed-down 50-percent-off sales approach. Providing shoppers with more value, rather than simply offering up cheap prices, is the real ticket. Signs are that even Wal-Mart, who led the way in deep discounting, is embracing the concept of value, as they open up a new, more luxurious store in Plano, Texas, offering a much wider selection of higher, but value-priced, products. Inevitably, retailers and marketers pay the price for an overstocked selling floor and deep discounts—

and that is corporate profits. They need to tap into other emotional drivers, and there are many discussed in the next chapter besides just offering up a sale that will stimulate shoppers and get them in the mood to spend money. These other emotional stimulants, while they may take a bit more planning, work, and strategy to implement, ultimately yield greater profits and more long-term business success.

Aerosoles

■ Where Value Is a Core Attribute of the Product and the Shopping Experience

Aerosoles, the shoe company famous for comfort, is not thought of as a discount retailer, along the lines of Payless or DSW, yet value is an essential quality associated with the brand. For Aerosoles value is not just a euphemism for cheap; it actually means what is says, giving more value to the consumer for the amount of money spent. Kimberley Grayson, senior vice president of marketing at Aerosoles, says, "For us a huge part of our success is the value, and we absolutely believe that value is not a price formula. It is the whole experience coming together to create value for her [the shopper]—great sales associates, wonderfully merchandised store, product that's at a quality level so that she's surprised at the price. She would have bought it even if it were expensive. So the whole experience is coming together to deliver value and a style that is trend right. She can see that by comparing a $60 or $70 pair of Aerosoles with other brands. Here she gets the same wonderfully styled product that she sees merchandised elsewhere at a much higher price and sold in an environment with far less service and support."

Taking a totally different angle from that of many marketers where exclusivity is valued, Aerosoles is motivated to get more people, rather than just a select few, wearing their shoes. The goal is to get happy shoppers who enjoy Aerosoles' extra level of comfort and the whole in-store shopping experience to pass the word along. Offering up their products at an attractive, affordable price is key to this strategy. "We have at our heart and the core of our concept that value is what we are all about, and we're going to pass that value back to the customer. Other companies build in higher margins than we do to fund their marketing initiatives. For us our best marketing initiative is word of mouth. Our goal is to get more shoes onto a woman's feet, so that she tells her friends and her family and the word starts to spread. That is powerful and we recognize that it's an important marketing element in addition to what we do with advertising and other forms of consumer marketing," Grayson says. Surely being in control of product design, buying materials in bulk, and selling them through multiple channels is important to the company's pricing model, but Aerosoles is driven by a mission to broaden the market for their products to more and more women who want stylish shoes served up with an extra measure of comfort.

"We have at our heart and the core of our concept that value is what we are all about, and we're going to pass that value back to the customer," says Kimberley Grayson, Aerosoles.

A central element in getting the word out about Aerosoles is the company's commitment to multichannel distribution, including wholesale through department stores and independent retailers, Internet, direct-mail catalog, and 126 branded retail stores in the United States and another 100 overseas. Grayson explains the rationale behind the company's branded stores: "Our first channel of distribution was wholesale through independent specialty stores, department and chain stores. Then we branched out into our own proprietary retail store in order to have a location where customers who were already loyal to the brand could come and find a wider selection of Aerosoles products, as well as give us a platform to branch beyond casual into dress shoes, sports shoes, tailored styles, and give her all these products together. We also want to be in markets where we did not have strong wholesale distribution, but mainly we wanted to accomplish more for our loyal customers and expand the presence of Aerosoles into new marketplaces."

The branded retail store isn't the primary communicator of brand values, however: the sales staff in their stores is. The layout, design, and ambiance of the stores promote the brand, but the sales associates add the missing ingredient that makes the brand personal. "A lot of women enjoy shopping for the complete Aerosoles experience. So the stores give us a greater breadth of assortment to be able to show, but the ability to talk to and educate consumers about our products and what makes them special is critical. So it's in what the sales associates bring into the environment that makes the whole experience really special. They add the energy," Grayson says.

Store design and location is selected to draw the customer into the store to interact with the staff and the products. "In our window displays and the interactive displays we put around the store, we want somebody to see the product and feel it with their eyes. We are very much a tactile product, so we have incredibly soft, flexible, comfortable shoes. We want that to come through in the visual imagery and stop the shopper in her tracks. We have only about eight seconds to get her as she walks past the storefront so we want something to capture her attention by sending a stylish message and pulling together a trend that is so visually compelling that we pull her into the store to give her some special messages about the product," Grayson explains.

The whole experience works to further the company's goals of getting more Aerosoles shoes on more women's feet. Grayson says, "We go for locations where we know that customers are shopping. We want it to be accessible to her, not in some exclusive area that's hard to get to or out of the way, but we expect our store to be a destination. Our stores are always inviting with an open door, both literally and figuratively, because if the weather is nice, we have our door open at all times. We want customers to come in and touch the product. We invite customers to come in and try the products on; in fact, some of our promotions revolve around try-on promotions. So we incent our shoppers to come in and have a dialogue with us, experience our products and our price point. Ultimately our goal is to make us accessible to all women and that is the real value."

CHAPTER FIVE

Emotion^2

PUSHING THE SHOPPERS' EMOTIONAL
HOT BUTTONS

Carrie: Honey, if it hurts so much, why are we going shopping?
Samantha: I have a broken toe, not a broken spirit.

FROM SEX AND THE CITY

The fourth and pivotal variable in the quantum theory of shopping is emotion-squared. Emotion plays off and magnifies all the other factors—Need, Features, Affordability—to make the item irresistible.

Propensity to buy = (Need + Features + Affordability) $\times$ Emotion^2

Making the impact of the emotional component even more important in the formula is that its value is squared or doubled. Retailers with their ongoing emphasis on the material goods or the merchandise they sell are in real and growing danger of ignoring or at least giving short shrift to this most crucial of all factors in the shopping formula. Why? Simply because it is a whole lot harder to transform the experience of shopping to make it delightful for the shopper than it is to simply order another truckload of stuff, price it cheap, and stock it on the shelves. A retail store is more than just a cash register and a bunch of merchandise displayed on shelves. It represents a shopping experience for the customer that is infinitely more than just going to a store and buying stuff. In this chapter we explore the transcendental nature of the shopping experience and how the shoppers' emotions dominate the buying decisions made in the store.

A retail store is a more than just a cash register and a bunch of merchandise displayed on shelves. It represents a shopping experience for the customer that is infinitely more than just going to a store and buying stuff.

Emotions Transform Need into Desire

As the shopping formula makes clear, shoppers' need in and of itself is only a small part of the reason why people buy. Rather, it is the impact of emotion and how the shopper interprets their emotional desire as a real and compelling need that ultimately tips the scale toward "buy." As we scan across the consumer landscape, there is one place we find that true need—shopping for a thing that is a necessity for contemporary life—plays virtually no role in the shopping formula and that is in the $1 trillion American luxury market.

There are lots of definitions floating around about what qualifies as "luxury" today. The word luxury comes with so much baggage that the image it conjures in people's minds may bear little or no resemblance to a clear and concise marketplace definition that people like me who study the luxury market try to propose. In my analysis of the luxury market I let the consumers define what luxury is for them, rather than applying some external, product-centric definition on the term. That makes luxury very subjective, because frankly it is very subjective. What I consider a luxury is very different from what you consider luxury or your neighbor considers luxury, and who can argue that each of our unique, subjective definitions of luxury is wrong? The consumers themselves are the final arbiter of what luxury is today, not some external authority like a designer, company marketer, advertiser, or anybody else.

Because it is so highly subjective, it is really hard to come up with a definition that fits all circumstances and all situations. However, in my work with luxury consumers and how they view the luxury products realm, the very best and most inclusive definition that I have discovered is that luxury is simply "more more," a consumer's phrase, not mine. Luxury is "more more," meaning it is more than anyone

---

SHOPPING FACTOID
Luxury Goods Market Potential Is $1 Trillion

One trillion dollars is an estimate of the amount luxury consumers spent in total buying luxury goods and services in 2005, based upon total purchase incidence and average amount spent by luxury households on specific luxury goods categories multiplied by the total number of affluent households in the U.S. economy (for this calculation we use just the number of affluent households with incomes over $100,000, or 17.8 million).

Luxury Market Potential in Millions

	2004	2005	Percentage change
Home	$313.8	$276.4	−11.9%
Personal	$107.9	$113.4	5.2%
Auto	$267.3	$266.0	−0.5%
Experiential	$209.1	$346.3	65.6%
Total	$898.0	$1,002.2	11.6%

Source: Unity Marketing, Luxury Report, 2006

needs, over the top more, the pinnacle more, the ultimate more, the extraordinary more. So in any class of goods you might look at, you find the discount or the value brands at Target, Wal-Mart, or Old Navy; and the normal, everyday, the regular brands at J.C. Penney's, Sears, or The Gap; the premium brands, i.e., items priced higher than the norm but not yet into the realm of luxury, like Ann Taylor, Banana Republic, and Talbots; and then luxury, at the "more more" range found in stores like Nordstrom, Neiman Marcus, Lord & Taylor, Saks Fifth Avenue, and Barneys. Personally I would class DKNY as luxury, yet there is even another realm above that brand in the Donna Karan line; maybe that is the luxe-luxury or the "more more and then some more" range.

So depending upon who you are and your particular vantage point, there inevitably will be overlap between products in one range or another, but the consensus definition, the one that best fits today's world of luxury, is that luxury is very definitely more than what anyone really needs. Therefore, we all might need a pair of jeans and we can buy a very good quality, long lasting, nationally recognized brand in the $50-$60 range and under. Nobody needs to pay $200 to $300 for a pair of jeans. Anyone can find perfectly good substitutes for far less, so who can argue that a pair of $200 Citizens of Humanity distressed jeans, with requisite holes adorning them, is anything but a luxury?

The luxury market ultimately is one driven solely and totally by desire, not need. Savvy retailers at all levels in the retailing sphere, from Wal-Mart and Target, J.C. Penney and The Gap, are taking a lead from the luxury marketers and retailers in order to move from their more or less needs-based retailing model into one driven by desire. Satisfying shopper desires, not their needs, is where the real serious money is to be made. It is tapping into the emotion behind all consumer purchases, from the most mundane to the most extraordinary, and appealing to shoppers' emotional desire, not the normal, physical, everyday need.

One important lesson we learn from luxury marketers is that they move their target customers up the ladder to greater and greater levels of luxury. They get you hooked at one level of luxury or wonderfulness, only to draw you to spend more at an even more wonderful or luxurious level. Ralph Lauren has got this luxury scale model down pat with his ultra-luxurious, over-the-top Runway Collection where outfits go for $3,000 and above; the luxury Black Label brand where cashmere sweaters retail for $700 or so; the Blue Label and Lauren brands in what one might call the premium range where you won't find cashmere but cottons, silks, and wools offered at competitive premium prices. So a shopper starts at the Blue Label level with a nicely styled silk knit sweater, only to be drawn up to the Black Label for something a little bit more special and luxurious. Maybe not a lot of shoppers that start at the Blue Label graduate all the way up to the Runway Collection, but no matter, they are still sporting one of the Ralph Lauren labels and living the Ralph Lauren lifestyle vicariously through his designs.

Colleen, the mother of two teenage daughters, describes how she got hooked on luxurious 400-count sheets, "One luxury that I recently discovered which is wonderful is 400-thread count sheets. I didn't think that sheets were a luxury, but these are a real luxury. I bought them on sale, so they were a pretty good deal. But they are so wonderful. These luxury sheets I didn't know about, then I got them and now I am hooked. For me they are a luxury that is essential too."

While luxury marketers lure shoppers up the luxury ladder, there is also a reverse trend going on with all things luxury inevitably losing some of their specialness, as more people become used to them. Luxury is in constant motion by being reinterpreted down from the classes to the masses. There is a natural gravitational pull with the transformation of luxury from the extraordinary to the ordinary. Colleen expresses this reinterpretation in the world of luxury sheets. What she once considered luxury, i.e., 400-thread count sheets, are now her ordinary, everyday sheets. When she wants to experience the same luxury thrill again in bedding as she did when she moved up to 400-thread count sheets, she is going to have to go for even more specialness, maybe 600-thread count Egyptian cotton sateen over a European goose down featherbed. Retailers thus must continue to enhance the level of luxury that they offer to move the needle from need to desire, where the real money lies. I call this process where retailers and marketers must continually inflate the luxury value of the goods and services they offer "luxflation," the process by which retailers and marketers can counteract the inevitable downward gravitational pull of luxury from the extraordinary to the ordinary.

Another important lesson from the luxury market about building shoppers' desire is to get to the root of why people want, crave, and have a passionate desire for more and more luxury.

Another important lesson from the luxury market about building shoppers' desire is to get to the root of why people want, crave, and have a passionate desire for more and more luxury. Surely, like Colleen's 400-thread count sheets, luxury satisfies our desire for creature comforts, a most powerful and compelling drive for all humans. However, at the luxury level it is even more than simply seeking more creature comfort.

For luxury consumers the desire for luxury is a reflection of their self-actualization needs. We touched upon this motivator in Chapter 2 in the discussion of Maslow's Hierarchy of Needs, but it is so profound in the luxury market that it is worth looking at again.

The need above all needs that luxury consumers most actively pursue is self-actualization, because they presumably have all the lower-level needs satisfied—physiological and safety needs most definitely; love and affection needs hopefully through their families because the vast majority of luxury consumers are married and have children; needs for esteem derived from accomplishment in their jobs and professions, because 90 percent of luxury consumers in American today arose from middle-class backgrounds and so are self-made. Their ultimate pursuit as humans and as shoppers is toward self-actualization, that personal transformation that helps people create a more idealized, self-actualized version of themselves.

Surely fashion has its own rewards, but my personal desire to dress fashionably, to enhance my figure by accenting the positives and disguising the negatives, to present a fashionable, contemporary, and youthful yet sophisticated image through my dress is actually a reflection of my self-actualization needs. I can clothe my body, and be super comfortable and warm in sweat pants and a hoodie. Heaven forbid that anyone besides my husband and sons see me dressed like that. The image I want to project to the world is a self-actualized version of me, dressed to the nines to reflect the person I ultimately want to be. It is that drive that powers me as a consumer of fashion magazines, fashion television, and most importantly, fashion apparel in the stores.

Fashion is my thing, but every shopper has that special self-actualized image that he or she is trying to create for his or her self. In discussions with many women, they often self-actualize through their home. Their homes, how their homes are decorated, cleaned, organized, and presented to the world, are their canvases for personal transformation, so their spending focuses on home-related things. Other women self-actualize through their children, so they shop for their own clothes at TJ Maxx or Kohl's, but spare no expense for fashion for their kids. Many men self-actualize through technology or technical accomplishments; thus, they buy new computers or new tools to help them self-actualize through these mediums. Further, most people have several areas in which they self-actualize, so while buying a new computer may not give me the same thrill as buying a new outfit, I self-actualize through my professional accomplishments and I need, or more correctly desire, the latest and greatest new computer system to help me achieve new levels of career transformation.

The most important lesson all retailers and marketers can learn by studying the luxury market is very simply, "as above, so below." Because luxury is in constant motion, pulled down by gravity from the extraordinary to the ordinary, we find that what was hot in the luxury market last year, last month, even yesterday, inevitably is what is hot in the mass market today and tomorrow. Thus the plasma screen televisions that only a few years ago were available only to the super-wealthy at a hefty $10,000 price tag today you can pick up for under $1,000 at Wal-Mart. If you want to know where the mass market will be moving in the next couple of years, watch the luxury market closely today in order to predict the future.

While material goods can help one achieve self-actualization and transformation, the true lasting, most profound changes come through experiences.

What I see so clearly taking precedence in the luxury market today that will inevitably hit the mass market consumers shortly is a continued pursuit of self-actualization through experiences. While material goods can help one achieve self-actualization and transformation, the true lasting, most profound changes come through experiences. Unity Marketing's Luxury Tracking Study, a quarterly survey conducted among 1,000 affluent consumers about their luxury purchases, has consistently found that luxury consumers gain their greatest luxury satisfaction from luxury experiences, like travel, dining, entertainment, sporting events, museums, spas, and other experiences, as opposed to home luxury purchases or personal luxury purchases, notably fashion, jewelry, and other personal luxuries.

Not just the luxury consumers, however, but the mass market consumers as a whole are going experiential. Psychologists Leaf Van Boven and Thomas Gilovich published a study about consumer happiness and satisfaction in the *Journal of Personality and Psychology* (vol. 85, no. 6, 2003) called "To Do or to Have? That is the question." In their research they never used the word "luxury" and they studied consumers across all income levels, not just the affluent, and they

Greatest Source of Luxury Satisfaction

From which do you derive your greatest source of luxury satisfaction and happiness?

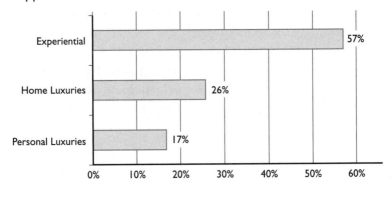

Source: Unity Marketing, Luxury Report 2006

found basically the same thing. They found consumers' greatest source of happiness did not derive from the material goods they bought, but from their acquisition of "life experiences." They write, "'The good life,' in other words, may be better lived by doing things than by having things."

These findings about the shift to experiences give a clear wake-up call to retailers and marketers everywhere. The goods they create and sell simply are not enough anymore for shoppers. They desire more fulfillment, more happiness, more personal transformation, and more self-actualization than material goods can ever provide. That is why at its most basic level, retailers must embrace an entirely new business paradigm that focuses on the shopping experience, not the things or merchandise that people shop for. The new experiential retailing paradigm transcends the material world into a whole new experiential realm.

That is why at its most basic level, retailers must embrace an entirely new business paradigm that focuses on the shopping experience, not the things or merchandise that people shop for. The new experiential retailing paradigm transcends the material world into a whole new experiential realm.

Nordstrom

■ In Thrilling the Shopper Emotionally, They Set the Standard for Experiential Shopping Today

When I talk to shoppers, I hear a lot about how people like this store and appreciate that store, but rarely do I hear someone say they "love" a particular store, and really mean it. Yet when the topic of Nordstrom comes up, "love it" is what you regularly hear. There is something about the Nordstrom shopping experience that is really magic and they seem to get it right consistently. Shoppers are just passionate about shopping there.

Here is how one enthusiastic Nordstrom shopper describes the shopping experience:

My favorite store is Nordstrom because it's an experience to walk through there. They usually have someone playing the piano. And everything is organized nicely, and they have wide aisles. And you can just walk through and listen to music and look at all their pretty things. Their shoe department is like no other. And I just think they have a great selection. Everyone who works there will do anything you need. They have great customer service. They don't have sales very often, but when they do, they're very good. If they don't have something in the store, they will find it for you. It is wonderful. And it's just an experience. It's relaxing. It just feels luxurious to go in there.

From Nordstrom's roots as a specialty shoe store founded by John Nordstrom in 1901 Seattle, today Nordstrom Inc. operates about

150 stores in 27 states, including 95 full-line specialty apparel stores, 49 Nordstrom's Rack stores specializing in off-price fashion, one free-standing shoe store, and two clearance stores. In 2000, the company acquired Façonnable, a chain of French fashion boutiques based in Nice, that today includes 32 international Façonnable boutiques primarily in Europe, and five U.S. shops.

While the company went public in 1971, it has remained committed to its founder's vision: to offer the customer the best possible service, selection, quality, and value. The exceptional level of customer service the store is famous for, along with the superb in-store experience shoppers enjoy, give meaning to this commitment. The results speak for themselves: Net sales in 2004 reached $7.13 billion, up 10.6 percent over the previous year. Their 2004 annual report credits the overall shopping experience: "Our continuous progress in delivering a quality shopping experience to our customers is resulting in increased value to our shareholders . . . Overall, 2004 was the best year in our company's history."

Explaining the company's marketing philosophy, executive vice president of marketing Linda Finn, in a recent interview with *Brand-Week* magazine (November 7, 2005), says, "We're proud of the fact that we have outperformed our peer group average for the past 29 consecutive months. We never take that for granted and are always trying to give our customers something new and a reason to buy." Both superior customer service and trend products are key elements to the company's success. In fact, the company views providing "compelling products" along with superior service as the foundation of the customer experience. That translates into Nordstrom presenting a continually changing assortment of fashion that their shoppers feel compelled to buy.

Their merchandising strategy, therefore, focuses on the customers' lifestyles, rather than individual product categories. For example, their woman's fashion home page gives shoppers choices of Narrative looks, which are described as "effortless fashions for work, for play, for evening, for day . . . beautifully styled, instantly gratifying;" Individualist, which presents a more contemporary fashion-forward selection of looks; and Encore, sophisticated styles for the plus-sized woman. "Customers want fashion and we strive to be a leader in the marketplace with products and trends. One of the core elements of what we do is give customers a reason to buy something new," says their annual report.

Nevertheless, while the company stresses the in-store experience, Nordstrom recognizes that today's shopper also wants other types of shopping experiences besides browsing through the store. Catalogs and, increasingly, the Internet offer at-home shopping convenience to the Nordstrom service mix. They have been one of the early pioneers in Internet retailing and have been enormously successful in converting browsers to buyers, not just in the store aisles, but online as well. Finn continues, "We've always believed that the store experience is critical to our success, so we have always been totally driven by word-of-mouth [advertising]; however, people are changing the way they communicate today." In 2004, Internet sales increased 53.1 percent, as they pursue a strategy to shift catalog customers to the Internet.

Based on the testimony of appreciative shoppers in discussion groups—"I love Nordstrom, that's my favorite," another shopper says—and as the company's financial results prove, Nordstrom is "delivering a great shopping experience . . . that's rewarding for so many customers," as their annual report states.

Emotions Touch Off and Magnify All the Other Factors in the Shopping Formula

As we have seen, emotion takes the lead in the quantum theory of shopping. The thrill people feel, their excitement, their longings, transform need into desire. Emotion plays up product features, making them appear even more attractive, more compelling, and more desirable. Moreover, emotion helps interpret price, either by making the shopper feel excited about finding a bargain or willing to stretch their budget to pay a price higher than they would like.

Propensity to buy = (Need + Features + Affordability) × Emotion^2

Let's look more closely at how emotion touches shoppers.

Product Features Touch Hot Buttons
to Spark Purchase

As we discussed in Chapter 3, few shoppers buy *because* of product features. Rather, the combination of specific product features spark purchases by touching off emotional hot buttons in the consumer. Therefore, how the product promises to deliver emotional rewards and benefits to the shopper needs to be the focus of all merchandising efforts for the retailer.

My husband, Greg, like the middle-aged men in my family and among my friends, simply hates clothes shopping. He tolerates my fashion addiction, but he has been totally lacking in any kind of interest or desire to shop for clothes, until recently when he discovered Lucky Brand Stores. He wandered into a store quite by accident on a shopping trip with our 15 year-old musician son who was drawn to a retro Bob Dylan t-shirt displayed in the window. From that day on, he was hooked. For him stepping through the door was like transportation back to the '60s in a time machine. The music was his, not our son's generation's music. The clothes and styles were his styles, though I am afraid to say that the fashion also appeals to our son, too, at $100 for a pair of jeans—moderately priced Old Navy jeans will never do for him now. He has bought logo sweatshirts, a corduroy jacket, t-shirts, jeans, even a scarf, and is a walking advertisement for the brand. Almost anything they offer up is his cup of tea—and, did I mention, the prices are hardly cheap, though not in the stratosphere either.

The product really touches all my husband's retro-hippie hot buttons, but the store environment as well as the young people who work in the store have consistently been exceptional. There are three stores in close proximity to our home and in every one they know him by name, remember his favorites and chat him up with news about the last retro rock' n' roll stars coming to town. In our travels we have also visited shops across the country and we have found the kids who work in the store are cool, super-friendly, and fun to shop with. Every one of them knows how to have a meaningful conversation with an adult—try to find that in some youth-skewing stores like Abercrombie—and they all will bend over backwards to help.

Finding Something Wonderful for Less Makes You Feel Like You Won the Lottery

As we explored in Chapter 4, the emotions sparked by finding a good deal can often be the only reason to buy, trumping need and features. For many, finding something cheap is all it takes to make a purchase. In Unity's recreational survey, 61 percent of shoppers agreed with the statement, "I often buy things I see on sale that I don't strictly need but are at such a good price that I can't pass them up."

Absolute affordability, i.e. whether or not a particular purchase fits into one's budget, is far less of an issue today than relative affordability, meaning, can I make that purchase fit into the budget? Emotions and feelings are the leverage factor that stretch and squeeze a particular purchase to fit the budget.

Discount shopping today is a competitive sport and the shopper who scores the most stuff for the least amount of money wins.

Shoppers get an absolute kick out of buying things for less. It is like they hit the lottery jackpot when they find a $500 jacket for $250. Discount shopping today is a competitive sport and the shopper who scores the most stuff for the least amount of money wins.

Admittedly, some shoppers are skeptical about too frequent and too rampant discounting. When it comes to my passion for fashion, I figure if it ends up on the sale rack, then it must not be too fashionable because nobody else wants it. Don't get me wrong, I will buy on sale, like the velvet three-quarter length coat I found at DKNY for more than $100 off the list price, but that isn't my primary or personal motivator. In fact, I tend to look askance at the sales rack because I just don't trust that the fashions I find there are as cutting edge as I want them to be. My thinking is if the styles moved so slowly that nobody else wanted to buy them, then why in the world should I buy them? It is a variation on the famous Groucho Marx line "I refuse to join a club that would have me as a member." If the price is too cheap, it simply can't be something that I would want.

SHOPPING FACTOID
Merchandise Determines the Store; Finding Bargains
Dominates When the Shopper Is In the Store

While merchandise-related features influence the shopper most in his or her selection of a store in which to shop, finding bargains and discounts is where they get the most joy when they are in the store shopping.

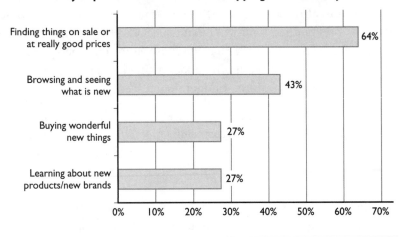

Very Important Activities When Shopping Recreationally

Source: Unity Marketing's Recreational Shopping Survey, 2006

Other shoppers also think that what's to be found in the bargain bin is more likely to be trash than treasure. For this affluent shopper sharing in the focus groups, bargains often aren't bargains at all because they are not as good as the full priced items. "I don't shop for bargains. To me, they don't hold up. So it's not a value there. For me when you pay more, normally it equates to a better quality, better service, and that's what I like." Another shopper who disdains the bargain aisles says, "You can pay more money, but then you are getting the value, as opposed to buying something cheaper. The cheaper stuff you may not like as much, so you don't use it and it becomes a waste. Or it just doesn't hold up so you have to buy it again and again."

Shoppers like me and some of the women in the focus groups, who are not necessarily hot for bargains, are the exception, though, not the rule. That is why the majority of retailers today play this factor up more than any other factor in the shopping formula. Dangling a 50 percent off price tag on merchandise that should never have been bought by the store's merchandisers in the first place can suddenly move the immovable, but the price retailers and marketers pay for pushing product out the doors with discounts is profit. How much better would it be to delight customers with wonderful merchandise that they are perfectly willing to pay full price for?

Retailers Can Play Off a Whole Host of Other Emotional Factors to Encourage Shoppers to Spend More

With their overriding emphasis on product and price, retailers often overlook the many varied dimensions of the shopping experience that they could use to play to the shoppers' emotions. For example, just as many shoppers (62 percent) agree with this statement, "I like to shop at certain stores because of the special treatment and services that I receive" as with this statement about the thrill of bargain shopping: "I often buy things on sale that I don't strictly need but are at such a good price that I can't pass them up" (61 percent). While sales and discounts draw people into stores, offering up a really special shopping environment every day, like Nordstrom does, is a powerful strategy to attract people to shop. Nearly 70 percent of people who love to shop agree with this statement, "I have a favorite store(s) that I regularly shop at because I find the shopping experience there very pleasant."

This is a wake-up call to retailers, large and small, to look beyond the obvious and tangible aspects of their stores like product and price to enhancing the shopping environment to make their store a destination where people enjoy shopping.

This is a wake-up call to retailers, large and small, to look beyond the obvious and tangible aspects of their stores like product and price to enhancing the shopping environment to make their store a destination where people enjoy shopping.

Customer Service Is All about Serving the Customer

Like the word quality when describing products, the concept of customer service means so many things to so many different people that it ultimately means absolutely nothing. From my perspective, customer service extends far beyond the way a store clerk treats the customer into all the many ways that stores, including the staff people, the stock people, the merchandisers, the janitors, store designers and managers, along with the physical store design and layout, signage, and atmosphere, as well as parking and location, serve the customer. Everything about the store and the shopping experience needs to be designed from the customers' point of view. It needs to be focused exclusively and primarily on satisfying the shoppers' personal desire. The best analogy I can think that describes truly outstanding customer service for retailers to aspire to is that found in a really good hotel.

Because I have such an active speaking schedule and the conference or the event planner solely determines the place where I stay, I experience an incredible mix of hotel experiences—the very good, the middle of the road, and sometimes the very bad. Let's face it, hotels make their money selling you a room, just like retailers make their money selling you stuff. The room, its amenities, and so on are important, but far beyond the room, most hotels realize their focus is not the room itself, but the way they sell you that room. Too few retailers have learned this lesson—that it isn't the product, but how they sell the product that really matters.

My husband and I recently stayed at two four-star, true luxury hotels in a single week, one hotel in Florida, which will remain nameless, and the other the Regent Beverly Wilshire in Beverly Hills. Both hotels compete in the same class and cater to the same luxury clientele, but there was a world of difference in the way we were treated as guests. The nameless Florida hotel staff gave off this attitude, "We are The ***** and aren't you the lucky ones to be staying here." Arriving at the hotel mid-afternoon and starving, we immediately went to the restaurant where $150 got us lunch (I had a glass of wine and my husband only iced tea, for which he had to ask the server several times to bring him sugar) and the view of the ocean, which really wasn't much to look at on the cloudy, wintry day we visited. The hotel room was acceptable, but on the small side. We basically were underwhelmed by this landmark hotel's service and the overall experience.

Everything about the store and the shopping experience needs to be designed from the customers' point of view. It needs to be focused exclusively and primarily on satisfying the shoppers' personal desire.

The Regent Beverly Hills was another story entirely. They are part of the Four Seasons chain, but we didn't check in with particularly high expectations after our Florida landmark hotel experience. We arrived at the hotel similarly famished after missing lunch, and got a great lunch in their dining room, served without missing a beat, and the price was in the much more reasonable $60 range. In addition, I had wonderful fun people-watching during lunch. People-watching in Beverly Hills beats looking at a gray overcast ocean in Florida any day.

Everyone at the Regent Beverly Hills across the board couldn't do enough to make us feel welcome, comfortable, and cared for and we put them through their paces having to get a suit cleaned and pressed for an early morning meeting. I needed to work with the business center for some last minute technical glitches in my computer presentation, which they handled expertly, and we even let the bell staff ship back materials left over from my presentation. They obviously could handle anything we threw at them with superb efficiency and a positive attitude. When we checked out, we asked about the price of our room and we could have stayed in a mid-range New York City hotel for about the same price. It was an experience that was totally remarkable—borrowing the phrase popularized by Seth Godin, author of *The Purple Cow: Transform Your Business by Being Remarkable,* denoting a word-of-mouth worthy experience. I simply do not understand why retail stores don't pay the kind of attention to serving their customer that a hotel of the Regent Beverly Hills caliber does. If I ran a retail store, the service at a hotel like Regent Beverly Hills would be the benchmark I would judge my level of customer service against. Of course, you would have to staff your store adequately with enough people to service the typical number of shoppers expected, but if you didn't have to mark all your products down to get those goods out the door and so could sell them at full list price, you might have enough money left to support ideal, rather than sheer minimum, staffing levels.

What shoppers are looking for from the people in the store is to feel special.

Maybe I aim a little too high to expect retail service levels to be on par with a Four Seasons hotel, but when I talk to shoppers, they draw the comparison with a good restaurant experience. Carol, a married professional in her 30s, describes the level of service she expects in a store: "You want to feel respected. If you are going to spend your valuable time in a store, you want to feel good and appreciated. You want to feel like a customer. You are choosing this store over other stores that you could have gone to, so you want to be treated as special. It's like when you walk into a restaurant. You don't want the waitress to be indifferent, and you don't want her walking over and asking if you need anything while you are having a conversation. But you want her to come back and warm up your coffee."

What shoppers are looking for from the people in the store is to feel special. Women, in particular, are the caregivers in the family and they tend to put their husbands, children, and everybody else first. So when they are shopping, out getting their retail therapy, they want someone to cater to their needs and desires. Another shopper says, "Service is service. They need to put service back into the experience. I am not going as far as to say the customer is always right, but they have to give you the service and put your needs first."

Putting Service Back into the
Shopping Experience

While the retail industry is moving more into the self-service realm with stores collocated in destination shopping malls, shoppers feel nostalgic for the old days when shopping was an event for which you got dressed up and went downtown for a full day of browsing, shopping, and experiencing. This Atlanta shopper longs for when you went downtown to shop: "I like more of the downtown-shopping atmosphere because you also have cafes and places where you can sit outdoors. It's more fun to people-watch while they're shopping—it is just more for recreational. It is more European style where you can shop and eat and be with friends. I think it's sad that downtown shopping is gone."

With the rise of the enclosed malls and so many shopping destinations scattered in the suburbs, the country is being blanketed over with retail sameness. This professional woman, who travels a lot for her job, goes to shopping malls as recreation when she is visiting new cities. She says, "When I traveled and I went to these malls—to kill time and get some exercise by walking around—I wouldn't know what city I was in. Every mall looked the same. And outside every mall there's Red Lobster, Olive Garden, and I'd look and sometimes I would think, where am I? I miss being able to go to downtown stores or boutiques or Main Street and get the feel of the city where I am."

Part of what is missing under the new self-service mall-based retailing paradigm is knowledgeable salespeople who really know their stuff. In our discussions with shoppers they talk about how nice it is to go into a store or a department in the store and have someone wait on you who knows the products, knows what they carry, and can advise you on what is the best item for you to buy. Too many retailers today staff their stores with minimum-wage part-time workers assigned to housewares one day and the jewelry counter the next. No wonder when a shopper asks a question she is confronted with blank stares.

For this shopper talking in the focus groups, good service means, "that the person who is in the department has been there and knows what they have and knows about the styles." Because merchandise is such a draw in the shopping formula, shoppers want sales help from people who know more than shoppers do about the merchandise. They want a greater level of merchandise expertise, style advice, brand referrals, and staff people who can truthfully answer questions about quality. Talking about Nordstrom, this shopper says, "I walk in there and the experience is special—it's so pleasant to be in there. The people are really helpful—especially if I go and I'm trying to buy something I don't know a lot about, like a shirt and tie for my husband. I can ask someone to help me find a tie that goes with this shirt. Those men that work in that department actually know what they're doing. And so I'm willing to pay a little bit more for that shirt and tie for that extra help, compared to when I'm in Macy's looking around for half an hour on my own."

Easton Town Center

■ Offers Alternative to Unwieldy Enclosed Malls, by Recreating
   Main-Street Feel

Located in the northeast part of Columbus, Ohio, Easton Town Center is one of the nation's premier town centers—a venue that combines the latest and greatest shopping with destination restaurants and entertainment venues in a thoroughly modern setting that hearkens back to Main Street shopping experiences, explains Barry Rosenberg, president of Steiner & Associates, a firm that develops town centers and currently manages Easton Town Center.

Easton Town Center is where people in and around Columbus go for a night on the town. It attracts people much like traditional downtowns did in the cities, when shopping, movies, and restaurants all were located in the downtown area where most people also lived and worked. That all changed as people moved to the suburbs and stores went into the malls. "When people moved out of the cities to the suburbs, then came the shopping mall. The mall, this big, huge enclosed environment, became the most efficient place to shop. But a disconnect occurred because the part of the entertainment component was left downtown and part of it was out-parceled outside of the mall. But the result is people don't go to the mall for fun and entertainment like they used to go downtown," explains Rosenberg.

The concept of the Town Center in general and Easton Town Center specifically is that it has all the components the downtown used to—shops, restaurants, jobs, homes, hotels, theatres, clubs, and more. "Easton Town Center shows the power of putting together that overall mix, essentially creating a real town center," he says.

Easton Town Center is anchored by Nordstrom, Macy's, Crate & Barrel, AMC Easton 30 Theaters, Life Time Fitness, Barnes & Noble, and The Cheesecake Factory, all of which illustrate the diversity of the concept. What the center puts back into this leisure time experience that is largely missing from other shopping environments are places that encourage and support social interaction—people meeting, talking, and sharing with other people. "What is missing today from our lives characterized by suburban sprawl are the meeting places, social gathering places that downtown used to offer. We have built walls around ourselves, but we crave places where we can get together. That's one reason a place like Starbucks has been so successful," Rosenberg says.

Easton Town Center offers a wide assortment of restaurant and dining experiences that bring people together, like the centrally located Brio Tuscan Grille restaurant, which borders the center's central park and fountain, and is the focal point of the entire center. "Strong public spaces are the most valuable real estate in America. You've got Central Park and Bryant Park in New York, Rittenhouse Square in Philadelphia, and Regents Park in London. Creating strong public spaces really becomes the anchor around which we create our retail environments," Rosenberg explains.

Also special to the Town Center concept is an emphasis on small specialty retailers. Traditional malls are anchored by major department store tenants, and specialty stores in between the anchors often are overlooked. At the Easton Town Center, shoppers can park close, if not right in front of, the specialty store where they want to shop. Given the overall design and layout, a small specialty store can make a powerful statement to passersby. "There is always something new and interesting around every corner. You get a sense of adventure strolling along the walkways," he says.

"We have to think about the shoppers' experience as soon as they get off the highway, where they park their car and how they walk into the project," says Barry Rosenberg, Steiner and Associates.

As the manager of a Town Center like Easton, Rosenberg and his company have to think of all the things great and small that make up the total shopping experience. That begins when the shopper gets off the highway. "We have to think about the shoppers' experience as soon as they get off the highway, where they park their car and how they walk into the project. It's a lot of little things, like our staircases where the steps aren't steep and the foot widths are longer than traditional stairs. And safety. We have call-for-assistance boxes where you can push a button and immediately someone comes on and answers you; meanwhile, a camera goes on so that we can make visual contact. Customer service is everybody's business, whether you work in security, are a janitor, or work in guest assistance. How you relate to the customer is very important to us. It is all these things that add up to creating a wonderful guest experience," Rosenberg says.

For the future, Rosenberg describes a vision of Easton Town Center that is even more town-centered, with a greater mix of stores, hotels, and residential to create a vibrant, coherent community. "We want to create an environment where people want to live so they can walk to the Starbucks, visit a restaurant, go to the movies. We are planning to add more residential to create that kind of community, that kind of experience. So it becomes a great place to have your office, your store. And it is a great place to stay in a hotel where you can walk across the street for dinner. And that brings a responsibility of giving back to the community, so we host the four biggest fund-raising events that take place in our area to raise money for youth and families."

Stores and Shopping Environments
Must Strive to be Shopper Friendly

In discussions with shoppers, the phrase "shopper friendly" emerged as a key value that shoppers desire. It's what stores like Nordstrom and Target have embraced as a core value, as well as shopping destinations like Easton Town Center. These shopper friendly destinations truly put the shopper at the center. They design the store not necessarily to maximize sales, though that is often the result, but to delight and entice the customer. They truly care about the customer, not by instituting policies where by rote staff members "greet" the customer, but by employing sales associates who want to take care of or serve the customer. They know their products, know the store, and will shop with the customer to make sure they find just what they are longing for.

This shopper describes the elements that make up good customer service—it is a standard that every shop can strive for through staff training, but more importantly, by hiring the right people in the first place: "Good customer service is all about help. I have no patience with stores where the salespeople are all over you when you come in the door. I want to know they are there if I need them, but I don't want them on top of me. I want to be able to get help if I need it."

CHAPTER SIX

Inner Life of Passionate Shoppers

THE FIELD GUIDE TO THE FIVE SHOPPING PERSONALITIES

"Human behavior flows from three main sources: desire, emotion, and knowledge."

PLATO

We have already met the passionate shopper—a person who is passionate about shopping and who loves to shop. Before we talk about how retailers can transform their stores into customer experiences, let's look more closely at these passionate shoppers to understand them better.

Who is the Passionate Shopper?

At some level most people like to shop and do it occasionally for fun or entertainment, whether it is going to the mall on a rainy weekend when no ball games are on television or heading out to Barnes & Noble for a latte and a browse on Sunday evening when all the other stores are closed. Nevertheless, not everybody says, "I enjoy shopping and think of it as a form of entertainment." In Unity Marketing's recreational shopping survey among middle- to upper-income shoppers (incomes $50,000 and above), only 55 percent of shoppers agreed with that statement. Another 20 percent of those surveyed were neutral toward that statement, meaning they neither agreed nor disagreed.

Among these neutral respondents to the previous statement, a majority agreed with at least one or more of these other statements:

- "I like to shop at certain stores because of the special treatment and services that I receive." (62 percent agreement)
- "I often buy things on sale that I don't strictly need but are at such a good price that I can't pass them up." (61 percent agreement)
- "I enjoy spending time browsing in different shops to see what they have and what is 'hot' right now." (60 percent agreement)

When we take the first group who believes that shopping is fun and add in those who are neutral to that statement but who agree with one of the others, we find that almost three-quarters (72 percent) of shoppers surveyed are classified as "passionate shoppers"—people who love to shop. Everyone else, the 28 percent who don't view shopping as fun, are defined as "regular shoppers."

One defining demographic characteristic of the passionate shopper is high household income. Unity's survey didn't include the 62.2 million U.S. households with incomes under $50,000 because these lower-income households have relatively low levels of disposable income and so are less likely to engage in shopping as a pastime. In fact, as household incomes rise so does people's enjoyment of shopping. Some 75 percent of shoppers surveyed with incomes of $150,000 or more are passionate shoppers, as compared with 69 percent of those with incomes $50,000 to $74,999; 70 percent of those $75,000 to $99,999; and 72 percent of those $100,000 to $149,999. The average income of a passionate shopper is $113,000 as compared with $108,700 for the regular shoppers' comparative group.

Another defining demographic characteristic of a passionate shopper is gender. Not unexpectedly, women are far more likely than men to love to shop. Some 70 percent of recreational shoppers are female, as compared with 30 percent who are men, but that gender breakdown doesn't tell the whole story. The fact is, among the middle- to upper-income shoppers surveyed, some 59 percent of men surveyed, or a clear majority, enjoy shopping and do it for fun. This compares to 79 percent of all women surveyed. So in both absolute and relative terms, women are more likely to love shopping, but even

SHOPPING FACTOID
Men Spend More Than Women When
Recreationally Shopping

Men who shop for fun spend 30 percent more on average per month than women do when recreationally shopping.

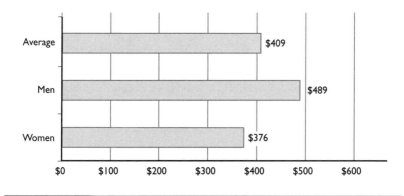

Source: Unity Marketing, Recreational Shopping Report, 2006

so, the majority of higher-income men are also predisposed to be passionate shoppers as well.

Being younger is also a defining characteristic of passionate shoppers. The typical passionate shopper is two-and-one-half years younger than the comparable regular shopper, with the average age of a passionate shopper being 42.9 years, as compared with 45.4 years for regular shoppers. With age, people's tendency to shop for fun and their level of spending when shopping recreationally declines.

To summarize the key demographic characteristics that distinguish the passionate shopper, they are:

- High income (average income $113,000)
- Female; though a majority (59 percent) of higher-income male shoppers are also classified as passionate shoppers, the male passionate shoppers spend more on average per month ($489) than women ($376)
- Youthful, under 45 years of age

SHOPPING FACTOIDS
Recreational Shoppers' Spending Declines with Age

Recreational shoppers aged 25 to 34 years spend 58 percent more per month when shopping for fun than those aged 55 to 64 years and 22 percent more per month than those aged 45 to 54 years.

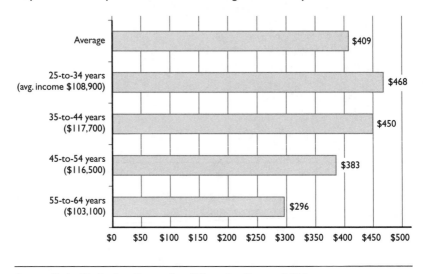

Source: Unity Marketing, Recreational Shopping Report, 2006

Passionate Shoppers Are Not All the Same

While passionate shoppers tend to share certain demographic characteristics, they are hardly a homogenous group of people with the same attitudes and motivations in their pursuit of shopping. Like some people favor football, others prefer baseball, and some go wild for basketball, different shoppers, all of whom are passionate about shopping as entertainment, get their kicks from shopping in different ways.

If we analyze the responses of all passionate shoppers to a series of 26 attitude statements and group them together according to the similarities or differences in their responses, five distinctive personalities of recreational shoppers emerge.

FIGURE 6.1 Recreational Shopper Personalities

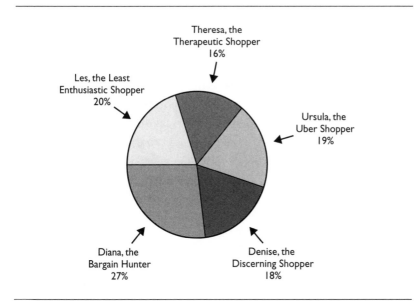

Diana, the Bargain Hunter,
Buys Only When the Price is Right

The largest personality segment found among passionate shoppers is Diana the bargain hunter supreme. Diana is the type of shopper that upon walking into the store immediately proceeds to the bargain bins. She gets her kicks out of the shopping game by scoring the most bargains. She is the type that rarely, if ever, pays full price and needs very little excuse to buy something she sees priced at a very deep discount, even if she doesn't have an immediate need for it.

Because she gets her thrill from finding a bargain, Diana gets stressed if she spends lots of time shopping and can't find any attractive sales. She regularly reads the newspapers watching for special sales events and is first in line when the store opens if they are having a big sale.

She tends to feel guilty if she actually has to pay full price, but she spends so much time in the store searching out bargains that she knows where she can score a big discount for most things. For Diana, shopping is a solitary pursuit. She'd rather shop alone because she is so driven in her passion for discounts. Shopping with others simply keeps her from her primary shopping pursuit: discounts.

Demographically, Diana is a prototypical passionate shopper in terms of average age, gender, and income. While this personality is dominated by women shoppers, some 28 percent of the Diana-type shoppers are men who go for bargains.

Because the promise of a deep discount is the only spur that Diana needs to make purchases, she actually spends 15 percent more per month when she shops for recreation than the average passionate shopper: $470 as compared with $409 among all passionate shoppers. She is a perfect example of a shopper who ultimately spends more money in pursuit of saving it.

Theresa, the Therapeutic Shopper, Escapes Her Humdrum Existence by Shopping

Theresa's motivation to shop is primarily a desire to escape from her day-to-day life. Shopping is a form of entertainment, a way she explores different sides of her personality and new aspects of herself. While she gets a thrill out of finding bargains and hunting for attractive prices, she is more of a browser than a buyer when she is shopping. What separates Theresa from the other shopping personalities is that she gets just as much enjoyment in browsing around a store than in actually making a purchase. She doesn't need to buy things to gain enjoyment and satisfaction from shopping.

In keeping with her propensity to browse, rather than buy, Theresa spends significantly less on recreational shopping purchases, $337 or 18 percent less than the passionate shopper average of $409.

Theresa looks for stores that offer special, inviting environments to pursue her shopping therapy. Her favorite shopping haunts are stores where she can find lots of things to look at, such as clothing and accessories stores, traditional department stores, discount department stores, and personal care, beauty, and cosmetics stores. When she shops, stores with a wide selection, unique products, and quality merchandise draw her.

Demographically, Theresa is predominately female—of this personality, only 10 percent are men—with an average age of 44 years, a few years older than the passionate shopper average of 42.8.

Ursula, the Uber Shopper, Is the Over-the-Top Shopper and the One Retailers Want to Invite into Their Stores

Ursula, the Uber Shopper, is at the top of the passionate shopping pyramid. She simply loves to shop and pursues shopping not just as therapy or a hobby, but almost as a profession. She is the go-to person when you want to know where to find a specific item, because Ursula spends lots of time in the stores checking the merchandise and looking for deals.

Unlike Theresa, Ursula doesn't just want to browse. Rather, Ursula gets her kicks out of buying wonderful things when she shops and, like Diana, she gets a thrill from finding the special, unique items she craves at a good price. Therefore, Ursula watches for sales, keeps her eyes on the Sunday supplements to find coupons, and is always on the lookout for a special sale where she might find great deals.

The stores she favors are those that offer wide merchandise selection and high-quality merchandise, but she also is an enthusiastic bargain hunter, so she is also looking for stores where she can get good prices. However, while she loves to bargain shop, she is perfectly willing to pay full price for something she loves. It's because Ursula is such a determined, experienced, and knowledgeable shopper that she knows where she is likely to find the best deals and get the most attractive prices.

The Ursula personality skews toward the female, but nearly one-fourth (24 percent) of the Ursula type are men. This segment is younger than the typical passionate shopper, average age 39 years as compared with 42.9 years. More GenXers (46 percent) than baby boomers (36 percent) make up this personality type. Ursula's average income is 7 percent higher than the typical recreational shopper, $121,000 vs. $113,000.

Given her greater passion for shopping and her higher income, Ursula spends the most when shopping, $613 in a typical month when recreationally shopping, or 50 percent more than the recreational shopper average of $409.

Denise, the Discerning Shopper, Has Been There and Done That, So Shopping is Not Such a Thrill Anymore

Denise just doesn't shop like she used to. The key feature that distinguishes Denise from the other personalities is that she is older, 45 years on average as compared with 42.9 years for the typical passionate shopper. Denise is far more likely to be a member of the Baby Boom generation, with 62 percent of this personality type being boomers as compared with 29 percent who are GenXers.

As an older, more mature woman, Denise is likely in her empty-nesting years, at a life-stage where she is down-sizing her life rather than acquiring more material goods. She has bought most of the material possessions she is likely ever to need, so buying something new is just not as compelling for Denise as it is for a young Ursula shopper.

Unlike Theresa, Ursula, and Diana, Denise is distinctly *not* motivated to buy based upon price. She doesn't shop the discount aisles first or spend lots of time looking for bargains. If she needs something or wants something, she pays full price and make the purchase most efficiently. Time, not money, is more valuable to Denise, and she knows shopping for discounts takes a lot of time.

Denise also isn't strongly motivated to browse a lot when she is in the stores. When she shops, she focuses on getting in and out of the store quickly, rather than spending lots of time in browse mode. In this sense Denise is opposite Theresa, because Denise gets her thrill from making the specific purchase she is interested in and not wasting time on unnecessary browsing and hunting for the item. Given her desire to find what she wants and get her mission accomplished quickly, Denise highly values good customer service and having sales people help her make the most efficient use of her time.

Denise has an average income of $113.6k, so she is just slightly above the recreational shopper average, yet she spends significantly less when she shops than is typical. Her recreational spending is 34 percent less than the average, $269 as compared with $409. While 68 percent of the Denise personality is female, about one-third (32 percent) are men (and so should actually be named Dennis, the Discerning Shopper).

Les, the Least Enthusiastic Shopper Who Still Enjoys Shopping

If Ursula is the over-the-top passionate shopper then Les is her polar opposite. While Les likes to shop for fun, he just isn't into shopping as much as the other personality types. Is it any wonder that men are the majority of the Les personality type, 56 percent, while women comprise 44 percent? Like Denise, the discerning shopper, Les also is not driven to find bargain prices, though he doesn't turn away from a good deal when he finds it. It is just that he does not actively pursue discount shopping as a passion like Diana or to a lesser extent Theresa or Ursula.

Les doesn't have a lot of spare time to shop and so he shops less frequently every month: 2.68 times for recreation, as compared with 4.9 times among all passionate shoppers. He also spends less when he shops for fun, $322 on average or 21 percent less than the $409 recreational shopper average. (Note: The average spending of all male passionate shoppers is $409 and higher than the average female. While men dominate in this personality type, men are scattered among the other personality types. So the typical male passionate shopper spends more than the typical female, but the Les personality, made up of a higher percentage of men, spends less.)

His average age is slightly higher than the passionate survey average (44 years) and the majority (51 percent) of the Les personality type is a baby boomer. His average income is slightly lower than the average, $110.2k as compared with $113k for all recreational shoppers.

FIGURE 6.2   Field Guide to the Five Recreational Shopper Personalities

	Theresa, the Therapeutic Shopper	Ursula, the Uber Shopper	Denise, the Discerning Shopper	Diana, the Bargain Hunter	Les, the Least Enthusiastic Recreational Shopper
Market Penetration	16%	19%	18%	27%	20%
Consumer Psychology	For Theresa shopping is retail therapy. She gets her therapeutic treatment from being in the store itself—browsing the aisles and looking at all the merchandise. Shopping is her escape from ordinary life and she really doesn't need to buy anything when she shops. She gets her kicks from simply browsing in the stores.	Ursula is the over-the-top enthusiastic shopper. She shops for fun, she shops for bargains, she shops for therapy, and she shops as a social occasion. She is the shopper who literally shops till she drops.	Denise is older than the typical recreational shopper and thus tends to have acquired lots of material goods in the course of her shopping career. As a result, she is more careful in her shopping choices and far less likely to buy based solely upon price.	The personality found most predominantly among recreational shoppers, comprising 27 percent of the total recreational shopping market, is Diana, the Bargain Huntress. Diana is always in search of the best price and it is the thought of finding a bargain that sets her shopper's heart aflutter.	Men are more likely to be Les, the Least Enthusiastic Shopper, thus the masculine name. Les shops for fun and gets pleasure out of the endeavor, but he is less enthusiastic overall about recreational shopping and will do something else more rewarding if given the opportunity.
Demographics	Male 10% Female 90%	Male 24% Female 76%	Male 32% Female 68%	Male 28% Female 72%	Male 56% Female 44%
Average Age. 42.9 years	44 years GenXer 33% Boomer 52%	39 years GenXer 46% Boomer 36%	45 years GenXer 29% Boomer 62%	42 years GenXer 31% Boomer 50%	44 years GenXer 37% Boomer 51%

FIGURE 6.2 Field Guide to the Five Recreational Shopper Personalities (continued)

	Theresa, the Therapeutic Shopper	Ursula, the Uber Shopper	Denise, the Discerning Shopper	Diana, the Bargain Hunter	Les, the Least Enthusiastic Recreational Shopper
Average Income $113,000	$111,800 (1.2% < avg.)	$121,000 (6.9% > avg.)	$113,600 (about avg.)	$109,500 (3.3% < avg.)	$110,200 (2.7% < avg.)
Shopping Frequency (Avg. per month) Necessities: 9.6 Recreational: 4.1	10.74 4.98	11.92 6.69	8.38 3.35	9.21 3.88	7.88 2.68
Total Spending (Avg. per month) Necessities: $749 Recreational: $409	$797 $337	$1,010 $613	$697 $269	$776 $470	$666 $322
Favorite Stores Recreational Shopping	Clothing & accessories (19%) Discount dept. store (19%) Traditional dept. store (13%)	Discount dept. store (19%) Clothing & accessories (16%) Traditional dept. store (13%)	Electronics/appliances (17%) Discount dept. store (16%) Clothing & accessories (11%)	Discount dept. store (21%) Clothing & accessories (12%) Electronics/appliances (10%)	Electronics/appliances (20%) Discount dept. store (20%) Nonstore retailers (9%)
Most Important Factors Influencing Where to Shop	Wide selection (23%) Unique merchandise (12%) Quality merchandise (11%)	Wide selection (22%) Quality merchandise (15%) Discount prices (11%)	Wide selection (26%) Discount prices (18%) Unique selection (9%)	Discount prices (21%) Wide selection (17%) Quality merchandise (10%)	Wide selection (27%) Discount prices (18%) Quality merchandise (10%)

Magnolia Audio Video

■ A Store with a Deep Understanding of Its Shoppers' Personalities

Best Buy, the parent company of Magnolia Audio Video, is a big-box specialty retailer of consumer electronics and entertainment products. In marketing circles, Best Buy is famous for their innovative use of consumer psychographics, in other words, identifying its target customers through personality profiling and attitude analysis. Best Buy's psychographic segmentation includes personalities like Buzz, a technically sophisticated early adopter who likes gadgets, and Jill, a busy mom who wants a kid-friendly store environment. Their Barry personality is a high-end luxury consumer who craves the latest and greatest. It is the Barry type of customer that Best Buy's Magnolia Audio Video standalone stores and its Magnolia Home Theater stores-within-a-store reach out to. Today Magnolia operates 20 free-standing stores and about 100 Best Buy stores within a store.

Jim Tweten, president of Magnolia Audio Video, explains the concept, "In a word, we sell home audio video experiences. We sell it all, from MP3 players, car audio, projection television, media rooms, PC media centers, high quality speakers, and receivers. And we put together home entertainment solutions, from design and installation." Magnolia traces its roots from Seattle in 1954, when Tweten's father opened the Magnolia Stationery store selling cards and pens and pencils. They branched into the camera business, and then into the hi-fi business in the mid-sixties, which is where they have remained ever since.

As a Seattle-based business, the Magnolia team was able to study Nordstrom up-close and personal, and benchmarked the Magnolia superior level of customer service against this industry leader. Magnolia combines superior levels of customer service with carefully edited selections of the highest quality products to deliver the ultimate in home entertainment solutions to its customers. "We have aspired to be like Nordstrom, from the standpoint of customer service—whatever is required to take care of the customer—as well as having the best, most premium products in one place. That's how we built our business. We are fanatical about dedication to customer service," Tweten explains.

"We are fanatical about dedication to customer service," says Jim Tweten, Magnolia Audio Video.

Tweten explains that customer service the Magnolia way is all about having a "genuine relationship with the customer that expresses passion and energy about the product and the experience." That dedication to service has become even more critical in the increasingly complex product world that Magnolia sells into. Tweten says, "It's become so complex to build and install entertainment systems. Today you can go into a home and people have six different remotes where you have to press one button only to get to another button. But we can program a universal remote so you can operate your systems with one remote, but customers need help setting that up. They also need service to wire up a system. So we do it all, from delivery, installation, programming. We deliver the ultimate experience. That is where we shine."

To attract the more discerning, upscale customers into the Magnolia Home Theaters within the Best Buy stores, the Magnolia stores are crafted to look more like a home environment than a retail store with couches and wall-to-wall carpeting. Walls define the Magnolia space, which is also set off with separate lighting and a unique sophisticated ambiance. The stores within a store are quieter so the shopper can listen to better speakers and appreciate the quality differences. The stores present high-quality products in a homelike systems setting, so the shopper can imagine the total experience. Tweten says, "We think the art of the demo is really important—to demonstrate the kind of music the customer likes so he or she can experience it in the store. We have sound rooms that the customer can experience because we think the sound is the emotion in the audio-video experience. So the art of the demo for us is to deliver an audio and video experience in an environment more like home."

Another key benefit of the Magnolia environment is that it draws women as well as men. "We think of our product, especially the thin panel TVs, as a fashion statement, as well as a fun movie and audio experience," Tweten says. "Women are more important than ever in driving the purchase decision when it comes to their homes." To this end Magnolia also sells furniture to compliment and house the entertainment equipment they offer.

The key word describing the Magnolia shopping experience is "premium" and that has guided their every step. Tweten sums up, "Magnolia is a boutique environment inside a big box retailer where we can demonstrate to our premium customer our premium goods in a premium environment. We provide a premium experience, which is how we differentiate ourselves from other retailers that just sell consumer electronics. Our focus has always been on the premium customer because we sell the best to people who want the best."

Part Two

SHOPS THAT POP!

Stores that Achieve the Ultimate

Consumer Experience

CHAPTER SEVEN

The Pop! Equation

"Whoever said things won't make you happy,
didn't know where to go shopping."
BO DEREK

In Part Two: Shops that Pop!—Stores that Achieve the Ultimate Consumer Experience, we turn our attention from the consumer to the stores themselves. Having explored the shopping equation—the factors that influence people to shop and buy—we focus on how stores create that special shopping experience. Stores that have it are what I call shops that pop.

Just like there is a formula for shopping—the quantum theory of shopping: $P = (N + F + A) \times E^2$—there is also an equation that defines the qualities and features of stores that make them pop. I call this the pop! equation and express it as specific qualities that distinguish and identify shops that offer superior shopping experiences. The pop! equation defines the unique way that retailers apply specific strategies and combine them to create a truly special, extraordinary shopping experience for the customer.

Shops that pop, like The Apple Store, Nell Hill's, Target, Godiva, Nordstrom, Aerosoles, Magnolia, Easton Town Center, and the others discussed in Part Two exhibit each of these qualities to a greater or lesser extent.

The pop! equation defines the unique way that retailers apply specific strategies and combine them to create a truly special, extraordinary shopping experience for the customer.

Those qualities that make up the pop! equation are:

- **Encourages high levels of customer involvement and interaction**—Shops that pop create a shopping environment that fully involves the shopper and engages them interactively in the shopping experience. Shoppers don't just browse the aisles and participate as passive observers. Shops that pop encourage customers to touch, feel, taste, try on, and participate in the store in a more involving way. Think of the difference between a store that posts signs saying "You broke it— You bought it!" as compared to a store that invites you to touch, feel, and explore, like Magnolia, where product demonstrations have been elevated to an art.
- **Evokes shopper curiosity**—Shops that pop excite consumer curiosity to explore and experience, from the shop windows and entrance through the different displays. They lure shoppers into the store and then to turn the next corner and walk down the next aisle to find that wonderful treasure just out of sight. Customers spend hours exploring the Easton Town Center just to make sure they don't miss anything exciting.
- **Has a contagious, electric quality**—Shops that pop exude energy and excitement that is contagious. Shoppers catch it and return again and again to the store to rev up their engines. The contagion also spreads through word of mouth to make the shop a destination for people in the community, the state, even across the country. It is this quality that makes a shop that pops a happening place, exciting to visit, and a thrill to participate in. Even for shoppers that are not all that into the category feel there is something in the store for them. The Apple Stores have this contagious quality in spades.
- **Presents a convergence between atmosphere, store design, and merchandise**—Shops that pop present a comprehensive

vision that captures all the tangible and intangible elements of the store in a unified whole. This quality of convergence extends far beyond a cookie-cutter, homogenized, neutralized shopping environment. These shops present distinctive points of view that tie together all the disparate elements of the store into one experience. The music, merchandise, service, design, and architecture work together to make Nordstrom a truly special place to shop.

- **Expresses an authentic concept**—Shops that pop are more than stores selling stuff; they are conceptually driven and reflect a visionary's values. A shop that pops transcends being just a store into a new realm of experience. Nell Hill's is an authentic expression of Mary Carol Garrity's personality and charm. That is what draws customers in, as much as the wonderful merchandise.

- **Priced right for the value**—Shops that pop have a carefully constructed pricing strategy based upon offering fair value delivered to the shopper for a reasonable price. That is, they try to maximize the value of the goods offered and price them right. Pricing is not about how low can you go, but how much value can you offer at a good and fair price to the shopper. Pricing, therefore, hinges upon the value for the shopper, not necessarily the money. Aerosoles packs their products with extra value at a great price, just like Godiva offers extra added value chocolate in affordably priced packages.

- **Offers an environment that is accessible, nonexclusive, and free from pretensions**—Shops that pop have all the preceding qualities, plus another essential feature—they are immediately accessible to everyone, free from pretensions of exclusivity or snobbishness. They know they are good, but rather than resting on their laurels and expecting everybody else to know it too, they are constantly reaching out, drawing people into their web with missionary zeal and self-effacing charm. It is all about making the shopper feel personally welcome, as every one of the stores we looked at so far do—The Apple Store, Nell Hill's, Target, Godiva, Aerosoles, Nordstrom, Easton Town Center, and Magnolia.

What's Next

Shops that pop have got the formula right. They deliver engaging shopping experiences to their customers that stimulate their curiosity, make them feel welcome, invite them to explore, and most importantly, encourage them to buy. In other words, they love their customers and make shopping there fun, which is absolutely contagious to the customers and in turn makes the customer love shopping there.

In the chapters that follow we explore each of the qualities that make up the pop! equation through case studies of retailers that are doing it right. We draw upon in-depth interviews conducted with retail leaders, both large and small, to understand how they work the magic in their store and what makes them pop for the shopper.

This leads us to Part Three where we pull the consumer insights and retailer case studies together into specific principles for retailers to create a pop experience in their shops.

Before we proceed, though, I'd like to share highlights of a discussion held with 12 small specialty retailers who shared their experiences in the retailing trenches.

Retailers Tell It Like It Is

"The car, the furniture, the wife, the children—everything has to be disposable. Because you see the main thing today is shopping."
ARTHUR MILLER

In my line of work, I spend a lot of time with retailers, from large national retailers to small, independent, often struggling mom-and-pops that are trying to eke out a living through their store. Having talked to so many retailers in so many different venues over the last decade, I felt confident in writing this book that I understood the fundamental issues challenging them—attracting and keeping customers coming into the store to buy—and the ultimate solution: align the store, its offerings, its environment, and its service with the expectations of the shoppers so that shopping there is a pleasure and delight, not a chore. However, because I am a researcher and turn first to research whenever I face a new challenge, I decided to do a bit more structured research with retailers so that this book would really address their issues. I sat down with a group of small independent retailers located in Columbus, Ohio, to understand their views of retailing, their problems, and their satisfactions.

A total of 12 owners of independent stores were recruited, with the majority of shop owners operating a single store and two participants operating stores in multiple retail locations. Store revenues ranged from $100,000 to $1 million or more and the owners' ages ranged from 35 years to 60-plus. Eight men and four women were included in the discussion group and the types of stores owned represented electronics, jewelry, gifts and home decor, t-shirts, women's apparel, furniture, toys, hobby store, video games, and florist. All participants were recruited based on their concern about the encroachment of national retailers, big boxes, and discounters in their local market area.

During the discussion group, Greg, the owner of a 3,500 sq. ft. toy store in business for 24 years, gave the most succinct summation of the challenges facing specialty retailers today:

> We all obviously have competitors. And I've noticed over the last ten years that Columbus is totally over-retailed. You can't go anyplace without finding stores and shops and shopping centers. And it's compounded by so much advertising and marketing from the big retailers about shopping and buy, buy, buy. I mean, shopping has become a national pastime and that's what people do for entertainment now. They go shopping and they spend money, and we're dealing with competition from everybody trying to get a piece of that pie . . . the money people are spending when they shop.
>
> So now my competition is not just other toy stores, but it's Wal-Mart and it's Target and it's everyplace where people go to spend money, because we all have a limited amount of money that we can spend. So competition is just growing everywhere.
>
> In my business, we look hard for things that are not going to show up in a lot of other stores so that we don't have to worry about price, but more and more of our manufacturers and suppliers are selling to more and more places, because they're trying to grow their business. So we'll buy something we think is absolutely unique, and before we know it, it's down in Target or it's someplace else. And then you have to compete on price and that sort of thing.

SHOPPING FACTOID

The business of retail, $3.06 trillion in 2002, is rapidly consolidating. In 1997, the 50 largest competitors in each retail sector made only 25.7 percent of the industry's total $2.5 trillion in sales. By 2002, nearly one-third of total retail sales (31.7 percent) were made by the top 50 biggest.

Concentration of Retail Sales

	Total Sales 2002 (× $1,000)	2002% Share 50 Largest Firms	Total Sales 1997 (× $1,000)	1997% Share 50 Largest Firms	Pct. Point Diff.
Total Retail	**$3,056,421,997**	**31.7%**	**$2,460,886,012**	**25.7%**	**6.0**
Motor vehicle & parts dealers	$801,740,162	12.1%	$645,367,776	6.7%	5.4
Furniture & home furnishings stores	$91,814,210	29.3%	$71,690,813	23.7%	5.6
Electronics & appliance stores	$82,228,017	65.4%	$68,561,331	54.1%	11.3
Building equipment/ hardware/garden centers	$246,560,851	46.2%	$227,566,101	34.5%	11.7
Food & beverage stores	$456,942,288	59.5%	$401,764,499	54.1%	5.4
Health & personal care stores	$177,947,091	63.5%	$117,700,863	60.4%	3.1
Gasoline stations	$249,141,412	33.2%	$198,165,786	28.2%	5.0
Clothing & clothing accessories stores	$167,934,068	55.1%	$136,397,645	49.7%	5.4
Sporting goods/ hobby/books/ music stores	$73,212,205	57.2%	$62,010,926	50.7%	6.5
General merchandise stores	$445,224,985	97.9%	$330,444,460	95.80%	2.1
Miscellaneous store retailers	$90,811,742	32.3%	$78,109,161	29.6%	2.7
Florists	$6,624,783	6.4%	$6,555,088	6.8%	−0.4
Office supplies/ stationery	$21,617,623	82.5%	$17,075,739	82.0%	0.5
Gift & novelty stores	$16,001,184	29.4%	$14,497,296	27.1%	2.3
Pet supplies	$7,592,596	63.4%	$5,492,749	52.9%	10.5
Art dealers	$4,236,526	28.9%	$3,000,798	28.2%	0.7
Nonstore retailers	$172,864,966	42.8%	$123,106,651	43.3%	−0.5

(continued)

The categories experiencing the most rapid consolidation include electronics and appliance stores, e.g., class of stores that includes Best Buy, Circuit City, Apple Stores, and so on; building equipment, hardware, and garden centers, e.g., Home Depot, Lowes, Ace Hardware, and so on; and pet supplies, e.g., PetSmart and Petco.

To date, certain retailing sectors have been largely immune from the consolidation trend, notably, florists, gift and novelty stores, art dealers, and furniture and home furnishings stores.

Prediction for the future: Furniture and home furnishings stores will be the next major sector to undergo major consolidation.

Source: Economic Census, 2002 and 1997, Dept. of Census

And for the manufacturers things have changed a lot. It's harder and harder for small, independent manufacturers who are making really unique and beautiful product to stay in business. They can't stay in business because manufacturers in China will copy it and make it for much less. It's become much more difficult to be in business than it was 25 years ago.

Toy shop owner Greg touched on many of the most confounding trends in retail today:

- Increased competition with more and more stores competing for shoppers' available discretionary funds, which aren't growing as fast as the competition for those funds is;
- Small retailers don't have the resources to go head-to-head with national retailers' national-sized advertising budgets to get attention and attract customers to the shop;
- Retailers' basic competitive strategy—stocking unique, different product—doesn't work anymore because the big-box retailers are sourcing virtually identical products overseas; and
- Smaller, independent manufacturers, who have traditionally relied upon small specialty retailers for distribution, can't depend upon them anymore. In response to their own com-

petitive pressures, manufacturers have to sell to a wider range of retailers as well as direct-to-consumers to stay afloat.

All in all this adds up to an incredibly challenging situation for retailers big and small, as well as for manufacturers that need to find sales outlets for their goods. Let's look more closely at how the retailers are responding to the new challenges.

Finding New Customers and Keeping Existing Ones Is Retailers' Key Challenge

Independent retailers express the number one business challenge they face: getting more customers and keeping the ones they already have. Greg, the toy store owner, explains the most important issue for him is "customers—maintaining customers, getting new customers, keeping customers that you get into your store." Becky, the owner of a specialty gift and home furnishings store, finds the same challenge: "It's getting more customers in the door, because once they come in, they will buy. But you got to get them into the door."

In their search for new customers, small retailers find that the old solutions, especially advertising in the local newspapers, Yellow pages, coupon-clipper venues and other locally targeted media, don't work any longer.

In their search for new customers, small retailers find that the old solutions, especially advertising in the local newspapers, Yellow Pages, coupon-clipper venues and other locally targeted media, don't work any longer. They feel they have no voice anymore to reach out to the potential shopper, tell their story, attract their attention, and draw them into the store to shop. Costs are one limiting factor, but that isn't the crux of the problem. Rather, advertising messages today are scattered widely across the consumer landscape and so they don't attract shoppers' attention anymore. Retailers are willing to spend money to advertise if it yields results, but it simply doesn't deliver any longer. As this video store owner says, "The problem is advertising isn't profitable. When I first started in business, you could put spots on WTBN [local television station] and conquer the world. Now you've got about 85,000 outlets that you need to be on to catch all the different segments of the market." The noise is deafening today and small retailers simply can't break through.

Just like the decision about where to advertise isn't clear-cut anymore, what the advertising message should be isn't as simple as it once was before merchants like Wal-Mart and Target launched major national campaigns developed by award-winning advertising agencies. Pam, the owner of a gifts and collectibles store, says, "I think it's really hard to advertise customer service. That's a really tough thing to do. The best thing to do is give your customers the best service they can get, and then you hope that they'll go out and tell a friend that, 'Hey, I was in this store and I got this great service. The people were so friendly and they were helpful. They wrapped my gift and they carried it out to my car and they did all these things for me.' That's one thing that most of us [small retailers] offer—spectacular customer service. But I can't advertise that on TV . . . You got to wait till the customer comes in then you can 'customer service' them to death. Ultimately we have to rely on word of mouth."

If stimulating word of mouth is the answer to the challenges of advertising, then retailers need to focus on making their shops word-of-mouth worthy—or remarkable in Seth Godin's terms. That means making the shopping experience truly exceptional, far beyond the expected in a delightful, engaging way.

Establishing a Dialogue with the Shopper— Both in Word and Deed—Gets the Message Across

In order to break through the advertising noise and create a meaningful relationship with shoppers, small retailers must tell a story about their store and their service. The story must delineate the differences between themselves and the competition. Then they have to back up their story with actions that validate those differences. Sherry, the co-owner of a specialty women's clothing store, who you'll hear more about later, says, "It's hard to explain to the customer why

I have a sweater in my store that looks very similar to the sweater she saw at Macy's, and the Macy's sweater was $99 and mine is $299. It's really difficult to make her understand that this is a handcrafted piece and all the work that goes into it." Sherry's solution is to sell very select lines of designer clothes and accessories that aren't available in any of the department stores or major chains.

Limited availability is also a hook for one furniture retailer. In a business increasingly impacted by competition from low-cost foreign imports, Mindy, who runs a family-owned furniture store, tries to anticipate the styles her customers want six to twelve months in advance, but only orders limited quantities in order to make those pieces on display all the more desirable. "When they [customers] say, 'Can't you order me one,' I tell them we don't want your neighbor to have the same thing that you just bought. So I'm not going to have that same item again." Mindy believes that, once customers understand, they appreciate the concept of limited availability. "Quality and uniqueness will always sell."

To be successful in a small retail store, the store owner and staff need to be constantly mixing it up with the consumer, talking with them, learning more about what they want, and then figuring out innovative, creative ways to deliver to the consumer.

To be successful in a small retail store, the store owner and staff need to be constantly mixing it up with the consumer, talking with them, learning more about what they want, and then figuring out innovative, creative ways to deliver to the consumer. The challenge of stocking a limited range of very selective products is that everybody who wants it can't necessarily have it. That can be frustrating to the shopper, but more importantly, if they are educated right, it can encourage them to shop more often and act faster if they see something that they want. Directly challenging the growing trend toward merchandise sameness and conformity—think the limited selection of styles and overstocking of those on display in the typical The Gap, Banana Republic, Ann Taylor store—Sherry the clothing boutique store owner has to educate her customers that wearing a mass retailers' fashion " uniform" is not the way to be fashionable or well-dressed, "How I market it to the customer is that there's a certain point when it's not fun and it's not fashionable to look like your best friend."

If the shopper is indeed convinced that buying that unique item is desirable, the challenge then becomes whether he or she is really willing to pay the premium that limited availability and production runs in the thousands, instead of the millions upon millions, requires. Keith, a music store owner facing pressures from national retailers Sam Ash Music and Guitar Center, says the improved quality of musical instruments available in these stores is squeezing him, even as the prices decline. He says Fender guitars used to cost $400, but "now they're $99 with an amplifier, because they're made in China. They're mass-produced." Keith is not impressed with the quality of the mass-produced guitar.

Mass-Market Retailers are the Biggest Competition Today

Given the high cost of running a small independent business—payroll and payroll taxes, benefits, other tax expenses, merchandise, shipping, utilities, and more—and the premium that customers must be charged because of those high fixed expenses, independent retailers find the mass merchants, big boxes, and national retail chains who can offer more for less are their biggest competitive headaches. Not only can the big boys directly import products at significant savings over the prices charged by smaller manufacturers, they can strike deals with major suppliers to move hot items. This takes the small, independent retailer completely out of the picture because they can't compete. The owner of a chain of local video game stores complains that national retailer GameStop gets special treatment from Electronic Art (EA), one of the leading suppliers of electronic games, so his store is left out when it comes to stocking the latest and greatest hot game on the day of official release. "[GameStop's] in bed with EA, so they get the game two days before every other retailer. That takes me and other small retailers like me out of the picture. If the game is out on the sixteenth and only GameStops got it, everybody else has it on the seventeenth or eighteenth, you've lost some business."

It is no wonder that large manufacturers give special treatment to large retailers. Keith, the music store owner, says, "Yamaha may discontinue a guitar, and they've got 5,000 of them in their warehouse, and they can make one call to Sam Ash, who can take them all. They'll sell them . . . at 20 cents on the dollar, and they're gone."

Independent Retailers Believe Service Distinguishes Them from the Mass Market

Recognizing that mass-market retailers are here to stay, independent retailers have made an uneasy peace with their presence. They place a lot of emphasis on the role of their superior levels of customer service to fight back at mass merchants' and big box retailers' onslaught. Joe, the owner of a 40-year-old florist shop, says, "The mass market doesn't even offer service . . . and that's where we have to come back in and do things, because 99.9 percent of everything that we sell is customized to a particular customer. I really take some pride in the fact that almost all of our stuff is customized to the particular sale." He goes on to explain that mass merchants and grocery stores, many of which today stock flowers, have expanded the overall market for fresh flowers. While they have undoubtedly taken away some of the "low-hanging" fruit in terms of the lower end of the flower market, they don't offer custom design services that are in demand for special occasions, weddings, funerals, and romance. The special services appeal to the higher-spending customer and so Joe, as a specialty florist, can focus on what he does best—custom flower design. (For more insight into the realm of the floral business in particular and opportunities in offering customized services to retail customers in general, see the profile of Tiger Lily in Charleston, South Carolina, in Chapter 10.)

Not only do independent retailers focus on customizing product to meet the shoppers' need, they also customize service.

Not only do independent retailers focus on customizing product to meet the shoppers' need, they also customize service. The same retail florist talks of his customers he calls "church ladies"—retired and often widowed women who want the most flower bang for their very limited bucks—and how he regularly customizes arrangements for them that meet their sense of value. He also is willing to work late to meet their last-minute demands. Another retailer notes, "We'll go into somebody's home and we'll provide them with the service of putting up their Christmas décor."

Additionally, independent retailers tend to focus on the little details of service that make the shopping experience more fun for the customer. One retailer regularly calls his own store to learn if his employees are answering the phone with a "happy voice." His secret of retail success is simple: "You have to have a happy voice. You have to be happier than the guy down the street. You have to smile more than the guy down the street."

Sherry, the clothing store owner, finds that encouraging her customers to take small fashion risks leads to repeat business: " I say to the customer, 'I know you never wear anything but black and tan, but let's try some pink, just a little bit, get a reaction from your friends and family.' I know she's going to get a positive reaction, because it's much more flattering and it's much more fun. And when she finds out she's having fun in it and people are complimenting her, then she's back to say, 'Okay, Sherry, now what new color can I try?'" She continues, "It's totally personal service. We put together the whole outfit and match the shoes, sweater, jewelry, handbag to make everything work. When she goes out my door, we want her to look and feel and hear from all her friends that she is a million-dollar picture. She can't get that at Macy's."

A home décor retailer reports building customer loyalty with little gestures that enhance the experience, such as carrying purchases to customers' cars. "I used to really think that it was all about the customer service, and it still is about service. I'll have repeat business often."

Programs to foster loyalty are another way that independent retailers can encourage return visits to their stores. Sherry offers a pay-for-enrollment club that gives its members a flat 20 percent discount on all clothes in the stores (details to follow in the profile of Sherry's store, Damsels in This Dress). Another retailer reports a unique program in which, if he or his store employees make a mistake that causes a customer to visit without being able to purchase their desired product, the store will give the customer $6 to cover gas and time. "If they come back again, I make my money."

Unfortunately, the focus on customer service can have a downside. One music store owner reports customers will come in to research items, then go home and buy them online. He says, "That isn't right to come into your store and waste your time. It is wrong for people to come into your store, tap your knowledge, and then go buy elsewhere."

What Small Specialty Retailers have to Offer May Not be What Everybody is Looking For

Finally, with the rapid rise of mass-market retailers who perpetuate an expectation of self-service in their stores, the culture of shopping in America is undergoing changes. As shoppers come to experience only self-service in stores, they don't know quite how to react in stores where a dedication to service is practiced. The retailers in the discussion group are confounded by this contradiction: that shoppers today are so jaded they don't trust when store service people are nice. A gift retailer with a store in the Easton Town Center (see Chapter 5) says the atmosphere is less personal in that store, as compared to her destination shop in small-town Worthington, Ohio, outside Columbus proper: "When people walk into that store [Easton Town Center], they do not want us to talk to them. They don't want us to greet them. There is no familiarity."

Online shopping also contributes to the culture of self-service shopping that runs counter to the personalized experience created by the independent retailer. "You just punch on the Internet, and you can come up with whatever, whoever it is, and for some people, that's all they're interested in. They're not interested in all the things that we are in business to offer them," says one retailer. This retailer continues, "We have to come to terms with that to keep from waking up in the middle of the night worrying about it, because there's not a damn thing any of us can do about it."

WHEN CUSTOMER SERVICE BECOMES
TOO MUCH OF A GOOD THING

While we are focusing on what retailers have to say about customer service, it is interesting to compare what shoppers said in the shopper discussion groups when customer service takes a turn for the worst. Like eating one piece of scrumptious Godiva chocolate is a true luxurious treat, eating a whole box is definitely too much of a good thing. Here is what shoppers have to say about when customer service crosses the line from friendly to overbearing:

- This shopper takes offense to over-personal sales personnel: "I was just at Anthropologie, and they knock on your dressing room door when you are getting changed and ask 'What is your name?' Then she says, 'Christi, is there anything else you'd like?' That bugs me. Like when I walk back in the store tomorrow, are you going to say, 'Hi, Christi?' No. It doesn't make me want to go to Anthropologie anymore."

- Another says, "I can't stand it when I'm in a store and four different people ask me, 'How are you?' and 'Can I help you?' You know, five feet ago, somebody already asked me that. I mean, it's very nice, but just let me alone."

- Another mentions that one store she visits has trained the sales personnel to say how good their jeans fit, but after you hear it a couple of times, it becomes really annoying. "I was going to mention that Abercrombie Kids' Stores have a new policy that they are supposed to ask—'Have you heard how good the jeans fit?' But they will tell you that every time you turn around. Five different people will hit you with that along the way. I think it is annoying."

Independent Retailers are Optimistic about the Future

In spite of all the challenges, independent retailers are optimistic about the need for their type of special retail experience in the changing marketplace. "I think that there will always be independent retailers," says one retailer in the group discussion. "I think the mall-ing and big-boxing of America is going to result in a backlash. I think there will be a backlash to this suburban sprawl . . . so it has to end someplace. What people want is a simpler, more old-fashioned style of life. We like small towns with trees and cars and shops." Another sums it up this way: "That's what we hunger for. That's what we want. We want the personal interaction with somebody in a store."

Independent retailers are flexible enough to respond to changing customer preferences: "We, as small business people, are going to change enough to stay satisfied with what we're doing. We'll reduce our inventory, we'll change our inventory, reduce our staff, increase our staff, move our locations, whatever, in order to meet what we perceive as the demand to satisfy us and the consumer."

Damsels in This Dress

■ Delivering Style to the Fashionista

Located in a quaint historic district of Worthington, Ohio, on the outskirts of Columbus, is an apparel store, Damsels in This Dress, which would fit right into the fashionista shopping districts of Soho. Sherry Keefe and her partner Alise Ghanem run a women's apparel and accessories store that showcases fashion from small designers and artisans. Nothing mass-produced comes in their doors. "The things we carry are custom ordered and usually we work with the designer to pick out colors and how we want things done. So it's really a collection of individual artisan designs with apparel and accessories that are not mass produced," Keefe explains. What she really sells is wearable art.

With uniqueness as the watchword, Keefe attracts women much like herself into her shop. "I wanted to offer the shopper a chance to create a unique look for herself, and I offer her a chance to work with somebody who has worked in the fashion industry for years and years to decide where to start and what colors to choose. My whole premise is I don't want to look like everybody else and that is who I attract— women who are tired of a cookie-cutter look and want to express their individual style," she says.

Keefe tantalizes her customers not just with great things, but also with great stories about where the items come from and how they are made. As Damsels in This Dress lends support to artisans and designers, the customers respond to support their artistic efforts. Keefe says, "It's developed into more than just finding cool things to wear. People are excited to learn about the designers and to know where these items are made and what goes into making them. I invite designers into my store to meet my customers and they really like that interaction. We've grown by leaps and bounds, way more than I ever imagined."

But Keefe's mission for Damsels is more than just unique, individualistic fashion. She delivers style to her customers, which is how fashion retailers can transcend selling just more things into a shopping experience. She explains, "As women mature, I think they want and deserve a look that is their own style. I tell my customers the best compliment anyone can give you is not that 'I love your blouse' or 'what great earrings' but 'I love your style.' It almost takes a more mature woman to have that sense of style. When you are in your twenties, you want to look cool for your friends. But when you reach a certain age, you just want to project that personal, unique style."

Toward the goal of helping her customers discover their individual style, Sherry sponsors events where the customer can work directly with the designer to create their own custom pair of earrings or a one-of-a-kind handbag by selecting their own zipper, pockets, leathers, and linings. She reaches out to the community with fashion shows and talks to women's groups about fashion. In these efforts she shares how specific fashion can fit into people's lives, how to coordinate looks, and how fabric affects style.

The ultimate expression of Keefe's outreach to her customers is the Damsel Divas club. Not just a loyalty discount program, though all members of the Damsel Divas club get an across-the-board 20 percent discount, the Damsel Divas get together for high tea and jewelry-making events and every year they go on a Damsel Divas' cruise. Keefe explains, "We never want to be the same as everybody else—not in our clothes, not in how we treat our customers, and certainly not in a same old run-of-the-mill loyalty program. So we decided to make it a club, so by creating Damsel Divas, it is that woman's club ... it belongs to her. It isn't mine, but it belongs to the woman who decides to join. She can participate as much or as little as she wants. The women love it."

"We never want to be the same as everybody else—not in our clothes, not in how we treat our customers and certainly not in a same old run-of-the-mill loyalty program," says Sherry Keefe, Damsels in This Dress.

As great as the merchandise she sells is and as engaging as the Damsel Divas club is to the customer, another critical element that makes Damsels in This Dress so successful is Keefe herself. I haven't had the pleasure of meeting Keefe's partner-in-crime Alise, but I feel that if Keefe likes her then I am sure to as well. Keefe has an irresistible personality, full of enthusiasm and excitement. She is the kind of person you just want to know and her inimitable personal style guarantees she will never shrink into the background and go unnoticed. She shares, "Anytime you have a customer who comes in your door and immediately gives you a hug because she is so happy being there, it is really special. I think your personality as a store owner can create whatever your imagination will allow you to create. So if you put your personality and your heart in a store, people recognize it by how things are displayed and the store is designed. But not only that, your aura creates a magical atmosphere for the customer just because you give of yourself."

Keefe's enthusiasm for her store, her products, her displays, and her customers is clearly contagious. Her final piece of advice to other retailers is to keep on dreaming. "It's always a challenge to come up with new ideas, but we never stop thinking. That's the whole key: imagination. Imagination is the key to success and the key to happiness. If you can imagine it, you can do it. You have to constantly be thinking, using your imagination and coming up with innovative ways to appeal to people so things don't grow stale and so they don't get bored. Because we put our hearts and our personalities into Damsel, it keeps people coming back, and it keeps things changing and different all the time."

CHAPTER EIGHT

Build Customer Involvement and Interaction

CREATE THE
ULTIMATE SHOPPING EXPERIENCE

"When the customer comes first, the customer will last."
ROBERT HALF

Having looked at the challenges of retailing today and explored the shoppers' experiences, this is the time to probe into exactly what it takes to succeed in retail now and into the future. The strategy is simple: Love your customers by making shopping in your store truly a special experience. The focus for retailing success in the future is not so much what you sell, but how you sell it.

The focus for retailing success in the future is not so much what you sell, but how you sell it.

Retailers, especially the small independent types who offer a limited range of merchandise in a limited space with a limited operating budget, recognize that their special shopping experience doesn't appeal to everybody. That is the role of mass retailers: to sell to the masses. What specialty retailers must focus on is the type of shopper that responds best to their unique combination of products and services. And that is largely the recreational shopper who shops for pure pleasure and fun. So the competitive secret for small specialty stores is to make shopping in their store fun.

SHOPPING FACTOIDS
Americans Have Extremely High Standards of Living

Home ownership (2004):	69 percent
Home ownership of married couple families:	84 percent

Households in 2001 with . . .

Ovens:	95 percent
Range:	99 percent
Refrigerator:	99.9 percent
Microwave oven:	86 percent
Dishwasher:	53 percent
Air-conditioning:	76 percent
Color television:	99 percent
Two or more color televisions:	72 percent
Cable/satellite antenna:	77 percent
VCR/DVD equipment:	77 percent
Personal computer:	56 percent
Cell/mobile phone:	53 percent

Source: U.S. Census Bureau, Statistical Abstract of the United States: 2006

These same principles apply to the big boys, too. In fact, they have enjoyed such dynamic growth over the last ten years that they are inevitably heading toward a growth plateau. Wal-Mart, the nation's largest retailer, found Christmas sales for the 2005 season disappointing at best. With only 2.2 percent same-store sales growth reported in December, this is Wal-Mart's poorest Christmas performance since 2000, despite early and aggressive discounting and marketing.

For the future, Wal-Mart, like many other big national retailers, will find that their favorite bag of sales-stimulating tricks—deep discounts, frequent sales, heavy advertising—is going to produce diminishing returns. American consumers, especially the dominant Baby Boom generation now aged 42 to 60 years, have been on a buying spree for the material trappings of 21st-century life. In fact, Americans have made huge strides in our standard of living since the postwar

'50s, but as a culture we have pretty well reached our zenith in terms of overall improvement of our standard of living. (See the factoid on the previous page.) Surely there are pockets of poverty and want in the culture, but overall the statistics that describe contemporary American life show little evidence of widespread privation.

With the number of The Gap stores reaching 1,239 in the states, The Gap is struggling with retrograde growth. Same store sales in November 2005 were down 5 percent and December's numbers were even more dismal, with a 10 percent drop. Their strategic solution to declining sales is to redesign the store. Their new prototype store jettisons the light blond floors, harsh lighting, and white wall board in favor of darker wood floors, couches, and coffee table waiting areas, new shopper-friendly fitting rooms, and movable walls that create a boutique feel inside the store. All that is well and good, but by simply redesigning the store space, they aren't necessarily going to create one of the magic elements that make a shop pop—customer involvement and interaction. The Gap has clearly taken its cue from Starbucks in creating a space that is inviting and comfortable for the customer but they need to bridge an even bigger gap—creating a community among their shoppers that engages the customer and makes them feel part of the brand, part of the store, and part of the total experience.

Barnes & Noble

■ Creating Community with the Customers by Feeding Their Minds and Their Bodies

Barnes & Noble stores have evolved far beyond being just a bookstore. Part music and video store, part bookstore, newsstand, and gift store, and most importantly for the caffeine-addicted, a café, a Barnes & Noble store becomes a favorite community center drawing people from all walks of life, all income levels, and different educational backgrounds. Steve Riggio, CEO of Barnes & Noble, Inc., says the current stores' culture grew from a vision they had in the mid-'70s for their lone Fifth Avenue New York store: to create a bookstore that was a nonintimidating place. "Our original vision and concept was rooted first in making them [Barnes & Noble bookstores] nonintimidating. Throughout the '80s, and then in the early '90s, we began to perfect the concept, and the store evolved from being nonintimidating to being welcome in a way that we never actually envisioned, and it grew. The community aspect of the store has grown many times since those days, to the point where people feel more comfortable being in a Barnes & Noble than in any other retail store. For some people, it's become like a second home. The cafés came in the early to mid-'90s, and I think they added that aspect of electricity, kinetic atmosphere, and community connection. People say 'Meet me at Barnes & Noble,' and customers in our store spend an average time of about an hour, which is much more than in any typical retail."

Through its unique configuration selling books, music, and movies that expand the mind and cafés that become social centers, Barnes & Noble has transcended the traditional confines of a retail store into something totally unique. It's a shop that pops. In keeping with their 'first you break all the rules' approach to retail, their stores are open seven days per week—Riggio tells me they were the first national retailer to do that—and extended hours, usually from 9 AM to 10 PM. Each store is designed individually to fit the local community, so Barnes & Noble rejects the cookie-cutter approach to store design that retailers with upwards of 800 separate stores typically resort to. "Every Barnes & Noble is different. That's perhaps one of the most interesting things about Barnes & Noble among big-box retailers or other specialty retailers. Even within a place like Manhattan, stores that are two blocks away from one another have different selections. So the managers are encouraged to do displays and feature titles that are unique to that community," Riggio explains.

To create an even more cohesive community feeling in each store, Barnes & Noble stores host special events including author appearances and readings, children's authors, and workshops. "These things add to the energy and life in the store, so there is always something going on in a Barnes & Noble . . . We wanted to make it a place where people enjoyed spending leisure time," Riggio adds.

In order to create a destination that appeals to the broadest cross section of people young and old, they designed a store where the customer determines the level of involvement they want to experience. With rows and rows of shelves and seating scattered throughout, the store encourages self-service browsing, but offers up expert levels of customer service for people who want help and guidance. Riggio explains, "When people ask for a book, our culture is to say 'yes' all of the time, whether we have it on the shelf or we have to mail it to their home. So while the store itself is designed for browsers, and we like people to come in and feel they can walk around without being interrupted, when they do need help, we're there. So it's a combination of laid back, built for browsers, but also high service. We have our stores staffed by very knowledgeable people and we've got great systems, so we can locate any book whether it is in the store or in our warehouse."

"These things add to the energy and life in the store, so there is always something going on in a Barnes & Noble . . . We wanted to make it a place where people enjoyed spending leisure time," says Steve Riggio.

Barnes & Noble plays a critical role in the communities that it serves. For the store's many loyal browsers, shoppers, and coffee tipplers, it provides a sense of belonging that is missing in so many other aspects of people's lives today. Riggio says, "Shopping certainly relieves people's sense of alienation and enables people to connect with others. What we did with the bookstores was way beyond anything done in retail, and it is far more than books. It's the total Barnes & Noble experience that is very, very special and hard to copy."

It achieves this by aspiring to be more than just a bookstore, and likewise what it offers its shoppers is aspirational as well. "The functional aspect of the store was to recognize that people had aspirations, and we could serve them by being an aspirational kind of experience. Booksellers themselves are autodidacts [I had to look up the definition of autodidact, and it means "somebody who has acquired a great deal of knowledge despite little or no formal education."]. The experience of working in a bookstore is an education in itself. So you've got this ongoing mix of ideas and community that is very hard to replicate in any other retail environment," Riggio concludes.

Maximize Customer Involvement by
Appealing to All the Senses

Barnes & Noble engages its customers in a multisensory way. They offer the latest books people are talking about, along with an engaging shopping environment, places to relax and browse, and a café that encourages people to spend even more time in the shop.

Shoppers come into the store with the potential to engage all five senses—sight, sound, tactile, taste, and smell. Too many stores play to only one or two of the potential points of involvement. The more sensory touchpoints a retailer can engage the customer in, the better their chances of building a true community with the customer.

The more sensory touchpoints a retailer can engage the customer in, the better their chances of building a true community with the customer.

When a store builds community with its customers, it isn't long before the customers themselves begin to build a community amongst themselves and that is when real magic happens. Sherry of Damsels in This Dress shop has her Damsels Divas club, a powerful form of community she is building among her customers. Hearkening to the power of the Red Hat Society, Damsels Divas creates a sense of belonging among her customers. Surely she rewards her paid members with a 20 percent discount across the board, but that isn't the driving force behind getting potential Divas to sign up.

People have a tremendous need today to connect with other people. Many of us derive our sense of community from our extended families, the workplace, our neighborhoods, and churches, but it is harder and harder to feel truly connected with others today as we spread out into the suburbs and live narrowly prescribed, overscheduled lives. I know for myself that I have thousands and thousands of acquaintances, but few people I am really close too. My life is entirely too busy to invest the time needed to build those connections, so I take what I can get on the fly. Many of those connections are established through the commercial realm; either I do business with them or they do business with me. My music teacher, my dermatologist, my hair stylist, my aesthetician, or Jan who runs my favorite fashion boutique and who I can always depend on to give me the right advice on fashion, are some of those people with whom I have built a limited sense of community and connection. The commercial nature of the relationship greases the wheels, but I truly believe that we have a meaningful connection where they have my best interests in mind. Many other women are just like me; they develop relationships with shopkeepers and other personal care providers as a substitute for deeper friendships that take more time to nurture and develop. As Sherry has discovered, women who like one particular store, its attitude, its image, its offerings are also likely to connect with each other. The store becomes the fulcrum for the community of shoppers which Sherry taps powerfully by sponsoring Damsel Divas cruises where like-minded women get a chance to dress up in Damsel outfits and have fun.

Nell Hill's Mary Carol Garrity has made creating an atmosphere that maximizes customer involvement a cornerstone of her marketing plan. How else to explain that she has built a very successful business based upon attracting shoppers who live over an hour away. Mary Carol sets the tone by spending 100 percent of her time in the store on the sales floor rubbing shoulders and chatting up the customers. Because Nell Hill's is a destination store in the true sense of the word, people who visit are not casual, but committed, having invested so much travel time just to get there. Because of that, they want to share their excitement with Mary Carol, her staff, and other shoppers in the store.

Shoppers come to Nell Hill's for the wonderful, innovative home furnishings offered, but they are equally drawn by the charged atmosphere, the warm welcome they get from the proprietor, and the chance to establish community with other shoppers in the store, as Mary Carol said shopping in her store is like a cocktail party without the alcohol. She carries that high level of customer involvement even into her personal life. She has opened her home up to her customers through regular open houses where they can tour her home and stop off by the tent out back and buy interesting items that aren't even featured in the store. Another hallmark of Mary Carol's customer involvement is doing special events outside the store. By reaching out into the community and going to them, not waiting for them to come to her store, Nell Hill's has attracted a passionate crowd of shoppers, near and far, who regularly visit her store to find out what's new, both in terms of merchandise and in Mary Carol's life as well.

Feast!

■ Feed Them and They Will Come

In a little corner of a market hall of independent food shops in Charlottesville, Virginia, home of Thomas Jefferson and the University of Virginia, is an artisan cheese and gourmet store called Feast! You have got to go out of your way to find it, but when you do it is an absolute delight for all your senses, but most especially the taste buds because everywhere you turn there are sample bowls to tempt you to try all the wonderful foods on display. Recognized as one of the top 20 cheese shops in America by *Saveur* magazine, Feast!'s founder, Kate Collier, and her husband, Eric Gertner, operate their store based upon a simple principle: "If someone asks about something, rather than tell them what it tastes like, we put it in their mouths."

> *"If someone asks about something, rather than tell them what it tastes like, we put it in their mouths" says Kate Collier, Feast!*

Food is so basic and sharing food such an important way to build community that Feast! takes advantage of that at every turn in the store. Collier explains, "One of our employees has been with us since we opened and he knows everybody's name and what they eat. So when they walk in, he says, 'Hi, Mr. Smith. Can I get you any more of that Stilton you tried last week?' That is one of our biggest hooks for customers. It feels like family when you come in there."

Customer service at Feast! means just that. They staff the store with friendly people who are food lovers. These are people who want to take care of the customer, give them a basket when their arms get full, and answer questions about specialty items such as herbal-infused vinegars, which may be unfamiliar to some. "One thing that my husband and I feel is very important is not to have a snooty gourmet food store," Collier says. "We look at it like welcoming guests into our home, instead of trying to sell them things. Our goal is not to upsell. Our goal is to make people feel comfortable so they want to come back regularly."

Feast! has come a long way since its founding in 2002. They expanded the business twice, the first time shortly after they opened with the addition of a gift store. That turned out to be a slight misstep for them because by adding gifts they shifted their focus away from what made them really special. Ultimately they shrunk the gift store back and opened a café instead which played to their strengths. "That [gifts] was not something that was our specialty, and so it wasn't extremely special. And so we really focused on what was special, which was expanding our meats, expanding our cheese, doing more produce. What really grew the business was adding that plus our café and lunch business."

Instead of offering hard goods, Feast! specializes in food baskets and boxes customizable by the gift giver. Rather than offering a preselected assortment of items in a gift basket, Feast! gives shoppers their own bag that they can fill up with what they want to put in a basket. "We used to have gift bags that we put together, but customers always wanted to take out a couple of things and add others. But you have to do what the customers want and are asking you for. So now they select their own stuff that we use to make into a basket. This has been a much bigger hit. They feel like they did the shopping, but they didn't have to do everything," Collier says. They also added Feast! branded items, like their signature pimento cheese, which makes their brand memorable. "For some reason people like to wear the Feast! name on their t-shirt. Customers keep buying our signature shirts and bibs, so we want to carry that as far as we can," Collier adds.

Feast!'s owners Collier and Gertner have created a shop that pops by delivering an excellent, high-quality product that is special and different from that found in grocery stores, adding the element of customer engagement by encouraging shoppers to taste and try before they buy—"We try to get it into their mouth"—and creating an atmosphere that invites the customers in. "When we designed the store, it was important to us that if we were going to be at this place all the time, we wanted it to feel like a place that we wanted to be. So we wanted to have great music, good lighting, good colors, and a vibrant staff. The staff is really special. They are young food lovers and have lots of creative energy. Fun is one of the things that makes the store have the good energy it has. And when we bake our molasses sugar cookies, the smell makes it comfortable, homey, and tantalizing as well," Collier concludes.

Building Customer Involvement Takes the Right People

Despite all the rhetoric in marketing circles about "belonging" to the brand and "connecting" with the brand, true connection can only occur between and among people. That is why brands that are people brands, brands like Martha Stewart, Donald Trump, Isaac Mizrahi, Nicole Miller, on and on, are ultimately so much more powerful in the marketplace than brands that do not have that personal connection. People relate to people, they build community with other people, they get involved with people. It is really hard to feel a personal connection to a thing or a branding concept.

People relate to people, they build community with other people, they get involved with people. It is really hard to feel a personal connection to a thing or a branding concept.

One of the most powerful elements in a store is the people who wait on you and service you in the store. Clearly, mass merchants with their do-it-yourself shopping philosophy are trying to move the needle in the other direction, away from the up-close and personal touch found in smaller, more personal shopping environments.

Nevertheless, shoppers everywhere long for that personal touch and feel nostalgic for the time when the people manning the stores really knew their stuff and could be a resource for the shopper to make sometimes confusing decisions, like "Will my guests prefer this soft goat cheese or the hard cheddar?" How much better life is when someone who really knows cheese—and you completely trust—can authoritatively and confidently recommend, "Let's do this one and that one, and why don't you add the pimento spread for people who might prefer something less stimulating. And can I show you a couple of wines that will pair wonderfully with the cheeses you've selected?" Yes, please! That is the ultimate level of customer involvement in the shopping experience. The shop puts my best interests first, because by putting me first they will build a loyal, devoted customer who will come back again and again. That is how a shop loves its customers: putting them first in all ways. Whether a shop sells food, home furnishings, clothes, books, DVDs, or anything else, customers crave involvement with people in the store who put the shoppers' interests first.

CHAPTER NINE

Evoke Shopper Curiosity

CREATE THE ULTIMATE
CUSTOMER EXPERIENCE

*"I love it when I catch someone's reaction at my stores,
when they turn a corner and come upon something unexpected.
Maybe it's something they didn't know they had to have until that
moment, or it's the way we've displayed something that's a little out
of the ordinary that they might be able to use in their decorating."*
MARY CAROL GARRITY OF NELL HILL'S

Curiosity may kill the cat, but it stimulates the shopper. Curiosity is what draws the shopper into the store, and pulls them down the aisle and around the corner to find wonderful, exciting, got-to-have things and experiences. Owing to our hunter-gatherer roots, people are programmed to notice changes, even subtle shifts, in their environment. Furthermore, because shopping hearkens back to our ancestors' hunting-and-gathering behavior, shops that pop evoke a powerful curiosity factor that attracts the shopper and keeps them looking—or more correctly, hunting—throughout the store.

Curiosity is what draws the shopper into the store, and pulls them down the aisle and around the corner to find wonderful, exciting, got-to-have things and experiences.

In Unity's survey of people who love to shop, we found that merchandise-related features were the most influential in determining the store where a person wants to shop. One of the chief merchandise-related features shoppers respond to is one that "always has something new, different, and interesting," right behind merchandise quality, wide selection, and unique merchandise and place to shop for many things. Shoppers respond to stores that change up their merchandise often. In discussion groups, a passionate recreational shopper expressed her preference for discounters like Marshalls and TJ Maxx: "There are a lot of stores that I favor because their merchandise changes a lot. Marshalls and TJ Maxx tend to have lots of different things like designer clothes all the time, but not at designer prices."

Shoppers are likely to shop more often in stores where merchandise moves in and out quickly. Retailers are rewarded when stock turns frequently because shoppers are powerfully stimulated to buy. Shoppers can't afford to pass something up that they want because if they wait it might not be there the next time, as Mary Carol Garrity says of her Nell Hill's shoppers: "People who shop here know that if they see it and they want it, they better buy it. It won't be here the next time they come."

However, actual stock movement can be real or virtual, an impression created by simply redoing displays and shifting merchandise around from place to place. Mary Carol calls her displays "my silent salespeople." Included among her staff are dedicated decorators who do nothing but displays all day long, bringing out new stock and moving around existing merchandise. It was the end of October when I touched base with Mary Carol and she told me that at that time they had already redone their Christmas displays three times after putting them up the first week in September. Constantly changing merchandise and displays is one of the prime features that make Nell Hill's pop.

Boxwoods Gardens & Gifts

■ A Curiously Different Gift Store

From the first moment you see Boxwoods Garden & Gifts located in Buckhead, Georgia, right outside of Atlanta, in a quaint suburban home with a cottage-like ambiance, Boxwoods evokes shopper curiosity. With its dense front garden and moss-covered patio, it simply invites you to stroll up the steps, open the front door, and come on inside. Once you get inside, it is more and more curious. In keeping with the cottage feel, the Boxwoods store is broken up into small intimate rooms, each showcasing different assortments of merchandise, like the fashion room and garden room. You simply can't stop wandering through, because it is a store made up of nooks and crannies filled to the brim with wonderful stuff. Dan Bellman, co-owner of Boxwoods Gardens & Gifts with his partner Randy Korando, says, "When people walk in, it's is either 'welcome to my nightmare,' or 'come on in to the dog-and-pony store.' We started off with just one side of the building, then we added glass conservatories and it grew and grew. My father says 'this is a gruesome business,' meaning we grew, then we grew some more.'"

From the beginning Bellman and Korando were aiming for a destination shop that was an experience. "We were hoping for a fun and friendly shopping experience that would serve to showcase unusual, one-of-a-kind items and that would also highlight our creative floral abilities." One of the more curious things about Boxwoods is their floral business is huge, but they don't sell one cut flower or arranged flower bouquet. The store actually grew out of the partners' landscaping business and Boxwoods' floral business is a natural outgrowth of that. They only sell living plants so all flowers are delivered in pots with their very own greenery. Bellman says, "The problem with cut flowers is that they have such a short shelf life. They last a couple of days, if you're lucky, a week, then you toss them out. We promote floral compositions, which is basically we take anything from an old sugar bowl, centerpiece, basket, whatever and fill it with plants, both flowering plants and greenery. We have done weddings with live plants where instead of spending $10,000 on flowers that just get thrown out, people wind up with planted compositions that they can take and plant in their yard to create a permanent memory."

With a focus on the unusual and unique, they use antiques and vintage furniture as store fixtures along with antique sconces, chandeliers, and other decorative accents, and everything is for sale. "We go to Europe on buying trips three to four times a year," Bellman explains about the store's merchandising. "By its very nature, what we bring back is old and antique stuff, so it is one of a kind and unique. And that's what our customers crave. We have what we call the cell phone network. When we get a shipment from Europe in, we don't even have time to get on the phone to call our customers to tell them because one customer will walk in on the morning a container comes in and three hours later we'll have the whole parking lot packed with people, because one girlfriend will call another and another." Now that is powerful word of mouth.

Boxwoods also stocks plenty of new giftware items, taking advantage of their Atlanta location to shop the huge Atlanta wholesale gift show every day from morning till night over the course of the show's ten-day run. "We go to every showroom we can. We look at everything. We try to find unique stuff and we create our own unique stuff in our plant department," Bellman says. Due to the store's heavy sales volume, difficulties in sourcing one-of-a-kind items, and the overall weakness of the dollar in overseas markets, Boxwoods' original plan for an even split between gifts, antiques, and plants has been adjusted toward more emphasis on gifts.

"We are big believers in finding product that looks like it should cost twice what it is selling for and that has definitely become part of the culture of our shop," says Dan Bellman, Boxwoods Gardens & Gifts.

But no matter what merchandise they are buying for their customers, the guiding principle in Boxwoods' merchandise selection, besides uniqueness, is value. "We're really big on bang for the buck. Both Randy and I by nature are frugal. We live a good lifestyle, but we do it with one eye toward value. We are big believers in finding product that looks like it should cost twice what it is selling for and that has definitely become part of the culture of our shop." They have benefited from improvements in manufactured products coming out of China and India. Bellman says, "Low price and high style have now converged so that we can offer our customers a superior look at a very competitive price."

Another curious feature that elevates Boxwoods Gardens & Gifts beyond the run-of-the- mill gift shop is a whole department dedicated to fashion accessories and handcrafted jewelry. At the suggestion of one of their longtime employees, Chris, they brought in an artist line of garden-themed jewelry. After this first success, they gave over a curio cabinet to Chris to stock up with more jewelry. "From what started in one little case, we've now turned over and devoted a whole room to what we call the girlie-girlie stuff which is jewelry, handbags, pashminas, cell phone holders. Randy and I don't do any of that buying because we wouldn't know where to begin," Bellman says. Fortunately for them, Chris does, because she has scored a real hit in the fashion accessories department offering high style and extremely good value. Commenting on the success of fashion sales, Dan says, "We just had somebody come in today and she bought 12 handbags. She found out about them from her friend who told her 'You can't believe the prices on these wonderful handbags.' So she came in and did all of her Christmas shopping for her nieces in our handbag department."

It is win-win all the way for Boxwoods Gardens & Gifts, for its owners, its employees, and its customers. It starts at the top and works its way throughout the whole atmosphere and culture of the store. "Our best assets are our employees, without question. Through both words and action we try to achieve a friendly and supportive atmosphere with our employees. This feeling that we refer to as being part of the Boxwoods' family is conveyed to our customers, who then feel like friends of the family. Many customers are really our friends. Like at Christmas time when retail is crazy, we have people bring us boxes of cookies or homemade cakes. It is amazing how nice they are and that they really feel that we're more than just a store. It is a good feeling for them; it's a good feeling for us. We're a very happy shop."

Evoke Curiosity by Exciting All the Senses

Both Nell Hill's and Boxwoods Gardens & Gifts are in the envious position of moving so much merchandise in and out of the store that getting customers curious about what's in stock is simply a natural outgrowth of that perpetual motion. Speaking of turnover, Bellman of Boxwoods says, "We do such a heavy volume for a little shop that things are constantly changing. And it becomes part of a cycle, where things move so quickly, people know that they have to buy it when they see it. And that gives us room to bring in more product. It kind of goes around and comes around."

Other stores have to stimulate that curiosity through other means and that is where imagination and creativity enter the picture. Sherry Keefe from Damsels in This Dress plays off their very traditional store façade and old-fashioned Midwestern small-town setting to bring an unexpected surprise to passersby. With extra attention to storefront windows displays, Keefe tantalizes the shopper to come inside and find out what all the excitement is about. Her aim: "We transform the charming old-world Worthington look and what the customer might expect to be very traditional because of where we are located into a very magical, interesting shopping experience."

Curiosity is heightened when confronted with the unexpected.

Curiosity is heightened when confronted with the unexpected. With a natural eye for color and a design flair picked up on the job as a visual merchandiser for Charming Shoppes—"I learned that by only changing a wall, you can up-sell 10 percent in one day"—Keefe creates excitement through color and unexpected props in the window. Inside the store she delivers on the window's promise by merchandising the rest of the store to perpetuate the mood. She explains a particularly successful program, "Last year I had a feather pink flamingo and ribbons hanging everywhere with different props that you might see in the tropics. Then I had a sign on the window that said, 'Love the Tropics? Come in and we have a tropical experience for you.' We served frozen daiquiris and played Jimmy Buffett music so people felt they were in paradise. And the displays and everything in the store reflected that. People come into my store because they want to see what kind of crazy thing we are doing now. They come into the store antici-pating something unusual, something different." No halfway measures at Damsels in This Dress. They go all out with their particular theme and by not compromising, they demand that people notice.

Just think about the window displays in the typical mall store. There they have a captive audience never indisposed by bad weather, cold, rain, or snow. Yet most mall store window displays are totally bland, unexciting, and definitely lacking in curiosity-building appeal. I think about the many challenges facing The Gap stores as they try to create a new shopping experience. One of the problems they face with their old store model is that they are totally predictable, exactly what you would expect, and that makes them inevitably boring. I have passed by The Gap store in my local mall many times more than I have stopped by to visit, and I am a perfectly satisfied Gap customer. It is just that I never feel like I have to stop in the store, because I know exactly what I am going to find if I venture in. No curiosity, so there is no reason to shop.

Barry Rosenberg, speaking about the Easton Town Center shopping environment, describes building the curiosity factor as the "serendipity experiences," those moments when things unexpectedly come together to delight and engage the shopper. Rosenberg explains, "We try to build adventure into shopping. It's like you look around a corner and you find something wonderful, like a fountain, that draws you. We always try to have something to look at, to experience, to draw you in." At Easton Town Center, those serendipity experiences might be a live jazz concert, strolling a local farmer's market or an art festival, Christmas caroling or just enjoying the extravagant Christmas decorations, or the fun of watching the pop-up fountains where the water unexpectedly shoots on and off to the delight of children in their bathing suits who come to play in the fountains on warm days.

"From the very first design brief that I wrote for the stores, I used the word 'serendipity,'" says Steve Riggio, Barnes & Noble.

Steve Riggio of Barnes & Noble uses the same word, serendipity, to explain how they build the curiosity factor into each Barnes & Noble store. "From the very first design brief that I wrote for the stores, I used the word 'serendipity.' What we wanted to do was design a store that is very well-organized, so that if people were looking for fiction or mystery or cookbooks or business books, we wanted the layout of the store to be very, very easy to understand. But within that organization, we wanted there to be a lot of nooks and crannies—we used to call them 'books and crannies'—where people could have a sense of privacy and a sense of being alone while they are exploring and bumping into something that they didn't know anything about. And the stores have lots of nooks and crannies, lots of places to sit down, and it's a place to discover things that you never knew existed." Surely for a book lover like me, what could be more curiosity-arousing than shelves and shelves of books?

CHAPTER TEN

Build a Contagious, Electric Quality in the Store

CREATE THE ULTIMATE CUSTOMER EXPERIENCE

"We see our customers as invited guests to a party, and we are the hosts. It's our job every day to make every important aspect of the customer experience a little bit better."

JEFF BEZOS, AMAZON.COM

Nell Hill's has got it. Barnes & Noble has got it. And the Apple Store has got it in spades. Each store is a shop that pops because they built a contagious, electric quality in their stores. The atmosphere is so kinetic it literally draws people into the store to find out what all the excitement is about. And it is contagious because people learn about the store largely through word-of-mouth, one customer telling another and another about the fun experience of shopping there.

A lot of retailers try to introduce electricity into the store through music and pulsating rhythms, but that becomes a little too desperate. They try with a little paint and polish to rev up the electricity, but that looks contrived. True shopping electricity, excitement, and contagious quality in a store derive from something far more basic than loud music or bright colors. Electricity arises organically and spreads throughout to the community to draw people in. Clearly, creating a shop with high levels of customer involvement and one that evokes shopper curiosity helps build the kinetic quality, but based upon the interviews with shopkeepers, they feel that their shops' electricity originates in the store staff members themselves and then jumps from person to person. People who work in the store are the source of electricity and their energy just radiates

outward to spark shoppers and continues to build into the community to make that shop a destination.

---

*True shopping electricity, excitement, and contagious quality in a store
derive from something far more basic than loud music or bright colors.
Electricity arises organically and spreads throughout to the community to draw people in.*

When asked what generates the kinetic quality at Boxwoods Gardens & Gifts, Dan Bellman says it comes from the salespeople: "Our
salespeople are excited about the merchandise we carry and that creates excitement for the customers." Magnolia's Jim Tweten credits
their highly trained, super-enthusiastic staff as the source of their
stores' high kilowatt electricity: "When there's a contact being made
[with the customer], our sales associates have the passion and excitement. That's the wow. That's the energy." The Apple Store's Genius
Bar staffed by all those geniuses magnetizes the customers and gets
them all worked up for more Apple computer experiences.

By harnessing the power of that electricity, retailers can see their
stores blossom with success which breeds more success. Barry Rosenberg of Easton Town Center pays tribute to the center's environment,
tenant mix, and that it offers interesting things to do and see as part
of the secret of the center's success, but he also recognizes that having
positively motivated and happy salespeople is another critical part of
the equation. "It all feeds off each other when a center like this becomes successful. A successful center attracts the top performing
stores in a market. And the top performing stores tend to get the best
associates. So the success feeds off itself," Rosenberg says.

The fact is you simply can't make the electricity happen—it must
grow organically through a whole combination of factors—and it
starts with the people themselves who provide the vital spark. It flows
from the top down, from the excitement and enthusiasm of the shop
owner to the staff, then ultimately to the shoppers. We've seen that
Nell Hill's Mary Carol Garrity never leaves the sale floor. "The energy
comes from the love of what you are doing. I think too many people
get caught up in the wrong thing. I love being out on the floor. I love
working with the customer. I love listening to what they're asking for

and what they're saying," Garrity says. That kind of enthusiasm simply is contagious.

The fact is you simply can't make the electricity happen—it must grow organically through a whole combination of factors—and it starts with the people themselves who provide the vital spark

---

Sherry Keefe of Damsels in This Dress completely concurs that it all starts at the top. "Your aura creates a magical atmosphere for the customer because you give of yourself. That is what makes business successful. Every day either Alise [co-owner] or I are in the store working with the customer, greeting the customer, making her feel important. That is the key thing to making it electrifying for the new customer or the customer that is returning time and time again." But she laments that it is hard to build that level of commitment to the customer and excitement about serving them among all of her employees. "Your best-case scenario is having your employees think like you do. That's the ultimate in importance."

Tiger Lily

■ A Shop that Blossoms with Beauty and Enthusiasm

While all the popping retailers I interviewed for this book were super-enthused about their business with electricity exuding throughout their interview, Manny Gonzales from Charleston, South Carolina's Tiger Lily, a flower shop with a difference, stands out in terms of high-voltage electricity. Gonzales runs Tiger Lily with his wife Clara, who was the flower enthusiast behind the venture. Gonzales came out of Marriott Hotels as director of catering, so he wasn't weighted down with traditional "florists' think" in running his business. In fact, he claims when he and Clara were operating Tiger Lily in traditional flower shop mold that they were headed for the poorhouse.

> *"And that's when we said, let's just be Tiger Lily and be the best that we can be and forget all about the rules that we're supposed to follow to be a florist . . . We decided we were going to be the best place to buy awesome flowers. That's it," says Manny Gonzales, Tiger Lily.*

"Originally we didn't know much about the business, but Clara had a flair for it, so we decided we could teach ourselves and scratch out a living. So we followed all the books that told us how to be a florist, and we just weren't that happy. After a couple of years, we had our backs to the wall and almost went out of business. And that's when we said, let's just be Tiger Lily and be the best that we can be and forget all about the rules that we're supposed to follow to be a florist. That's when we dropped 'florist' from our name and got rid of the balloons, the toys, the cards, the plastic buckets, the daisies and the carnations, and somebody taking telephone orders. We decided we were going to be the best place to buy awesome flowers. That's it. So we just brought in the best flowers we could possibly find, got the best designers we could find and we just try to blow people away every time they walk in the door. We just celebrated our tenth anniversary and it is going real well," Gonzales says.

Gonzales explains that a major boost to Tiger Lily's success was getting rid of the crutch that the floral wire services represented. "The best payoff we got was withdrawing from the wire services where you pick a picture out of the book, you call a florist in New York, and they make the arrangement to match the book. To me it was our major source of mediocrity, and mediocrity is a four-letter word around here. Yet so many florists feel that the wire service is their lifeline and their major source of sales. We try to be different. We try to be awesome. How can you do that when you're following a book? And so at the time we decided to cut the wire services, they accounted for a third of our business. But we didn't like the quality. The book tells you how to be a mediocre florist. How can you be special and different if you're doing what everybody else is doing?" Gonzales explains.

In cutting the umbilical cord to the florists' business that the wire services represent, they were left to stand on their own, create their own unique vision in order to grow their business. It was a brave and bold move, but one that has paid off many times over for Tiger Lily as they morphed from being an ordinary run-of-the-mill florist to being flower superstars.

"The quality of what we were doing just took off because when you sent an arrangement out that had Tiger Lily on it, it wasn't a picture from a book. It was the vision of a designer. And the customer says, 'That's cool, that's different.' It immediately separated Tiger Lily from what everybody else was doing. And it really gave us the freedom to do what we believed in, and that's our vision, which is 'killer flowers' and 'killer service' that goes above and beyond, exceeding your expectations every time," Gonzales continues.

These are quite ambitious goals but their track record attests to the fact that Tiger Lily is doing it. They have been voted Best Florist in Charleston every year from 2000 to 2005. They were named Charleston's Small Business of the Year in 2004. *Elegant Bride* magazine said Tiger Lily is "one of America's Best Wedding Flower Designers," and they were just featured in *Southern Living* magazine in December 2005 in *South Carolina People and Places*. In 2006, *Florist's Review,* a national trade magazine, selected Tiger Lily as America's Best Florist, Runner-up.

With those accolades confirming their strategy, they decided to use their rewards as the key message to build the brand identity for Tiger Lily. Gonzales says, "That gave us the confidence to say, 'I'm not going to say we're the best because we try to be as good as we can be every day.' But if you [the customers] are saying we are the best, then I'm going to let that be known. So we put that on our vans, in our sale collateral, on our labels. And people started calling us because they wanted the best in town. There was a real need for special attention, special flowers, and special focus on what people say is important. Our sales have just gone through the roof every year since."

The electricity at Tiger Lily comes partly from this iron-willed commitment to being the best of the best, but it also comes from the electricity of being surrounded by flowers upon entering the store. "When people come in our front door, they basically run into 2,000 flowers. You smell them. You can touch them. You can pick them up. And if that isn't good enough, we will take you into the back and show you two walk-in coolers full of flowers and 20 people working with flowers going to hotels or for weddings. There is a whole floral kalei-doscope around you," Gonzales says.

He goes on to describe the energy in Tiger Lily's flower studio like that found in a gourmet restaurant. "If you were to stop and think about a florist, you'd probably think of a quiet, peaceful place. But around here is it like walking into a kitchen of a five-star restaurant and all the energy. That's why people buy flowers. They're not buying flowers so much for the colors. They're buying the energy. And we want them to get a taste of that energy when they come in." As an encouragement for shoppers to come into the store and partake of that floral-energy boost, Tiger Lily offers a half-price discount on all flowers shoppers pick out for themselves.

Perhaps one of the most challenging aspects of Tiger Lily's business, yet what makes them draw deep within their own creative reserves, is the customized nature of their business. Each design is unique, depending upon the needs of the customer, what flowers are available that day, how much they want to spend, and the creativity of the designer. "Value is a real buzz word for us. We're not the cheapest, but we want to be the best and offer the best value. Because I come from a food and beverage background, I see lots of parallels between the two businesses. Most florists out there are offering cheap fast food, but people want gourmet dining. We want to be the gourmet florist. The value's there because we aren't making floral arrangements, we are fulfilling your floral fantasies. People will spend $250 on an arrangement and call us the next day to say how unbelievable it was."

Electricity Starts with the People, Then Spreads from There

Ultimately the electricity must come from within. You can't design it, you can't merchandise it, and you can't paint it on or pump it in. It has to arise from the people who work in your store and who provide that personal face for the shopper. In researching this book, I visited lots and lots of stores, as you can imagine. Very few actually lived up to the standards I set for a shop that pops. One store in particular was a total disappointment, yet it came with glowing recommendations from printed reviews and the Fodor's Guide, my personal favorite when I travel. The store was located in New York, elegantly appointed and carefully designed. It offered a wide range of merchandise from fashion, beauty, home, baby, and gifts. It offered the shopper experiences, not just merchandise, with a gourmet café serving lunch and a beauty salon-day spa solving all the other problems of the harried shopper. Problem was, this store, as nice as it was, absolutely sucked all the oxygen out of my body and left me gasping for air. There was no excitement, no energy, no electricity, just deadly, dull boredom. I still haven't figured out what exactly was missing, except it had no soul—that hard-to-define, comes-from-within quality that is uniquely human, electrifying, and contagious.

I still haven't figured out what exactly was missing, except it had no soul—that hard-to-define, comes-from-within quality that is uniquely human, electrifying, and contagious.

So if electricity comes from the soul, that soul only comes from the people. With all the energy emitting from Tiger Lily, Manny credits his people as the ultimate source of his shop's electricity. "I think the number one thing that I do is I hire people who are truly engaged in what they do—people who can work with flowers for eight hours and then have a box of flowers come in and still say, 'wow, that's beautiful.' Even after a full day, they still have that passion. And that energy really sets a standard for the other designers in the shop, and they feed off of it. So there's a lot of energy back there [in the design room]. And then again I like to have folks come in the back room and get a wisp of that energy."

CHAPTER ELEVEN

Create Convergence in Atmosphere, Store Design, and Merchandise

CREATE THE ULTIMATE CUSTOMER EXPERIENCE

"People want to shop; it's in our genes. We are a social species. From our days as hunters and gatherers, we have needed to be around others. Thus the market is not just a place to exchange goods and money. It is also a place to see and be seen."

PACO UNDERHILL IN THE *NEW YORK TIMES*, NOVEMBER 24, 2002

"THE RETURN OF THE SHOPPER"

Another attribute that characterizes a retail shop that pops is the convergence between the store's atmosphere, its design, and its merchandise offerings. It involves creating a unified store environment in the design, layout, architectural elements, space and paths through the store, and the atmosphere of the store, including lighting, music, and scent most prominently. These factors are then connected with the merchandise offered, including how it is displayed, presented, organized, and offered up for sale. Through an emphasis on these more or less objective physical elements that characterize a store, shop owners can exert a powerful influence on shoppers in order to touch them emotionally and influence them to buy. However, there is an elusive, transcendent quality to this connection between the physical and emotional, which is where the magic happens.

Whenever a question comes up related to the physical design of a store environment, my personal go-to guy is architect Ken Nisch, chairman of JGA, a Southfield, Michigan-based group that has become one of the nation's leading retail design, brand strategy, and architectural firms. With a client list a mile long, including such popping retailers as Hot Topic, Diesel, Godiva Chocolatier, J. Jill, Levenger, Brookstone, Mikasa, Saks Department Store Group, Rainforest Café, Coca-Cola, The North Face, Hershey's, and Tommy Hilfiger to name a few, Nisch describes his firm as "a retail branding and environmental design company that focuses on transactional companies, such as retail stores, restaurants, theme parks, airline terminals, banks, and hospitals—any place where money and experience or products changes hands." That means he is concerned with far more than buildings or the bricks and mortar traditionally associated with architecture, but with digital experiences and other experiences delivered by media such as print communications and in-store pop-up environments.

Nisch explains that what makes this convergence factor between the atmosphere, the design, and the merchandise work in the retail environment is when the store is "full of places that unexpectedly meet your expectations, versus an environment like The Gap which is full of expected places that meet your expectations. The key is to create environments filled with places of unexpected difference just to keep the customer engaged." This paradoxical idea of meeting shoppers' expectations by creating the unexpected is what extraordinary stores like Boxwoods Gardens & Gifts, Damsels in This Dress, Nell Hill's, and Barnes & Noble have done.

Nisch describes this as paradox environments, as opposed to parallel environments, where the shopper has come to expect the expected and be overcome with boredom in the process. "Customers are increasingly fatigued with parallel environments. I think of Ralph Lauren or Talbots as being parallel—the store, the merchandise, the marketing, the branding are all absolutely consistent. Versus a store like Anthropologie, which is an example of the paradoxical in retail—relatively expensive merchandise in a flea market environment so you can create a mix-and-match look. You never see a table in the middle with one sweater in four different colors with pants to match, such as at Talbots. In Anthropologie you see fashion and home together with things mix and match, all different sizes, and accessories hanging around. It makes you feel like you discovered the environment. Shoppers who openly seek self-expression through shopping feel that they created the outfit, rather than it was created for them. This explains why retailers like The Gap are having such a tough time—they don't offer their shoppers creativity or self-expression."

Metropark, a chain of some 20 lifestyle stores located in malls, targets young adults by "blending fashion, music, and art to offer a rare and inspiring shopping experience. Part club, part street boutique . . . We're not your typical mall store, so expect the unexpected at Metropark!" their Web site (*www.metroparkusa.com*) proclaims. Nisch points to Metropark's pet department as a way to use merchandise to deliver the unexpected. He calls the pet department an "interrupter that is a category or product grouping that is totally unexpected in the environment. It's the 'bucket of cold water' that makes you all of a sudden reconnect with the environment. By throwing in something that is totally unexpected like doggie owner and pet sweaters that say 'Bitch,' all of a sudden the shopper is reengaged and reconnected. You can create that with some synergy or relationships, or with some shock value or interruption that gets you to rethink," Nisch explains.

The future success of retailers will be found when they offer up the unexpected in interesting, stimulating, and exciting ways.

It takes a certain kind of shopper to thrive in these parallel environments. They must have confidence and sophistication in order to put the look together and create their own self-expression, as opposed to shopping in a parallel environment where it is all put together for you. Therefore, the Anthropologie or Metropark experience isn't for everyone, just like the Talbots or The Gap experience isn't right for all, but increasingly in today's consumer-empowered marketplace, shoppers are rising to the challenge that a paradox environment presents. They are more knowledgeable, more experienced, more sophisticated. Yesterday's shoppers might have wanted the comfort and confidence that parallel environments, like Talbots or The Gap, offered, but today they want something more. The future success of retailers will be found when they offer up the unexpected in interesting, stimulating, and exciting ways.

Shoppers Hate Clutter, but They Love
Discovering Treasures among the Trash

Paradox is the operative word when you talk to shoppers about what they like and dislike in a shopping environment. While they overwhelmingly hate clutter in a store, they want to shop in an environment that offers them lots to see, lots to explore, lots of stuff; in other words, they want lots of good clutter, instead of bad clutter. According to the passionate shoppers we talked to, the department stores in general, and Macy's in particular, are among the leading culprits in filling up their stores with bad clutter. Talking about her experience shopping in Macy's, Sharon, a 40-something recreational shopper, says, "One problem I have [when shopping at Macy's] is how many items of clothing can they shove on a floor rack? You go into Nordstrom, and there's six shirts hanging on a rack, but you go into Macy's and the on the same rack you find 75. This is just organized chaos . . . They could be the same exact pieces of clothing, but if they are all shoved in there, the clothes are all over and look messy . . . It's a turnoff. It almost feels like a fire sale."

In Macy's with their overcrowded racks, she can't discern what the store really is all about. "I like to go into a department store and go to the section I am interested in and browse it without having to fight to make room. I like to know if I walk in, I can see what they have and then decide whether to stay or not."

Given shoppers' complaints about the negative shopping experience in stores like Macy's, is it any wonder that the traditional department store sector of the retail market is tanking? From 1994 to 2005, the retail sales in the GAFO classification of stores, which the Census Bureau defines as furniture and home furnishing stores, electronics and appliance stores, clothing and clothing accessories stores, sporting goods, hobby, book and music stores, general merchandise stores (e.g., department stores, discount department stores, warehouse clubs, superstores, etc.), and office supply, stationery and gift stores, grew over 70 percent, from $611.2 billion to $1,061.8 billion in 2005, while the traditional department store sector actually declined 3 percent, from $89.4 billion in 1994 to $86.7 billion in 2005. With such a dismal track record, the question really is why have so many department stores simply ignored the comments from their shoppers? Why have they continued to do more of the same and not gone about a wholesale remodeling and redesign effort to enhance the overall shopping experience in their store? It doesn't take a genius to figure out that that doesn't make sense—but it was the genius Einstein who defined insanity as "doing the same thing over and over again and expecting different results."

"Nothing dumbs people's perceptions of you down more than saying, 'I'm going to the mall today.' It sounds like you need to get a life," says Ken Nisch, JGA.

Of course, not every department store is going down without a fight. Nisch shares an innovative new prototype design effort JGA performed for Parisian, a department store chain of 40 stores located in the Southeast and Midwest that is part of the Saks Department Store Group. The new Parisian store was unveiled in the fall of 2005 in Memphis, Tennessee. The objective for developing the Parisian "store of the future" was to reinvent the department store experience by creating a "full-flavored, event-driven experiential marketplace appealing to all the senses." Nisch explains, "We wanted to design a store based around 'things I can do today,' so it might be have my fortune told, get a mini-facial, sample food in the restaurant. We recognized that if you can build a reason for people to be there, people will shop, but shopping can't be the only reason to be there." So the new Parisian store has an open floor plan that is flexible enough to expand and contract merchandising areas and to create event marketing opportunities and trend zones. A two-story atrium that brings in natural light becomes the focal point for the shopping experience that features a revolutionary beauty and wellness hub on the store's first floor. Commenting on why shopping itself can't be the single focus in the Parisian store, Nisch says, "Nothing dumbs people's perceptions of you down more than saying, 'I'm going to the mall today.' It sounds like you need to get a life." So in answer to that, the Parisian prototype store emphasizes experiences, not necessarily merchandise. Their goal was to 'reinvent and reclaim the excitement of the department store itself,' and through an inno-

vative combination of design, merchandising, and atmospherics they
have achieved that ambitious goal.

The Store Becomes a New Multimedia, Interactive Advertisement for the Brand

One of the more predominant trends in retail over the past ten
or so years has been that the number of marketing and brand companies that used to sell exclusively through third parties have expanded
their business model and opened dedicated or captive retail stores of
their own. Part of the reason behind this trend is that traditional
brand advertising is no longer delivering the right branding experience to the consumer. So instead of dropping a couple of million on
a Super Bowl ad that people only see once, marketers invest in
opening a retail store where people can touch, feel, and interact up-
close and personal with the brand every time they shop. At once it
gives a brand company better payback on their investment and a
fully engaging branding experience.

The new Hershey's store in New York's Times Square becomes
much more than simply a store; it is a living, breathing ad for the
brand. Nisch says, "People are segmenting their portfolio into stores
that on a four-wall basis make money; stores that on a contribution
level make money; and influencer stores that while often being
financially viable serve a purpose beyond the purely transactional.
Influencer stores are viewed as alternative media or what is called
below-the-line marketing. It's taking money out of traditional advertising and putting it into what Procter & Gamble calls the First Moment
of Truth—those first three-to-seven seconds when the shopper con-
fronts the product on the shelf into the marketing proposition of
communication options. For brand marketers the magic increasingly
is moving away from traditional advertising, because of diffusion or
changes and lack of freshness, into other things like a store experience or blogs and other things. The Hershey's Times Square store is
one of those examples of an influencer store that is both a commercial and a branding success."

The objective of the Hershey's Times Square store was to infuse
the warmth and nostalgia of the Hershey brand into the unique New

York Times Square attitude that Nisch describes as "creating an immersive retail experience." In keeping with that Times Square point of view, the 215-foot tall, 60-foot wide Hershey store façade is the largest permanent fixture ever constructed in Times Square with its stunning wow factor. Against a clean white "candy factory"' backdrop the store is decorated with iconic brand packaging and nostalgic advertising art. A Wall of Brands showcases key company brands in varied sized cubes that take on each brand's unique color and graphic cues. Shoppers' favorite brands—the Hershey's Bar, Hershey's Kisses, and Reese Peanut Butter Cup—get special attention. The result is "the authentic character of the interior and interactive focal features create a chocolate experience representing the brand's unique legacy."

In summing up the power of the Hershey's Times Square store in building and perpetuating brand identity, Nisch says, "Influencer stores like the Hershey's store are about changing people's perception of the brand by creating an experience, or what some people call atmospherics. If you look at the space, there are a series of intangible elements that add up to changing perception that traditional media just can't deliver because digital media, however visually exciting, can't deliver across five senses. And where traditional media falls short the most is that it can't create a social or community aspect of the experience. The customers are often the best salespeople in the world. But if you cannot be intuitive, interactive, or communicative, this feature is lost."

The Store Is about Creating Points of Customer Interaction

Designing a store is ultimately about creating points of customer interaction with the products for sale. Nisch distinguishes between passive interaction and a more active, involving interaction that ultimately leads the customer toward self-expression and creativity. "Some categories have what I call passive interaction, so for example if I am buying a flat screen television there is a more passive interaction than if I am buying fragrance that I touch, and feel, put on, and smell. It's the difference between a more personal purchase and one that is about self-expression, as opposed to a television, which is mostly about receiving output. If the sale involves self-expression of creativity, you want to design lots of interactivity. If it doesn't involve self-expression, you may not find interactivity as highly effective in increasing customer interest."

Nisch goes on to explain that more and more products are moving toward self-expression as a means to differentiate them in the marketplace, so stores, even more passive interaction stores, must be designed to increase customer involvement. He points to the new way cosmetics are sold—at the end of the counter, rather than across the counter—as one of the more important trends in customer involvement. "The simple things are going to be more important in the future, like how to get somebody to pick it up, try it on, and react to trying it on. In recent work we did in the cosmetics area we found that the best way to shape and organize the transaction isn't over the counter, but it is best done off the corners of the counter, where the salesperson stands next to or beside the customer." [Note: "Over the counter" in this case refers to the traditional means of selling to customers across a display counter with the salesperson behind and the customer in front.] "This increases the potential of somebody interacting with you. It's going to radically change businesses that have been traditionally done over the counter, including jewelry or cosmetics. We even see it in restaurants where they put the kitchen out front versus hidden in the back. People don't want the beginning and the end. They want to see the middle."

Another highly interactive retail environment that JGA was involved with creating was a flagship store for the cataloger Soft Surroundings in St. Louis, Missouri. Founded by Robin Sheldon, Soft Surroundings got its start in direct mail in 1999, and was based upon a simple premise: "We target busy women of all ages—especially those who need to take a moment for themselves to renew their bodies as well as their spirits," according to the company's Web site (*www.softsurroundings.com*). Offering a selection of comfortable and comforting fashion, bedding, linens, and other high-touch products, along with cosmetics, skincare, aromatherapy, and other anti-stress goods, a cozy/cuddle rating distinguishes Soft Surroundings clothing from "so soft" to "heavenly soft" to the "ultimate softness."

The retail store, as Nisch explains, has to reflect the brand's dedication to comfort and relaxation. "The store is organized around life experiences, around the bath, the bedroom, the living room. And literally you go into the store and you are encouraged to just touch and feel the merchandise. There is lots of seating designed into the store. The fitting rooms are very much like a place where you like to be seen wearing the merchandise, not just trying it on. People can spend three hours in the store, trying on clothes, talking to the other customers and sitting in the various settings. People can interact with peer endorsers, rather than just staff."

People Add the Life into Retail

While Nisch's firm designs shopping spaces that create an atmosphere that builds interactivity with the product, the success of bringing these elements together to make a truly distinctive shopping environment is ultimately all about the people who fill the space. Commenting on the vital force that people play in the shopping environment, Nisch says, "Think of The Apple Store. The environment in itself isn't very interesting if you went into the store before it opens. But what is interesting is what happens when the store opens. It brings people together. They are full of people who want to get their Apple fix and they want to be around other people who are getting their Apple fix too. So they have become a kind of cultural magnet. It's become something like a club and that is a new category in retail. It used to be that lifestyle retail was considered the ultimate. But now it is concept retail, shops like American Girl Place or Apple or Selfridges. These are stores that are on top of the retail pyramid that have built a community. You become part of the community."

"As we need less or want less, stores that figure out how to make you go there—where buying becomes secondary to the experience but not the focus of the experience—are going to be important places," says Ken Nisch, JGA.

The ultimate trick for retail shopkeepers, designers, and planners, according to Nisch, is to draw people to the store for the experience, rather than just to shop. Shopping becomes part of or in addition to the experience. He says, "The argument becomes 'I go, therefore I buy,' rather than 'I buy, therefore I go.' As we need less or want less, stores that figure out how to make you go there—where buying becomes secondary to the experience but not the focus of the experience—are going to be important places. It's what Starbucks has figured out. Buying a cup of coffee is just the price of admission to the experience which is the community. And it is what Apple has. Apple Stores really don't have that much to buy, but they are packing the aisles so full of people you can't even walk through. And the end results is the Apple Stores are doing huge amounts of business on top of it all."

Another store that puts the customer experience before sales is Cabela's, the destination store for the outdoorsman—and woman.

Cabela's

■ It Takes a Big Store to Be the World's Outfitter for the Great Outdoors

Not far from my home along Interstate 78 in Hamburg, Pennsylvania, is Cabela's newest and, reputedly, one of their biggest stores at 1.25 million square feet. Cabela's tag line is the "World's Foremost Outfitter" and its stores, according to Dennis Highby, CEO, Cabela's, target "people that are active in the outdoors—with a passion for the sports of hunting, fishing, camping, hiking—and who have a need for outdoor gear."

You probably have guessed that I am not the typical kind of shopper that Cabela's attracts. My idea of an outdoor experience is a walk in the park and the extent of my outdoors outfit is a pair of sneakers and sun hat. But when I visit a Cabela's store, there is no question that serious shopping is going on inside. Cabela's is a dynamic, exciting, electric shopping environment even for someone who isn't passionate about hunting and fishing and the outdoors lifestyle. Nevertheless, one of the characteristics of a shop that pops is that even people who are not all that into the category get excited shopping in the store.

What makes the Cabela's shopping experience special is that their stores—which the company more correctly terms "retail showrooms"—are a show, as much theatre and museum as a destination shop. With 14 mammoth-sized stores scattered across the country in carefully selected locations based upon where the customers of the company's direct-marketing catalog sales congregate, Cabela's showrooms are a true destination. While each store is custom designed for the interests of its local clientele, they share key features. The focal point of each store is the conservation mountain that arises out of the floor, stretches to the ceiling, and displays dioramas of big game animals people rarely get to see in the wild. However, this is a mountain strictly for looking, not climbing. About the store's wildlife displays, Highby says, "The towering conservation mountain sets the tone the instant people set foot in the store that this is really someplace special. We decorate the stores with the type of merchandise and type of experiences our customers enjoy. So we have a waterfall . . . a big aquarium . . . trophy animals on display that people long to have the opportunity to hunt. We decorate the stores the way our customers envision that Cabela's is all about."

"When people go to our stores they expect a lot, and we deliver a lot. People have never seen things like what we display in a retail store," says Dennis Highby, Cabela's.

For example, in their Hamburg store, there is a room devoted to white tail deer and another major display of African animals. These wildlife displays are really breathtaking and would fit right into any major natural history museum. Cabela's was founded originally as a direct marketer, but they have built the Cabela's destination stores as a means to deepen their shoppers'—70 percent of which are men—connection to the brand. Highby says, "Adding these destination retail stores creates so much excitement when people who have enjoyed our catalogs and have a passion for the type of product that we sell visit. They flock to our stores and once they get here, the stores turn out to be exactly what the customer hopes they would be. They have an immense selection that the competition can't compete with. When they get into our stores, they feel comfortable because the ambiance is what they expect and the stores look like they expect them to look."

Cabela's truly epitomizes convergence in atmosphere, store design and merchandise. "Cabela's stands for what sportsmen are all about," Highby explains. "There is a mystique about Cabela's, almost a cult following like you see with Harley Davidson. When people go to our stores they expect a lot, and we deliver a lot. People have never seen things like what we display in a retail store, for instance our gun library. They don't get a chance to see trophy animals like they see in our stores. They enjoy the aquarium. It's a favorite with kids. In fact, one thing we cater to are schools in proximity to our stores. We have regular programs where we bring students in to educate them about conservation."

It is Cabela's dedication to educating the consumer about wildlife and the outdoors that adds power to the "mystique of Cabela's," as Highby describes it. "When people first come into the store, so many say, 'I have to go get my camera.' It just blows them away. And we have many people who want to work here because they are excited to stand and visit with the customers and talk about things they are so passionate about. It's more than selling."

That is ultimately the secret of Cabela's success. They are about a lot more than just selling merchandise and it shows throughout the store and in all the customers' interaction with staff. So if you happen to see a sign off the highway to a Cabela's store, even if you think they have nothing in there for you, I encourage you to stop. It is well worth a visit, even if you don't know the difference between the fly on a pair of jeans and the one used for fishing.

CHAPTER TWELVE

Develop an Authentic Concept with Long-Lasting Value

CREATE THE ULTIMATE SHOPPING EXPERIENCE

"Capital isn't that important in business.
Experience isn't that important. You can get both of these things.
What is important is ideas."

HARVEY S. FIRESTONE

Among those qualities that characterize a shop that pops—one that makes a true emotional connection with the shopper—is the realization of an authentic vision for the store that works for today and can carry the store into the future. It requires an adherence and strict dedication to the original concept, but it must also allow for growth, change, modification, and adjustment as needed. It's how Barnes & Noble can grow from a single New York bookstore specializing in textbooks into a chain of over 800 superstores as the result of a very simple but overreaching concept: to create a nonintimidating bookstore environment for everyone. It's how Manny Gonzales of Charleston, South Carolina's Tiger Lily can throw out the rulebook on how to operate a florist shop in order to be "the best place to buy awesome flowers." It's why Kate Collier's Feast! in Charlottesville, Virginia, can abandon its expansion into traditional gift business to remain grounded in what they do the absolute best: artisanal cheese and meats that also make great gifts.

Prairie Edge

■ Where the Shopper Experiences a Vanishing Culture

Finding the right words to describe the Prairie Edge Trading Company and Galleries shopping experience is a challenge. For me, a native easterner, it is so exotic, so romantic, so Old West, so Native American, so historic that I don't have the vocabulary to explain how much the experience of visiting Prairie Edge in Rapid City, South Dakota, moves me. Rapid City is just a hop, skip, and a jump away from Mount Rushmore, with its flag-waving red, white, and blue vision of the American presidency embodied in Washington, Jefferson, Lincoln, and Theodore Roosevelt. It is the other side of that mountain, figuratively, the one that pictures Lakota leader Crazy Horse pointing to his people's land, which he is said to have defined as "My lands are where my dead lie buried," that so powerfully affects me. Prairie Edge invites you to touch, feel, explore, and discover the native culture that was almost lost to us and that even today clings close to the edge of survival.

Prairie Edge has a vital role to play in supporting and building that native culture by offering Native American reproductions, crafts, and craft supplies, Native American-themed books and authentic tribal music, and original art for sale. Prairie Edge, in turn, pays a fair market price to the native craftsmen and women who supply the store with these unique, often rare, and precious items. Prairie Edge was founded in the early 1980s by Ray Hildebrand and his wife Rita, who turned to raising buffalo on their cattle ranch because the native animals were better suited to the harsh South Dakota environment. This sparked Hildebrand's interest in the traditions and culture of the Northern Plains Indians. The original concept for the store, as described on the company's Web site (*www.prairieedge.com*) is:

- To educate the public about and preserve the heritage and culture of the Northern Plains Indians.
- To provide Northern Plains Indian artists and craftspeople an outlet, at a fair price to them, for their finest work which reflects their heritage and culture.

Describing how that mission is transformed into the retail environment, Prairie Edge's general manager Dan Tibby says, "We are a retail store, so we need to pay our bills, but half of our mission is the ability to educate the visiting public. We're a museum where you get to touch. We're certainly a retail outlet, but it is more than that . . . we're a spiritual store with a museum feeling to it."

"We're a museum where you get to touch. We're certainly a retail outlet, but it is more than that . . . we're a spiritual store with a museum feeling to it," says Dan Tibby, Prairie Edge.

But the educational experiences don't take place just from viewing the artifacts; the Prairie Edge staff members are also entrusted with that role. "We are constantly educating ourselves because not only do we have customers who come in who need to learn, but we do tour groups for bus companies and we do a tremendous number of school tours that come through. There are so many old ideas about Native American culture that are false that we feel it's our responsibility to give people an idea of what Native American culture really is, both as far as traditional native culture and modern Native American culture as well. Our employees are the driving force in the company, both the staff people and the artists we employ, who have a tremendous amount of freedom to express their vision."

Along with Prairie Edge's dedication to promoting and preserving the native culture is an unwavering respect for the artifacts and items they sell. Prairie Edge isn't just selling objects; they are selling pieces of history and art. "In all the years I have worked here, we've had things come in to make available to the public that you swear are the best of the best. It's just something so above and beyond that you feel bad even putting a price tag on it. And while our job is to sell those best of the best things, you almost don't want them to be sold because you want everyone who comes in to have the opportunity to see something that fantastic. It goes beyond a business-customer relationship. This is all about family and all about friends. Our customers appreciate when we let them know that this is something worth viewing, even if they have no interest in buying it or not. There's zero pressure to sell it to any individual," Tibby explains.

The store's atmosphere and design furthers the shoppers' personal experience with Native American culture. They play native music in the background and throughout the day some of the staff members burn sage in a small ceremony to take out negative energy. The result is that shoppers have a multisensory experience of the sights, sounds, and smells that typify the native experience. Dan says, "When you walk in the door, the visual presentation is absolutely overwhelming. But as a person continues to go through the building, and we have three floors in a National Historic Register building dating from 1886, every one of your senses is tapped. So you might come to an area with a strong smell of smoke from the leather artifacts. And the candle room is filled with the tannic smell of medicinal plants. It is a whole assault on your senses. And it makes people want to learn more because when the customer asks the questions, they have a real interest so there is an opportunity to expand their knowledge. With so much to see and experience in the store, we will have people who spend three or four hours here and they say as they are leaving, 'We'll be back tomorrow because we didn't see it all.'"

For the future, Prairie Edge is committed to not just looking back at the historical native culture, but to helping propel native artists and craftspeople into the future with a viable outlet for their artwork. "We are blessed to have artists who are so historically correct in what they do, but we also have some fairly young artists too. This new group of native artists is offering less traditional and more contemporary pieces, which are very exciting. It is important for the next generation to step in and get involved with the arts too. So we are always looking, including the employees, for new artists with enough differences in their styles to just keep it shaken up and fascinating for our customers."

The Vision Gives Soul to the Store and Makes It Important to the Customers

All the shopkeepers interviewed here express big visions, yet they execute those big visions in very small incremental steps, day in and day out giving those visions life, body, and soul. For Sherry Keefe in her Worthington, Ohio, Damsels in This Dress shop it means the difference between creating a store that sells unique fashions and accessories—a worthy cause and perfectly acceptable vision for a retail shop, but not a concept that pops—versus the kind of retail vision that she has created, which is to help her customers discover their inner diva, their own personal fashion and style.

For Barry Rosenberg's Steiner & Associates it means creating a true destination for things to do and see that people living in the Columbus, Ohio, area can experience, as opposed to just developing another strip-mall or shopping center. Barry describes the big vision as creating a place that becomes part of the community: "It really has to become part of the community. And in order to have that kind of value, the property [Easton Town Center] has to give back to the community and truly become the focal point for the community."

"You've got to build a reason for people to be there, and then they will shop. But shopping CAN'T be the reason to be there," says Ken Nisch, JGA.

These are the kinds of big visions that lead to longevity and true success. As Ken Nisch of design firm JGA stressed in Chapter 11, "You've got to build a reason for people to be there, and then they will shop. But shopping CAN'T be the reason to be there." The vision or the concept, then, becomes the reason to be there and it's got to have authenticity and value far beyond simply selling stuff. At its heart, a shop has to do something truly important and meaningful for the shopper.

Colonial Williamsburg Marketplace

■ Setting the Standard for a Museum Shop

Virtually every one of the thousands upon thousands of museums across America operate gift stores. With a few notable exceptions, like the Metropolitan Museum of New York, Museum of Modern Art (MoMA) also in New York, the Museum of Fine Arts, Boston, and the Art Institute of Chicago, most museum gift shops are pretty bland affairs.

One museum shop that stands above many of the others is the Colonial Williamsburg Marketplace, operated by the Colonial Williamsburg Foundation. Perhaps because Colonial Williamsburg is such a nontraditional, extraordinary museum is one of the reasons their museum shop, more accurately their shops, so far exceed one's expectations. There are actually 24 stores, according to Tammy Kersey, who works for the Colonial Williamsburg Foundation products division and is the person directly responsible for all retail stores, the catalog, the Web site, and the backend operations that support the above. Our focus here is the three brand stores that operate in the Merchant Square area of Williamsburg. They are Williamsburg at Home, the new home furnishings store that includes a Design Studio where interior designers can create custom designs; the Craft House, which focuses on gifts, tabletop, jewelry, ceramics, and other smaller items, which is the direct descendant of the original Craft House at the Inn store founded in 1936 and now relocated to the Merchant Square; and Celebrations, the headquarters for seasonal and holiday decorations which is so intimately tied to Williamsburg, along with garden and kitchen items.

While there is some overlap in merchandise and categories in each store, Kersey explains that each store represents a unique shopping experience in the Merchant Square central location. "It used to be frustrating for customers to fall in love with a bedding pattern and buy it in blue at the Craft House, but then go to another store and find it in a parchment color that they liked better. So we started to redefine each of the three stores as part of moving them into Merchant Square to give them unique personalities that would work together to complete the shopping experience, but be different in each location," Kersey says.

It is hard to get a handle on all that the Williamsburg product program entails because it is so vast. The products program itself was started in the 1930s when John D. Rockefeller, Jr., the mover and shaker behind the restoration of Colonial Williamsburg, was told that the tableware for the refurbishment of Williamsburg's Raleigh Tavern would have to be made from modern commercial patterns, because suitable reproductions didn't exist. That led Mr. Rockefeller to commission the Josiah Wedgwood and Sons Company to reproduce chinaware from actual china fragments excavated on the tavern site. He envisioned that "the purposes of education might be furthered by the sale of this ware" to the public.

Today the Colonial Williamsburg Foundation licenses over 50 manufacturers to develop and produce 4,000 products sold under the WILLIAMSBURG brand name. The sale of these products helps support The Colonial Williamsburg Foundation as keeper of 4,000 historic acres with 88 original 18th-century buildings, 225 authentic period rooms, three world class museums, and an 18th-century plantation.

The primary goal of the Colonial Williamsburg products program is as ambitious as the overall museum's scope requires: "Through our product licensing and marketing endeavors, we celebrate the origin of American style and the inventiveness of the American spirit . . . All WILLIAMSBURG products are reproduced from, or inspired by the Colonial Williamsburg Foundation's world-renowned collections of 18th and 19th-century antiques. Through the sale of WILLIAMSBURG products and all of our marketing endeavors, we celebrate the origin of American style and the inventiveness of the American spirit by promoting an understanding and appreciation of traditional design," explains the Colonial Williamsburg Web site (*www.williamsburgmarketplace.com*).

This dedication to the creativity of the American spirit from its European roots in the 18th century through today is reflected in important design elements in the new Williamsburg at Home store. In closing the original Craft House in the Inn store and moving it into the new locations in Marketplace Square, in true historical fashion, they moved some of the architectural elements from the Craft

House in the Inn store and installed them into the home store. For example, the fireplace mantels that decorate Williamsburg at Home are all from the original store, as are the arched doorways and some of the window frames. "They were carefully removed, then used there. We have brass plaques that have an engraved image of the old store with dates and original location. We felt this was important because the Craft House at the Inn was the original store that lots of customers thought of first when thinking of shopping in Williamsburg. It was sad to leave there so we wanted to take a part of the personality, a part of the history and connection with the Craft House at the Inn and create a wonderful new shopping venue today but with roots from the past."

Apparently this transition from the old to the new has been successful, according to Kersey, who shares how customers feel more comfortable and at home in the Williamsburg at Home store than they felt in the Craft House at the Inn which had a much stronger museum-like atmosphere. "When we opened Williamsburg at Home, we were transitioning from Craft House at the Inn where people would walk into that store, and they loved it. They thought it was beautiful, but they were afraid to touch anything. And in Williamsburg at Home, we immediately were seeing people getting on the bed with the cell phone, calling somebody. They felt like they could go and grab a pillow from one area of the store to see if it worked with something else on display. And in Craft House at the Inn, nobody would ever do that," Kersey says.

"We try to offer our guests more than just products. We offer some extra piece of knowledge like we do in decorating class or other special touches that make their visit more memorable," says Tammy Kersey, Colonial Williamsburg Foundation.

Balancing the challenges of operating a true museum environment where it is strictly "hands-off" and a retail store where touching and feeling is encouraged can be daunting, but the staff in the three branded stores accomplish this by involving the customer in learning experiences and hands-on demonstrations. Kersey says, "Celebrations is a great example of how we bridge the gap from museum to store with lots of decorating demonstrations taking place impromptu in the store, where a sales associate might put together an apple cone and be able to talk to the customer about tips for making it. We also have in-store kiosks in Celebrations and the Craft Store that might have demonstrations showing on the screen about different ideas for holidays and spring. And our sales consultants in the Williamsburg at Home store know how to work with the customer to pull together a room. We want our customers to be comfortable within the store instead of just walking through and looking but then moving on." One of the keys to shopper ease in the store environment is the genuine level of friendliness and courtesy you get from the moment you walk in the door. After visiting the historic areas where costumed hosts and hostesses are always chatting up the guests, the feeling coming into the store isn't all that different, even if the sales associates are dressed in contemporary garb. "We try to offer our guests more than just products. We offer some extra piece of knowledge like we do in decorating class or other special touches that make their visit more memorable."

After all, when you shop in any one of the Colonial Williamsburg stores, you are looking to take home a personal connection with the town, a memento that will bring back the memories of your visit. From authentic replicas to interpretations of designs in the Colonial Williamsburg collection, all the products sold carry a touch of Williamsburg hospitality and authenticity. "When Craft House started in 1937, everything that was sold was a reproduction or an interpretation of a reproduction. Today, our licensed products still have an educational mission, like we might take an image from a print in the collection and use that to create a fabric. Our customers look at it as having a piece of Williamsburg to take home. For our home designs, we have maintained specific elements, but updated for how people live today. So people can bring that piece of Williamsburg and that piece of history into their home in a way that is comfortable to live with today," Kersey explains.

Authentic Vision Transforms a Store into a Shop that Pops

Striving for more authenticity, pushing the envelope, and expanding the boundaries from a store that sells stuff into something much more meaningful is one of the secrets of transforming a plain vanilla store into one that pops. It is in recognizing that nobody needs any of the stuff you are selling anyway that the shop owner finds the freedom to explore the boundaries of what a store can aspire to be. It's not about selling clothes, but helping the customer achieve a personal style. It's not selling a flower arrangement, but the very ultimate in floral expression. It's not selling television sets, but home entertainment systems that stimulate the imagination. It's not selling Indian tchotchkes, but presenting the unique story of the native peoples through art and artifacts. It's not selling tourist souvenirs but presenting 21st-century Americans with a taste of 18th-century colonial America that the founding fathers would have known and recognized.

Striving for more authenticity, pushing the envelope, and expanding the boundaries from a store that sells stuff into something much more meaningful is one of the secrets of transforming a plain vanilla store into one that pops.

That is the kind of big vision that inspires the shopkeepers who create shops that make a true, lasting, and deeply meaningful connection with the shoppers. It's the vision that gives people a reason to come to the store and experience the store, so that they can, as a by-product of being there, also shop and do their part in perpetuating the vision for the next generation of shoppers.

CHAPTER THIRTEEN

Develop a Price/Value Model that Favors the Shopper

CREATE THE ULTIMATE SHOPPING EXPERIENCE

"People don't necessarily want to spend less—they want to pay less."
KEN NISCH, JGA

Figuring out an effective price/value model in a retail business can be a key stumbling block. It is not easy to find a way to price one's merchandise low enough to make the shoppers take notice, yet high enough so the shopkeeper can pay the rent, buy more merchandise, cover payroll and employee benefits, pay the taxes, and then take home a little bit of something extra for themselves— also known as profit.

It is no wonder that finding the right price/value model is difficult, because the shoppers are so profoundly confused and confusing. On the one hand, everybody hears about the boom in the luxury market and how retailers offering up goods at the very top of the pricing pyramid are making money hand over fist. Having studied the luxury market seriously over the past five or so years, I can assure you that this is nonsense. Luxury-goods retailing is just as difficult, challenging, and potentially thankless as any other kind of retailing, but no matter, often the media is guilty of spreading the idea that luxury retailing is booming across the board.

At the other end of the spectrum, retailers feel the pinch from the discount retailers—everyone from Wal-Mart, Kmart, Target, and the rest—to the dollar stores, outlet centers, and all the other retailers that ostensibly offer up more for less. The fact that three out of the five different passionate shopper personalities discussed in Chapter 6—Diana the Bargain Huntress, Theresa the Therapeutic Shopper, and Ursula the Uber Shopper—are so strongly motivated to look first to the sales and discount racks means that discounting at retail works today.

However, for all those retailers who feel that the only way to compete is to sell on the cheap, I say nonsense. You simply aren't working hard enough to give shoppers other reasons to visit your store and buy up your stuff. Discount prices have become the one-size-fits-all retailing strategy that has spread throughout the retail landscape. It is dumbed-down retailing. Sure, if you make it cheap enough, somebody is likely to buy it, but that isn't good business. Few retailers can match item for item the deep discounts available to mass merchants who can buy in bulk, ship stock out of a central warehouse, and benefit from the volume. The majority of retailers are stuck trying to eke out a living in a world gone mad for the cheap.

Give shoppers another reason to shop rather than the promise of cheap.

Here's a suggestion: give shoppers another reason to shop rather than the promise of cheap. I firmly believe in giving the shopper more for less, but not ridiculously less, just reasonably less. In the work I do with luxury marketers, my pricing recommendation is a simple three-to-two ratio. That is, give the customers three times more value over the ordinary, everyday brand, but only charge them two times the everyday price. It's a pricing strategy that is simple and easy, and it works. Shoppers today want more value, but people aren't fools. They know what things are worth, especially the active passionate shoppers who take shopping very seriously. What they really want is something that looks like a $100 item actually priced at $75. Sure, some people will only buy that thing if it is marked down a couple of times over to $20, but many more will recognize that if the price is too cheap, then it might not be worth paying for at any price. People know that there is a price for value and shopkeepers need to turn their focus to delivering more value, not necessarily offering up the cheapest price.

When it comes to developing a pricing strategy for a retail store today, it isn't about the money but the meaning, and the meaning is delivered through the value of the product. We need to keep the quantum theory of shopping formula firmly in mind.

$$P = (N + F + A) \times E^2$$

The P equals propensity to buy as a function of the sum of Need plus Features plus Affordability times Emotion-squared. The retailer who plays to the other factors in the equation besides affordability and price is able to get a fair price for the goods they sell, but the key is playing up the other factors, like need and desire, product features, and emotion. If someone wants something badly enough, he or she will pay for it. The key is to make them want it badly enough.

Pricing Is All About Enhancing the Value, rather than Marking Down Dollars

Ken Nisch, chairman of design firm JGA, who shares his point of view in Chapter 11, has an interesting perspective on the pricing/value equation. He says, "People don't necessarily want to spend less. They want to pay less. Lower income people may well be as concerned with paying less as with getting more. But for the more upscale customer, they are just more focused on not spending less, but paying less. So they want to buy the best, and they are willing to pay for the best, but they just want to buy it at the right price. That is why the Costco phenomenon works for these people, but it isn't even on the radar of lower-income people."

Costco is famous for targeting affluent shoppers with deeply discounted luxury goods with selected items from heritage luxury brands. A recent search of the Costco Web site turned up items from Bulgari, Cartier, Dolce & Gabbana, Prada, Patek Phillippe, Yves Saint Laurent, and Van Cleef & Arpels. While many of the prices for these items are hardly cheap—the YSL bags start just under $500 and range to $1,500—they are attractive when considering the price one would pay in a branded boutique. When you shop at Costco, you are assured you are getting value regardless of the actual price, whether it is the six-carat yellow diamond ring for $99,999 or the one-carat number for just under $4,000. Of course, Nisch notes that a diamond engagement ring from Costco doesn't send the same message as one from Tiffany or Cartier. "For certain things in their [affluent shoppers'] life, a Costco engagement ring is still not a good idea, or roses from Costco on Valentine's Day. If it's for me, I'm all about paying less. If it's for you, I only will pay less if I can get away with it," Nisch explains.

That is why a retailer like Tiger Lily with their commitment to the absolutely best flowers can charge what they want, because their customers want, and expect, the best and they are willing to pay for the best. On the other hand, Manny Gonzales gives walk-in shoppers a real incentive to buy—half price all the time, every day on all those absolutely best flowers when they are bought by the stem or the handful. Explaining the mind behind the madness, Gonzales says, "Flowers are expensive and people don't know how long they will last. They don't know the difference between a snapdragon and a daffodil. So we take the risk out of it for them. But then three years later, they can't live without flowers in their house. They become flower fanatics. We got them hooked. So that is where my half-price specials come in. Flowers aren't just for the elite, they are for everybody."

Prairie Edge doesn't have to resort to discounting to sell its unique, handcrafted Native American arts. They simply have to tell the story of how these rare and wonderful items are made and what they mean in order to command a fair and reasonable price for these goods that lets both the store and the artist make a living. Dan Tibby explains, "We don't draw the select high-end clients that are common in Santa Fe or New York. We are located in Rapid City, after all, but what we do try to do is pay all of our artists, whether they are native or non-native, a very fair price for the things they do. We don't do anywhere near a full markup on the items. But what we are able to do is price our Native American artwork from a third or so less than they would find in Santa Fe. So people from all over the world will fly into Rapid City when they have a large decorating project to do because they know they can come in here and get the finest quality artwork for a fair price. The logic behind it is simple. If we raised our retail prices, obviously we would sell fewer pieces over the course of the year and our intent is to sell for each artist as many of his or her pieces as we can, so we can continually reorder. So it may mean a smaller profit for the store, but that is just part of the equation." For Prairie Edge the meaning is in the artwork itself, and the prices they charge, while competitive in the marketplace, do not in any way compromise the meaning. The key is communicating with the customer and helping them to understand the meaning.

Tammy Kersey at Colonial Williamsburg Foundation also says her customers want to become a part of the meaning behind the products by supporting the foundation, and buying from her stores and catalog, rather than chasing the cheapest price found elsewhere. "With our licensed product, people might find it in another catalog where somebody has undercut our prices. They might call us and say they want to buy it from us, but this other catalog has it cheaper. We'll honor the price in favor of our customer, but it is interesting how people have a connection with Colonial Williamsburg. They want to buy it from us because it is full of national history that is special to Williamsburg. They aren't necessarily looking for the lower price," she says.

For Sherry Keefe at Damsels in This Dress, telling the story behind the products adds the value and ultimately makes the customer willing to pay the price because she understands the value that is delivered. Keefe explains, "I give the customer quality, and I use the word quality because customers value quality. Certainly they can go into a major department store and buy a black turtleneck for $10. I have to show them why they should come to me a buy a black turtleneck for $80. It's because of the quality of the fabric, the quality of design, and how it fits the body. My designers are designing for women's bodies. They aren't running things through a computer cut because they are not designing mass production." Keefe doesn't simply charge the highest prices around; she offers extra incentive to buy these very special high quality things from her store through her Damsels Diva club where members who pay a nominal annual fee get a flat 20-percent discount off everything in the store. The idea is to build involvement and commitment from the customers to what Damsels in This Dress is selling: personalized style delivered through superior quality fashion.

The secret of finding the right price/value relationship is pretty simple ultimately if you move beyond the dollars. It is a function of communicating the meaning, i.e., the value to the shopper and finding the kind of shopper that responds to your special meaning, who values your values. If all they want is the cheapest, i.e., cheap is their meaning, then clearly they aren't going to buy into your particular meaning proposition, but if they value the most beautiful exquisite flowers, the authentic Native American art, Colonial Williamsburg's mission, or finding a unique personal style, then they are going to pay the premium that these special retailers ask. In turn these special retailers give back to their customers by assuring them that they are asking a fair price that is in line with the values that are delivered. They even have special programs where the shopper can get more for less. The key to success in the realm of pricing is in the story telling about the meaning, and to learn more about that, the television shopping channel QVC is one of the best in storytelling.

QVC

■ Expert Storytellers with Quality, Value, and Convenience
in their Name

I have never made a secret of my passion for television shopping. It's not that I buy a lot of stuff off the air, though I probably average one or two purchases per month, mostly cosmetics; it is just that television shopping shows are entertaining and a whole lot more upbeat than the depressing 24/7 television news programs about war, crime, and other atrocities people do to other people. That is the reason why a television marketer like QVC pops. They have combined the best of television entertainment with shopping to create a new type of interactive shopping experience you can do in one of the most comfortable environments—your home. Doug Rose, vice president of merchandising and brand development at QVC, says the emphasis for their network is entertainment first and foremost. "Ultimately we are really in the entertainment business. We compete not just with other retailers, but mostly with other television shows like CSI or Larry King. Our sense of things is the customer we want to serve is a person for whom shopping is entertainment and so our whole mission in life is to entertain through shopping. I think other retailers would be well-served if they thought of their competition not so much as other stores but other entertainment choices."

QVC is true *retailtainment*—what many other retailers only dream about being as shoppers increasingly turn experiential. Rose and his colleagues at QVC understand that if they don't satisfy the shopper's desire for entertainment, they lose. That shopper will tune out today and likely will never come back, because it is the entertainment value, pure and simple, that makes them tune in in the first place. "In any typical hour we know between 5,000 and 15,000 people will order something from us. But in that same hour, about 100 times that audience is watching. So like any direct response business, only about one to two percent of the watchers are going to order. But we have got to entertain and inform those other 98 to 99 percent."

"I think other retailers would be well-served if they thought of their competition not so much as other stores but other entertainment choices," says Doug Rose, QVC

"The difference between QVC and a lot of other companies that are selling things on broadcast television is that we are really less concerned with how many items we sell. We are far more concerned with how many customers trust QVC and so the customer is far more important than the item," Rose continues. "This is a company that is building trust first and foremost, while we are hopefully persuading a small fraction of our audience to actually order something."

With a focus on entertaining and building a trust relationship with the QVC audience, the company takes a different tack when it comes to the selling process. Rather than trying simply to sell more stuff, they demand more of the process than that. Rose says, "Most direct marketing companies tend not to think the way we do. They tend to think that their job is to sell as much of whatever, say a tape recorder, as fast as they can. And when you begin to think that way, it affects everything you do. It affects the tone of voice you use. It affects the speed with which you talk. It affects the pricing promotional handles that you use. It affects the degree to which you invest in the customer experience. Ultimately all you care about is the fact that the customer has made the purchase, not how happy she is with the tape recorder when she gets it home. You are done, mission accomplished with the sale. Our feeling is if that is all we have done, we have failed."

QVC acknowledges that the key point of difference that QVC offers is its unique customer experiences, rather than product, which is something that many other retailers need to become attuned to. Shoppers can find all kinds of the same product everywhere, so the shopping experience itself becomes a retailer's competitive edge. "People today—and this is a statement not just about QVC customers, but consumers in general—they are beginning to realize that the items are oftentimes not the point of differentiation between one store and another. It is the experience of the store and the overall environment. It's the quality of the sales help. It's the confidence in knowing that if you have a problem or question, you can always take it back or send it back. So more and more the quality of the service experience is outweighing the nuances of product differentiation. We understand that our customers are shopping everywhere and they can find the same or very similar products everywhere. We must select product that stands up to the scrutiny of a very demanding audience. They may have been shopping at Bed Bath & Beyond this morning, then shopping at Bloomingdale's and Costco this afternoon and on amazon.com tonight. Our customers are everywhere and they are avid and very skilled shoppers. That's a tough audience, so it keeps us honest," Rose explains.

In terms of QVC's pricing strategies, they are careful not to stress sales, but special offers available for a limited time and at a specially configured price. The use of the word *value* in the QVC name, therefore, is not just a euphemism for bargain or discount, but that they deliver true value for the money. Rose says, "We don't encourage promotional thinking that in order to drive viewers to our shows we have to give them a bribe, like a coupon or discount. We try to give them another advantage, because getting into discount thinking is a very dangerous precedent. If they could change the world tomorrow, the first thing most department stores would do is eliminate 24-hour sales events, coupons, and discounts. Because everybody else is doing it and because they did it last year, they are caught in a trap. We've been fortunate to never get into that trap. Of course, we have promotional strategies like our Today's Special Value on QVC, where you are seeing a unique item created for that event. It's never been priced lower than you are seeing it today. It is a unique configuration that we hope our customers will like. But it's a different mentality than a markdown."

Ultimately the reason why QVC pops is because of how effectively they connect with their consumers. While they offer alternative channels to facilitate shopping, like QVC.com, along with a few outlet stores, the real secret of success for QVC is how effectively they utilize the strengths of the medium of television to reach out and connect with their audience of passionate shoppers. "Because we are in the entertainment business, watching our shows must be entertaining. It should be enjoyable and when we are doing it well, it should be educational. You should learn something after having watched, whether or not you ordered an item," Rose says.

The presentation of products on QVC is critical to sales success. The QVC spokesperson usually works with a guest from the company whose products are featured. The guests, often product inventors or creators, bring excitement and enthusiasm to the air, while the spokesperson keeps the show moving with commentary on what is truly unique and special about what is offered. They also regularly invite viewers in for testimonial chats about the products. These testimonials are not scripted and the callers are not paid. Testimonials bring third-party credibility to the air. Rose explains, "People begin to understand pretty quickly that these are legitimate real-life people just like me who have either had a good experience or are excited about getting this package they just bought. And our broadcast strategies are always intended to be very intimate. We don't want to give shoppers the sense that they are lost in an ocean of viewers. We'd rather have the viewer feel as though this is a one-on-one experience. The host is speaking directly to the guest, one-on-one. The guest and host are speaking directly to the camera in a very familiar way. We like to have the viewing experience feel as though you are witnessing two neighbors talking over the backyard fence."

Rose concludes that the key challenge for QVC is to keep on entertaining their audience of recreational shoppers with unique new products that offer a difference. "Our single biggest challenge and so much of our effort as an organization is spent on maintaining interest. We want to maintain a viewing audience that is engaged and interested and we want to be able to earn their trust someday. We want them to get to know us better. So we work hard at determining the proper pacing for an hour, whether this item needs more than a full eight minutes to explain it properly. And we consciously, strategically try to avoid becoming predictable. We are often asked why we don't anchor shows, like cosmetics or Craftsman tools, more regularly. That is a very deliberate strategy. We don't want to give people the sense that they can predict what is going to be on. We want to breed a sense of curiosity about what is going on because so much of our viewing audience is channel surfers. Our best customers are people who are sampling us all the time."

Does Internet Shopping Pop?

The qualities and attributes that define a shop that pops— customer involvement, shopper curiosity, electricity, convergence, authenticity, value, and accessibility—are not inconsistent with the Internet mode of shopping. However, I simply don't think we know enough about the medium of Internet shopping today to design Internet shopping experiences that truly pop. Other technology-enhanced shopping experiences, television, most notably, have got a history over half a century in terms of people building confidence with the medium and knowing how to use it. If you think back, both Lucy Ricardo of "I Love Lucy" and Ralph Kramden of "The Honey-mooners," were early pioneers of television home shopping, with Lucy selling her special recipe salad dressing on air and Ralph making a commercial for his "Handy Housewife Helper" kitchen gadget. As a culture we have a deep understanding of how television broadcast works and how to maximize it as a sales tool, thus explaining how the folks at QVC and other home television networks have developed and honed their sophisticated sales approach. By contrast, Internet e-commerce was invented yesterday. We just aren't there yet with the Internet, but I am confident that the day will come— and it won't take nearly as long to develop as television shopping did.

The key features missing from the Internet shopping medium today that television has corralled, are those that are people dependent. As we have seen, it is the people in the store, both the customers and the service staff members, who are the prime catalysts for the involvement, curiosity, and electricity factors. That is hard to supply over the Internet, but no doubt it will evolve. I am amazed at how our children have seamlessly migrated to the Internet for communicating with their friends. They have embraced the medium as their own and maintain real-time connections with their extensive network of friends through their IM lists (Instant Messenger). While my hat is off to innovative Internet retailers like Amazon and eBay, I don't think a true Internet shop that pops is here yet. As good as some of the Internet e-commerce sites are, they just don't compare to shopping experiences like Feast!, Cabela's, Nell Hill's, Tiger Lily, or even QVC. All signs point to the fact that the Internet can be just as emotionally involving and personally compelling as a shopping medium as television, catalogs, and in-store can be, but we adults in business need to see it more in the way that our kids do to make it really come to life for shopping.

CHAPTER FOURTEEN

Make Your Store Immediately Accessible and Nonexclusive

CREATE THE ULTIMATE SHOPPING EXPERIENCE

"I don't want my books to exclude anyone, but if they have to, then I would rather they excluded the people who feel they are too smart for them!"

NICK HORNBY, AUTHOR

Along with all the other features that characterize retail environments that are an ultimate shopping experience—a shop that pops—is another critical quality. Shops that pop are highly accessible, nonexclusive, and totally free from pretension. It is easy to identify stores that express the opposite of these popping qualities because they are inaccessible, exclusive, and give off a pretentious feel; they are profoundly uncomfortable. You don't feel welcome; you don't feel like you belong. On the contrary, you feel like you've got to prove something in order to measure up.

Stores that are accessible, nonexclusive, and free from pretensions are simply comfortable, welcoming, nice places to visit. You feel like you belong, as if the store is a place for you, that you are wanted and valued for the time you spend shopping. They make you feel at home, rather than like a visitor. We have heard frequently from the shopkeepers interviewed that their customers are like family or really good, close friends. There is a personal relationship between the shopper and the shopkeeper that just can't be faked. The shopkeeper really cares and the shopper knows that and craves to be taken care of.

Unfortunately in the luxury realm, exclusivity is often touted as a quality that luxury brands must aspire to. My research into the mindset of luxury consumers finds quite the opposite. Exclusivity is a feature of luxury shopping that falls right to the bottom of the list of desired features, along with status and social standing, when luxury shoppers are asked about motivators for making a luxury purchase. American luxury consumers, a highly democratic lot who truly believe that luxury is for everyone and different for everyone, don't place much value on exclusivity. After all, exclusivity is all about exclusion and excluding someone or some group of people. In the luxury realm it traces its roots from the Old World and European aristocracy where luxury was something that only the rich and titled folks could have and the common folk couldn't. Note also that the European luxury brands are the biggest proponents of exclusivity as a core luxury branding value, which is one reason why many European luxury brands aren't growing quite as fast in the U.S. market as they do in Europe or Japan. Exclusivity is more of a turn-off than a turn-on to Americans.

While exclusivity ruffles Americans' feathers, we highly value individuality and uniqueness, so we really don't care whether something is exclusive, so much as we want something that is very special and unique and that expresses one's individuality. Americans' quest for individuality is often mistaken for exclusivity. They are very different concepts and they come from different cultural ideals, yet they can appear on the surface as very close indeed. In distinguishing between the two—exclusivity and individuality—I like to think of the difference between a Do Not Enter sign, which signifies the message of a store that values exclusivity, versus a sign that says Turn Here for a wonderful, personal, individual experience. The concept of individuality, making your store more special, more personal, more individual for the shopper, is a way of turning the concept of exclusivity positive. It implies an idea similar to exclusivity—that the store is a place not for everyone, but for those special people who really can appreciate it—but it does it in a much more welcoming and personal way.

Saks Fifth Avenue

■ Where the "Ladies that Lunch" and the Hoi Polloi Rub
Shoulders Comfortably

Of all the grand dames of luxury retail up and down New York's
Fifth Avenue, Saks Fifth Avenue stands apart as a store that doesn't
take itself too seriously, unlike some of its equally tony neighbors.
While it has a demanding mission and maintains the highest ideals
for its products and services, it is a welcoming, fun, and comfortable
place to shop no matter how deep your pockets. Saks Fifth Avenue is
a store that has a wonderful story to tell and wants to tell it to those
people who will appreciate it. After all, as Kimberly Grabel, vice president of marketing at Saks Fifth Avenue, explains, being an accessible, nonexclusive, unpretentious store goes right back to its roots,
"Back in 1924 when Saks Fifth Avenue was founded, the original
vision was to create a luxury emporium of truly high-end products of
all types, which was really unheard of in its day. The idea of a giant
store, an emporium dedicated to this world of luxury products was
quite unique at the time. So when the store first opened, it functioned
almost as a theatre, a museum with a mix of customers, some of whom
came and spent substantially on high-end product and some of whom
just came to look."

Ever since its founding Saks has embraced the idea that nurtur-
ing and serving both lookers and buyers was a good idea. Grabel says,
"Saks has seen its role as one of retail inspiration, as well as aspiration.
Years ago it was a family outing to come to this big emporium. And it
was really not even so much about what you were shopping for or
what you were taking home, but it was to experience all these wonderful products in a wonderful setting. That was part of the theatre and
the magic that some retail has lost today. But for Saks, today we see
people of all levels of income who want to look upon and get inspired by the things they find in the store."

This makes doubly good sense today because the rich and super-
rich don't necessarily wear uniforms anymore that signal their status.
Affluent shoppers with means are just as likely to turn up at Saks'
door in jeans and sneakers as in an Armani suit. Grabel shares a story

about how their open-door approach paid off big time in serving an underdressed, but very well-off shopper. "Wealth today looks very different than it did in the past, especially since the dot com movement. You can't judge people by what they are wearing, and that has been a message that we've long trained. In our San Francisco store a guy showed up in the front of the store with his bike, looking like a bike messenger. Our store manager told him he couldn't come in with the bike, but he found a place where the bike rider could safely store his bike. Don't you know the guy who looked like a messenger boy went over to the jewelry counter and bought a $10,000 Chopard watch. So you can't judge anyone and we teach our associates that."

"The bigger thing that keeps us from pretension is that the people who work at Saks really love fashion, and they really love product. And when you love what you do, and you love what you're selling, you like talking about it to anyone," says Kimberly Grabel, Saks Fifth Avenue.

Training sales associates not to judge a book by its cover alone won't do the trick to keep Saks free from pretension. Grabel points to the personality and passion of the Saks' staff as being a critical factor in the mix. "The bigger thing that keeps us from pretension is that the people who work at Saks really love fashion, and they really love product. And when you love what you do, and you love what you're selling, you like talking about it to anyone. And so when I'm over in the store, I just watch our associates engage any and everyone. And it's their enthusiasm for their product that shines through. For example, this Christmas we had an absolutely beautiful Loro Piana scarf on display. Everyone who came into the store went over to look at it because it was so stunning. And about half the people would look at the price tag, gasp, and start talking amongst themselves, but the saleslady was there and she would engage them. She would talk to them about how it is made and it was just very interesting. It was almost like we were going back to our heritage and our roots of just having this fabulous product and celebrating it. Whether someone wants to go home with it or not is their personal choice, but we're happy to tell you about it because we think it's fascinating the way Loro Piana makes scarves. And that, I think, is the vibe that you get at Saks."

One of the secrets of Saks Fifth Avenue's success is their deep understanding of the psychology of selling luxury goods. Luxury goods have an important story to tell and in order for shoppers to appreciate those luxury goods, they need to understand the story. People need to understand why a $5,000 Vuitton suit costs so much. They need the story about how it is constructed unlike any other suit in the world. Therefore, Saks is a consummate storyteller, telling stories in all kinds of ways, through their windows, their in-store displays, their catalogs and Web site, via the sales associates, and in the New York flagship store through their fabulous historical architecture. Grabel explains, "What draws shoppers in typically, even it they are just walking down Fifth Avenue, are the windows and then once you get into the store and see the presentations, it really draws you in. It's that kind of drama that separates Saks from the rest of the pack of luxury retailers. There's this combination of understatement, but also a touch of drama that makes it more theatrical, more spectacular to walk into. But then after that initial wow impact, it is followed by interaction with our sales associate, because this is not a self-serve environment. This is an environment of consultation, of really getting to know and understand the customer. It is all about that conversation with the customer."

So a trip to Saks is fun for the shopper, whether looker or buyer. Grabel says, "We like talking about our products. It brings the customer, whoever the customer is, into this world of luxury and this world of best-of-the-best product. And whether they go out with something or not, it's been fun for them. And that is the whole idea."

Toward delivering a more fun-filled luxury shopping experience, Saks Fifth Avenue continues to expand its experiential offerings. The New York store has just opened three new restaurants, one called HTwo, which presents bottled water from all over the world; another is a cocktail bar and then Charbonnel et Walker, which is a chocolate café where shoppers can sample chocolates from a conveyor belt like you see in sushi places. They are also launching a new store-in-a-store concept for home called Flair. Grabel explains, "Flair is a shop in Milan run by a husband and wife. It is really . . . eclectic, and interesting to the customer. It's an experience to go into the boutique and see what's there and explore and discover. I think these zones of discovery like Flair are really important to making retail fun again."

Making the Shopping Experience More Personal Every Way Every Day

When it comes to creating a shopping environment that is accessible, it all boils down to sending the powerful message that you are welcome here. Making someone feel welcome is about structuring the interaction in such a way that it meets the other person's needs, targets their wants, and satisfies their expectations. The more personal and individualistic you can make that interaction, the better. Recall that most of Tiger Lily's business is purely customized flower arrangements to the customers' specifications. Your store doesn't have to create personalized, customized products in order to make their services more specialized and personal for the shopper. Damsels in This Dress puts ready-made clothes together in unique and personalized ways in order to help the customer discover her personal and individual style. Bluemercury personalizes the shopper's experience by helping her find just the right beauty product that works for her skin and lifestyle.

Bluemercury

■ Personalizing the Shopping Experience

Described on their Web site as a "luxury apothecary and spa chain," Georgetown, DC–based Bluemercury makes beauty products shopping personal by offering up not just customized spa services, but customized beauty routines as well. Founder Marla Malcolm Beck explains how personalization sets her shop apart from the traditional way people shop for cosmetics: "We are really trying to deliver very high customer service in the purchase of cosmetics. If you look at the department stores and the way their cosmetics departments are structured, it is all brand by brand. And employees are paid by the brand. So if you go to the Clinique counter in Macy's or Neiman Marcus, they are going to sell you Clinique products, period. Whereas our staff are trained in every brand and don't have compensation based by brand. So when a customer walks in the door and says, 'I need a new face cream,' we look at all the brands to find the one that is best for that client. In a department store, on the other hand, there might be a product at another counter a couple of feet away that would work better for that client, but the salesperson won't recommend it."

In the world of cosmetics retailing, selling across brands is a pretty revolutionary concept, but one that only makes a world of sense for the customer. Sephora, the cosmetics retail chain owned by luxury leader LVMH, offers up a similar broad mix of brands, but as Beck explains, Sephora is a self-service concept and doesn't embrace the high customer service levels you can find at Bluemercury. The difference is not so much what they sell, but how they sell it. That all comes down to the 200 staff members who service Bluemercury's customers in its 13 locations. Beck says, "The first thing is about hiring the right people. We take our hiring very seriously. All of our staff absolutely adores beauty products. We ask questions in the interviews that reveal if somebody loves products, and if they love products, they also must love helping people find products."

Her hiring policy is simplicity itself. "I interview everybody to see if they are real. I can usually tell right away if someone's friendly or pretentious. We don't hire pretentious people," Beck continues. These staff members become the catalyst that sparks the contagious excitement found in every Bluemercury store. "It's all about loving products. Everyone's excited about what comes in new. If you love new products and a customer comes in asking what is new, our staff knows and is excited about it. That's what is contagious. After all it's a product category that people love to shop in. It's like a candy store for adult women. That's what gets them going."

Because selling beauty products is so highly personal, the Bluemercury store design and layout also creates a sense of intimacy between the shopper and the sales professional. "Our staff doesn't stand behind the counters; they stand in front of them. So the store is designed for us to shop with the client. We try to break down a lot of barriers in that sense. We make all of the products accessible, so everything on the shelf is tagged with prices so the client can shop on their own if they want to. And we're there to help them if they want.

And the lighting is real critical to us, because we're showing people foundation and makeup colors. The lighting has to be good so people don't look different at home than they do in our store."

"Our staff doesn't stand behind the counters; they stand in front of them. So the store is designed for us to shop with the client. We try to break down a lot of barriers in that sense," says Marla Malcolm Beck, Bluemercury.

The level of intimacy that Bluemercury creates with its customers translates into a deep, heartfelt devotion among its shoppers. Beck explains, "The kinds of products we carry help people solve problems that are very personal. So someone might come in with acne, and if we can prescribe products that really solve their acne problem, the word of mouth is unbelievable. You can get a customer for life if you can fix a personal care problem for them."

Bluemercury works hard to build and maintain their shoppers' trust through personalized product recommendations and beauty regimes. It starts with a passion for beauty products, but the staff members are all carefully trained to be the experts across categories and brands. "We have an extreme focus on being experts at what we do and being known as experts. All of our staff is focused on knowing more every day, learning more—training. We also truly believe that honesty is always the best policy. We will tell you if something isn't for you, and we stand by that. A customer might ask a staff member how they like something, and they might say, 'I don't like that product as much as I like this one.' We take it to the extreme, where if we're not sure that that Bumble & Bumble [hair care] product is right for you, we would prefer that you take home a sample and try it, rather than spend your money on something that's not going to work for you. It's not a focus of trying to get that sale that day. We know our clients will come back to us. So it's really the honesty and a true drive to helping you find the right thing," Beck says.

Furthermore, the way the Bluemercury folks find out about how new product lines work is equally intimate: they personally test each one. Beck says, "We are stringent about high-quality merchandising. We try not to go on trend. For example, a product might be hot just because it is hot. We are strict in merchandising a line. It has to be high quality; it has to have staying power; it has to have beautiful, functional packaging. We don't just pick up anything to be trendy with some new ingredient we don't believe in. For example, we have $250 skincare creams that we think are worth it and we have $10 skincare creams that we think are worth it for the price. We won't take on a luxury skincare line just because it is high priced and trendy. We must feel and believe it is worth the price."

Part Three

HOW TO CREATE
A SHOP THAT POPS

CHAPTER FIFTEEN

Principles for Creating the Ultimate Shopping Experience

"Clear your mind of can't."

DR. SAMUEL JOHNSON

Now we have arrived at the part of this book where we put together the learning from the consumers and insights from retailers to present ideas, strategies, and tactics that retailers, big and small, can put to work in their stores to create ultimate shopping experiences. With these principles for creating a shopping experience put to work, you can transform your store from ordinary to extraordinary. The key word for retailers is transformation. You must first accept that the continued survival of your store, let alone future success, depends upon your commitment to change. In addition, it must be transformation, not just a minor makeover. It means examining everything about your store and its operation and reconfiguring it, not for your personal convenience or pleasure, but according to the needs, wants, and desires of the customer. The shopper must be the focus of all retailing objectives. Decisions must be made according to what is best for the shopper, not what works best for the store staff. If something doesn't work for the shopper, then you need to undertake the hard work of making it right for the shopper. With the shopper going more and more experiential, retailers can't leave anything up to chance or miss an opportunity to make shopping in their store even more fun and delightful.

The Rules of Shopping and Retail have Changed—You Have to Change With Them

I spend a lot of time with retailers, both large corporate giants and small independents, and while both the big boys of retail and the mom-and-pops are equally confounded by the dramatic changes taking place in their businesses, the big retailers have more resources to call upon to manage change. The small independents are really out on a limb with very little support to see themselves through these tough times. Many small independents blame all their problems on competition from big boxes and their favorite solution usually involves a two-pronged approach: beat the big boxes with superior customer service and stock more products that the big boxes don't carry. The reality, however, is a product differentiation strategy is getting less and less effective, because shoppers today can find almost any product or a perfectly acceptable substitute almost anywhere. Product alone isn't enough.

But the reality is a product differentiation strategy is getting less and less effective, because shoppers today can find almost any product or a perfectly acceptable substitute almost anywhere. Product alone isn't enough.

Challenged retailers are getting closer when they see superior customer service as key, but they need to vastly expand their definition and conception of customer service, take it up more than a few notches into a whole new dimension of serving the customer. As a researcher, the phrase "customer service" gives me the willies, just like the term "quality" does, because it lacks clarity and precision. The idea of good customer service covers such a wide range of experiences and is so personal—what is good to one person might not be good at all to another—that the phrase is rendered virtually meaningless. As we take our learning from the research among shoppers and retailers and turn it into strategies for success, we will try to explore the full scope and dimension of how good customer service at retail must be transformed into an experience for the shopper.

However, the real problem facing retailers today is not competition from better capitalized, better managed, better merchandised, better located, and bigger stores. It is from the changes taking place among shoppers. Customers are demanding more out of the time they spend shopping in stores than just buying more stuff, whether they get it cheap or not. They want payback in terms of more recreation, more entertainment, and lots more fun. This trend will continue to be magnified in the future so making shopping fun in your store is the ultimate prescription for success and in the chapters that follow we will provide key principles retailers can put to work to make shopping a truly exciting experience.

Review of the Major Research Findings

Before moving onto the principles for retailers to make their shops pop, we should review the key findings from the research because the recommendations that follow all are grounded in this research.

Shopper Findings

While need, product features, and affordability influence shoppers, emotions mean the most when shoppers decide to buy. We've seen that the quantum theory of shopping is the formula that defines shoppers' propensity to buy as the sum of need plus features plus affordability multiplied by emotion-squared.

Propensity to buy = (Need + Features + Affordability) × Emotion^2

Emotion magnifies and accentuates each of the other factors in the shopping equation, so that high emotion toward a particular product category can stimulate desire to buy, even if actual need is very low; high emotion can make certain product features that much more desirable and so increase likelihood to purchase; high emotion can make a shoppers' budget stretch to afford a particularly high-desire item or, conversely, if the price is so attractively low and the shopper gets the emotional thrill of finding a bargain, it can stimulate purchase when need and features aren't all that stimulating.

Retailers can play off each of these factors toward the ultimate goal of getting a shopper to buy; however, the factor with the highest potential payoff for the retailer is shopper emotion, because this is the factor that overwhelmingly dominates the purchase. Some retailers emphasize needed items, but in today's consumer marketplace, things that are purchased primarily out of need, not desire, tend to be commoditized and sold primarily on price. It is far better to sell to consumer desire, which is emotionally driven and not as influenced by price.

Product features in and of themselves don't make a shopper buy, but they can make an item appear more or less appealing based upon the added-value features the product offers. Affordability is the favorite hot button pushed by many retailers today in response to the success of discount retailers like Wal-Mart, but few retailers can sustain a profitable business selling only to the lowest common denominator—cheap price. They have got to offer something else besides low price. For retailers who want to compete, playing to shoppers' emotion is the best way to generate sales and build a profitable, successful retailing business.

Need stimulates shopping trips, while desire drives purchases.

Specific needs for goods stimulate more shopping trips, whether it is a gallon of milk, tank of gasoline, or prescription refill. These needs-based shopping trips get shoppers out and into the store, but they are rarely undertaken for pleasure. However, when retailers who traditionally sell to needs can make their shopping experience fun, think Trader Joe's, Whole Foods, and Wegman's, they can really clean up. (To my knowledge, nobody has done a "Whole Foods" model in drugstores/pharmacies, which is a wide open opportunity.)

Always keep in mind, though, that one person's need is another's luxury. Need is highly personal and categories that seem totally discretionary can be perceived by the shopper as a necessity under certain circumstances. One way shoppers transform desire into need is by using justifiers that give the shopper permission to buy. Justifiers are those little excuses we give ourselves that say it is alright to splurge on that special something. That might be a personal reward for some professional or personal accomplishment, a stress reducer, something for the home that will make it more comfortable, more homey, more pleasant to be in, or something to reduce boredom.

Self-actualization and personal transformation are shoppers' ultimate desire. When we study the dimensions of the various justifiers shoppers use to give themselves permission to buy, one macro overriding desire emerges as dominant: shoppers buy in order to improve the quality of their life in some meaningful, measurable way. This may be by acquiring new knowledge, achieving improved health and vitality, spiritual enrichment, emotional satisfaction, and rewards from our social connections. Psychologist Abraham Maslow defines the ultimate expression of one's desire to improve the quality of their life as self-actualization and personal transformation.

True physical need—food, clothing, shelter—more often sends us to the store, but higher level needs—improving the quality of life—directs more of our spending. Most recreational shopping today is primarily a drive toward self-actualization and it will continue to be the dominant motivator for consumers when they shop. Their greatest desire will be to buy goods and services that in some way offer the prospect of personal transformation, of helping the individual create a new more idealized self.

Retailers must recognize that the shoppers in their stores are not just people looking to buy more stuff, but people in pursuit of personal transformation and a new more idealized self. The goal then for retailers today is to help their shoppers transform themselves. That will create a loyal shopper who will return to the store again and again, because personal transformation is not a once-and-done thing, it is a perpetual, never-ending process.

Shoppers buy products for the emotional experiences those products promise to deliver. In the new experiential world of shopping, the role of the product is to stimulate shoppers' emotion and get them to pick up the item, put it in their basket, and take it to the register. It is not the thing itself that people buy, but the promise of how that thing will perform emotionally and experientially for them. The concept of product performance, which comes so naturally to us when we think about things that have gears and switches like cars, watches, and television sets, is largely overlooked when it comes to things that primarily deliver or perform emotionally. Yet it is through this concept of product performance that a material good is translated into an experience.

Products *perform* in many different ways, not just in the physical or mechanical realm, but they also are expected to perform on the emotional and experiential level. Fashion brands perform by making the wearer look and feel good. For the shopper the level of performance from a fashion purchase is not unlike the expectation of performance in buying a new dishwasher. In the new world of experiential shopping, all products must *do* (i.e., active verb), rather than simply *be* (i.e., passive noun).

Expectation of finding high quality products is one of the performance values that shoppers place a high emphasis on when choosing a store in which to shop. They want to shop where quality is high. Quality is a subjective term, however, so marketers and retailers have to understand the range of quality dimensions about which their shoppers make judgments and buying decisions. Then they need to make sure that they continue to enhance the quality, adding more and more value where the shopper believes that quality resides.

Shoppers are attracted to 'bling'—Added-value features that make items special and promise more emotional rewards. When it comes to selecting one item over another, the one that has unique product features that make the item distinctive, unique, individual, worthy of notice, remarkable in some special way is the one that will be bought. The fact is a product in a store has but a split second of time to attract attention and reel in the shopper to take a closer look. The bling factor, that special something that makes an impression, is how an individual product can stand out.

The product itself can incorporate the bling through color, style, design, added features, and so on, or it can be crafted through in-store displays and attention-grabbing presentations. The bling factor is what transforms the ordinary product into the extraordinary and justifies the consumer paying significantly more for that extra special version. The bling factor plays to shopper emotions. It is what touches specific personal hot buttons for the shopper. They don't buy an item *because* it's got bling, or is of outstanding quality, made by this or that designer, or any other specific feature. They buy the product for the specific performance attributes it promises to deliver, whether those attributes are mechanical, like when buying a dishwasher, or emotional, when buying fashion.

Finding a bargain gives shoppers a big emotional boost. The affordability hot button is the one that retailers and marketers push most aggressively and most consistently today in order to stimulate shoppers to make purchases. The reason that they rely upon cheap price so frequently is that it works like a charm. Nearly two-thirds of recreational shoppers (61 percent) agree with the statement, "I often buy things I see on sale that I don't strictly need, but are at such a good price that I can't pass them up." It is the price, and oftentimes the price alone, that moves the shopper to buy. Even affluent luxury shoppers who can afford to pay full price are powerfully stimulated to buy based upon reduced price.

Today rather than being something to hide, discount shopping is cool and what cool people do. Buying stuff on sale, using cheap price as a justifier to buy something you don't need, and the sheer thrill of scoring a great price are primary drivers for shoppers today. Bragging rights come from saving, not spending money. This is a real turnaround from the conspicuous consumption days of the '90s. Because so many people don't need to save the money and have plenty of extra to spend, the true challenge comes from finding it for less.

When viewed through the lens of the retailer, this passion for cheap is both blessing and curse. The simple fact is the majority of shoppers responds and responds very strongly to the sales lure. As shoppers learn more about the markdown tactics of retailers (and it takes lots of experience to learn the drill), however, they come to expect deeper and deeper discounts. Where 10 or 20 percent off might have given shoppers a thrill before, today they want 50 or even 60 percent off. Shoppers have been trained to expect deeper discounts, so they are discouraged to ever pay full price except in very rare circumstances. Retailers need to explore other ways to stimulate the shopper beyond the dumbed-down 50 percent off sales approach. Inevitably, retailers and manufacturers pay the price for an overstocked selling floor and deep discounts. They need to tap into other emotional drivers, and there are many besides just offering a sale, that stimulate shoppers and get them in the mood to spend money.

Shopper-friendly stores play to the emotions. As the shopping equation makes clear, shoppers' need in and of itself is only a small part of the reason why people buy. Rather, it is the impact of emotion and how the shopper interprets their emotional desire as a real and compelling need that ultimately tips the scale toward buy. Across the retailing landscape, the luxury market ultimately is one driven solely and totally by desire, not need. Savvy retailers at all levels in the retailing sphere, from Wal-Mart and Target, JC Penney and The Gap, are taking a lead from luxury marketers and retailers in order to move from their more or less needs-based retailing model into one driven by desire. Satisfying shopper desires is where the real serious money is to be made. It is tapping into the emotion behind all consumer purchases, from the most mundane to the most luxurious, and finding out what is the real emotional desire, not the normal, physical, everyday need.

In their search for emotional fulfillment, shoppers often find that the goods they buy simply fall short of delivering the ultimate experience they crave. They desire more fulfillment, more happiness, more personal transformation, more self-actualization than material goods can ever provide. That is why at its most basic level retailers must embrace an entirely new business paradigm that focuses on the shopping experience, not a business model focused on the things or merchandise that people shop for. The new experiential retailing paradigm must transform the material world into a whole new experiential realm.

In their search for emotional satisfaction, shoppers turn to the store and the shopping experience. Creating a shopper-friendly store, even more a store where the shopper is exulted and loved, becomes critically important. Everything about the store and the shopping experience needs to be designed from the customers' point of view. It needs to be focused exclusively and primarily on satisfying the shoppers' personal desire.

While the retail industry is moving more into the self-service realm with stores collocated in destination shopping malls, shoppers feel nostalgic for the old days when shopping was an event where you went downtown for a full day of browsing, shopping, and experiencing. An important piece that is missing under the new self-service mall-based retailing paradigm is knowledgeable salespeople who really know their stuff.

Shopper-friendly stores become shopping destinations because they truly put the shopper first and foremost in the operations of the store. The store is designed not necessarily to maximize sales, though that is often the result, but to delight and entice the customer. Stores that are shopper-friendly truly care about the customer, not by instituting policies where by rote staff members greet the customer, but by employing sales associates who want to take care of and serve the customer. The service people must know their products, know the store, and be willing to shop with the customer to make sure they find just what they are longing for.

There's a new way of segmenting the retailing market: People who love shopping. Every once in a while everybody shops for entertainment or fun. Not all people, however, say, "I enjoy shopping and think of it as a form of entertainment." About 70 percent of middle-income to affluent shoppers (i.e., incomes of $50,000 and above with discretionary money to spend for shopping) are defined as "passionate shoppers"—people who love to shop. These shoppers are distinguished demographically as being more likely to be female, more affluent, and skewing toward a younger age range (25–45 years). These shoppers, who are passionate about shopping, offer the best opportunity for retailers who sell discretionary or luxury goods and play to shopper emotions.

When the passionate shopper segment is further analyzed, five different personalities distinguished by different motivations and shopping behaviors are found. The personality found most predominantly among these shoppers, comprising 27 percent of the total recreational shopping market, is Diana, the Bargain Hunter. Diana is always in search of the best price and the thought of finding a bargain sets her shopper's heart aflutter.

The next most widely found passionate shopper is Les, the Least Enthusiastic Shopper. Men are more likely to be of this personality type, thus the masculine name. Les shops for fun and gets pleasure out of the endeavor, but he is less enthusiastic overall about recreational shopping and will do something else more rewarding if he is given the opportunity. About 20 percent of the recreational shoppers are of the Les personality.

Ursula, the Uber-Shopper, is the third most widely dispersed shopper, comprising about 19 percent of the passionate shoppers. Ursula is the over-the-top enthusiastic shopper. She shops for fun, she shops for bargains, she shops for therapy, and she shops as a social occasion. She is the shopper who shops till she drops, literally.

Denise, the Discerning Shopper, makes up about 18 percent of the passionate shopper market. Denise is older than the typical recreational shopper and thus tends to have acquired lots of material goods in the course of her shopping career. As a result, she is more careful in her shopping choices and far less likely to buy based solely upon price.

Finally, there is Theresa, the Therapeutic Shopper. Theresa goes shopping for retail therapy. She gets her therapeutic treatment from being in the store itself, browsing the aisles, and looking at all the merchandise. For Theresa, shopping is her escape from ordinary life and she really doesn't need to buy anything when she shops. She gets her kicks from simply browsing in the stores.

By understanding the different mindsets found among shoppers, retailers get an edge up in delivering the kind of shopping experiences that their primary shoppers desire. Therefore, if a retailer wants to attract more Ursulas, they can play up the social component of shopping, making friends with their clientele and helping her fulfill her shopping fantasies. If a retailer wants more Denise's, they need to play to her long experience as a shopper and offer her only the best, and not try to stimulate her with discounts because discounts don't really work for a Denise-type shopper.

Retailer Findings

Retailers face big challenges due to the growing demand of shoppers for new experiences. Small independent retailers face challenges that while not unique to small specialty stores, are more confounding to them than to better capitalized, better staffed, and larger retailers. Among the key challenges they face are increased competition with more and more stores competing for shoppers' available discretionary funds. Retail competition is growing faster than consumers' discretionary budgets, so the battle for the share of the shoppers' wallets is becoming heated. Most small retailers don't have the resources to go head-to-head with national retailers' national-sized advertising budgets to get attention and attract customers to the shop.

The specialty retailers' basic competitive strategy—stocking unique, different product—doesn't work anymore because the big box retailers are sourcing virtually identical products at cheaper prices. Smaller, independent manufacturers who have relied upon small specialty retailers for distribution can't depend solely upon them anymore, so in response to their own competitive pressures, manufacturers have to sell to a wider range of retailers and direct-to-consumers to stay afloat. All in all this adds up to an incredibly challenging situation for retailers big and small, as well as for manufacturers that need to find more sales outlets for their goods.

Retailers' primary business challenge is getting more customers and keeping the ones they already have. Independent retailers express the number one business challenge they face: getting more customers and keeping the ones they already have. In their search for new customers, small retailers find that the old solutions, especially advertising in the local newspapers, Yellow Pages, coupon clipper-venues, and other locally targeted media, don't work any longer. They feel they have no voice anymore, no way to reach out to the potential shopper, tell their story, attract their attention, and draw them into the store to shop. Costs are one limiting factor, but that isn't the crux of the problem. Rather, advertising messages scattered widely across the consumer landscape don't attract shoppers' attention anymore. Retailers are willing to spend money to advertise if it yields results, but it simply doesn't deliver any longer.

Because of the challenges of deciding where to advertise and what the advertising message should be, more small retailers are turning to word of mouth advertising as their primary vehicle. However, if stimulating word of mouth is the answer to their advertising challenges, then retailers need to focus on making their shops word-of-mouth-worthy—or "remarkable" in Seth Godin's terms—and that means making the shopping experience truly exceptional, far beyond expectations, totally unexpected in a delightful way.

Providing superior levels of customer service is retailers' favorite way to distinguish themselves from the competition. Retailers place a lot of emphasis on the role of their superior levels of customer service to fight back at mass merchants' and big-box retailers' onslaught. Not only do independent retailers focus on customizing product to meet the shoppers' need, they also customize service. Additionally, independent retailers tend to focus on the little details of service that make the shopping experience more fun for the customer.

Retailers that put the customer first to make shopping an experience share seven distinctive qualities, called the pop! equation. Shops that pop, like The Apple Store, Nell Hill's, Target, Godiva, Nordstrom, Bluemercury, Saks Fifth Avenue, and Easton Town Center, and the others profiled throughout this book, share a set of specific qualities. The pop! equation defines the unique way that retailers apply specific strategies and combine them together to create a truly special, extraordinary shopping experience for the customer. The specific qualities that make up the pop equation are:

- High levels of customer involvement and interaction (Chapter 8)
- Evokes shopper curiosity (Chapter 9)
- Have a contagious, electric quality (Chapter 10)
- Converges atmosphere, store design, and merchandise (Chapter 11)
- Authentic concept (Chapter 12)
- Right pricing for value (Chapter 13)
- Accessible, nonexclusive, and free from pretensions (Chapter 14)

What's Next

Shoppers today want more, lots more, than what is typically found in most stores that line the malls, fill up the strip malls, or stand alone as big-box behemoths. Shoppers today want more when they shop than just to go out and buy stuff; they want shopping to be a fun, engaging, and delightful experience. Otherwise, why waste their increasingly precious time walking through the mall or browsing the aisles of some nondescript store? They want a payback from the shopping experience that is more than stuff in a bag. They want to be entertained, to have fun.

Shoppers today want more when they shop than just to go out and buy stuff; they want shopping to be a fun, engaging, and delightful experience.

The principles about how to transform the retail shopping environment from the ordinary to the extraordinary follow in Chapter 16 and beyond. They are divided by category: people-related principles, product principles, pricing principles, promotion principles, and place (design) principles. After the discussion of each of the principles, I have added some questions and activities that you can do to help you put these transforming principles to work in your store.

The recommendations are drawn from all the research and interviews conducted with retailers who have created wonderful shopping environments that pop for the shopper. It may be a bit much to have you do them all, but it is my sincere hope that every one of you will take a few of these powerful principles for transforming the retail store into a shopping experience and put them to work right away in your store. The ultimate survival of your store may be at stake.

Because shoppers today demand more, retailers who offer them an alternative, one where shoppers can find great stuff at a reasonable price in a store where it is fun to shop, will survive—even thrive—in the future. From my many discussions with shoppers, I sense a feeling of profound disappointment about most of the shopping choices they have. They are looking for an alternative that can become a destination for them, a place where they really love to shop, not just another store where they have to shop. They want more and the recommendations and principles that follow ensure that you deliver them more.

CHAPTER SIXTEEN

People Principles that Transform the Retail Store into a Shopping Experience

"Dealing with people is probably the biggest problem you face, especially if you are in business. Yes, and that is also true if you are a housewife, architect, or engineer."

DALE CARNEGIE

When it comes to retail, people are number one. They are at the heart of the formula for retail success. The quantum theory of shopping that explains consumers' propensity to buy—Propensity to buy = (Need + Features + Affordability) × Emotion^2—places the emphasis of shoppers' behavior on emotion, a purely and exclusively human quality. While other inanimate objects and external factors may play on people's emotions, what most strongly impacts people's emotions and feelings are other people, their reaction, and their own emotions. In order to achieve maximum success, retailers must manage their shoppers' emotional responses, insuring that their in-store experience is a happy, pleasant, positive, emotionally uplifting one. The single most important factor in making sure people are emotionally satisfied comes through that uniquely human person-to-person interaction. Everything else—pricing, product, promotion, place/store design—pales in comparison to the people principles.

The essential people factors that transform shopping from the ordinary to the extraordinary are illustrated through the pop equation, those seven factors that characterize truly special shopping experiences—customer involvement; shopper curiosity; contagious quality; convergence in atmosphere, design, and merchandise; authenticity; right price/value relationship; and accessibility. Shops that pop put the shopper at the center of the store. Everything else is designed and managed to enhance the shoppers' experience.

The single most important factor in making sure people are emotionally satisfied comes through that uniquely human person-to-person interaction.

That is why if you are a retailer and you want to make your store a true destination for shoppers then the first and most important thing you must address are the people principles. Every other concern in running a successful retail operation is secondary to the people and that is how a store, no matter what your specific business, what you sell, or what your local competitive environment is, can ultimately succeed: Place the shopper first in your store.

People Principle #1: Pick Your Profession Carefully

Following a recent speech, I was talking with a group of retailers when I shared my belief about the two hardest professions in the world: nursing and retailing. As I was going on about how similar these two professions really are, both centered around taking care of people at their point of need and when they are likely not at their personal best, one of the retailers said, "That's right! I used to be a nurse, then I decided to try a second career in retailing. And both jobs really are the same." Ultimately, the retailer's job is about taking care of the customers, making them feel good and enhancing the quality of the customers' lives through the products and services that you deliver to them—just like a nurse who takes care of patients and gives them the medicine and care that makes them feel better.

If we look across all the successful retailers profiled here, and most especially the small independent retailers, like Mary Carol Garrity from Nell Hill's, Manny Gonzales and Tiger Lily, Sherry Keefe with Damsels in this Dress, Kate Collier and Feast!, and Dan Bellman of Boxwoods, we find, first and foremost, retailers with a passion for people. Surely they also have a strong affinity for the products they sell, but what comes across in talking to each of these retailing entrepreneurs is that no matter what business they are in or what products they are selling, from home furnishings to fashion to plants or flowers or cheese, what is the most important element to each and every one of them is their connection with other people, and that passion extends to both the customers and their staff. While Mary Carol Garrity grew up in a family of retail merchants, all the other retailing entrepreneurs came to retailing from other professions: Manny Gonzales was in hospitality and food service, Sherry was a visual merchandiser, Kate Collier's background was restaurants and her husband and business partner's was music, and Dan Bellman was a business consultant who helped turn around troubled businesses such as apartment complexes and dry cleaning businesses. They all recognize that at its core their retail business is a people business; what they are selling is purely secondary to that. As Bellman with his extensive business background says, "It's all business. It doesn't matter if you're selling two-by-fours, as I did as a kid because my dad was in the lumber business, or running a manufacturing company where you're selling widgets, or trying to help a company build Domino's Pizza stores. It is all about people."

If you are a person who likes the things that you are selling more than the people you are selling it to or with, then your retail enterprise is headed for disaster.

An unfortunate fact of the retail business is that there is a relatively low cost of entry, so just about anybody with a minimum of capital can get started in some kind of retail enterprise. That tends to let people into retailing who are totally unsuited for it, so people who really like home decorating open a home furnishings store, or people who like plants open a garden center, or people who like clothes open a fashion boutique, all with the flawed assumption that their primary business focus in retail is around the products they sell. That is a huge mistake. If you are a person who likes the things that you are selling *more* than the people you are selling it to or with, then your retail enterprise is headed for disaster. Mary Carol Garrity of Nell Hill's says, "I have observed a lot of people get into a retail store, like a home accessories store, because they love to decorate. That is a terrible mistake. I got in because I love retail, not because I love to decorate. I'm a people person and that is what I love about retail."

While success at retail does involve some level of product knowledge and expertise, you really can get that product knowledge on the job—and when all else fails, you can fake it. Gonzales is very modest about the extent of his flower knowledge prior to opening Tiger Lily, as he explains: "I have a secret to share with you. I'd never buy my wife flowers before we opened the shop up. I was one of the most flower-ignorant guys out there. But now I am so excited when I see wonderful things come in. So now we get these fellows who come in— mechanics and electricians—in their big pickup trucks. And they see me as a regular guy who can talk about football and fishing and then get really excited about flowers. And these guys get excited too. In fact, I have one customer who's a boxing coach. He comes in every week to buy flowers. Flowers are awesome. Flowers are for everybody."

So like Gonzales, anybody can pick up product knowledge on the job, but what you have got to start your retail business with and what you can't ever fake is really caring about the customer. Gonzales has an excitement about flowers and a passion to share those wonderful good feelings that flowers impart with his pickup truck buddies. Yes, he cares about the flowers, but more importantly he cares about the customer and wants to share his good feelings with them. The same thing goes for all the other entrepreneurs. They want to enhance their customers' quality of life, to make it more meaningful, more enjoyable, more fun by sharing their wonderful home furnishings (Nell Hill's), wonderful fashions (Damsels in this Dress), wonderful gifts and decorative accents (Boxwoods), or wonderful foods (Feast!) with them.

People Principle #2: Pick Your Staff Very Carefully

The people you hire to work in your store are there primarily to support the overall objective of the store, which is about taking care of the customer. Your staff members must be as equally people-pleasing and people-oriented as you are. Of course, there are support positions in any business that involve a minimum of people interaction, so their people orientation doesn't have to be as great, but for any staff position that involves significant customer interaction, you have got to hire someone for his or her people-passion as well.

Personally, I am not a big believer in psychological testing for many employment situations, but in the realm of retail, I make an exception, because the ability to work and feel with people is so fundamentally critical in the retail store. The Myers-Briggs system is one of the popular pre-employment tests in use today. It is based upon a four-part system that identifies basic dimensions of human personality:

- **Energizing preferences:** Extroverting (E) or Introverting (I)
  - Extroverting people get energy from other people, activities, and things they do.
  - Introverting people get energy from their inner world of ideas and thoughts.
- **Information-gathering preferences:** Sensing (S) or Intuiting (N)
  - Sensing people get information from their five senses and focus on what is.
  - Intuiting people are intoned with a sixth sense of hunches, insights and focus on what might be.
- **Decision making preferences:** Thinking (T) or Feeling (F)
  - Thinking people make decisions in a logical, objective way.
  - Feeling people make decisions in a personal, values-oriented way.
- **Lifestyle orientation:** Judging (J) or Perceiving (P)
  - Judging people live in an organized, planned way.
  - Perceiving people are more spontaneous and flexible.

(Definitions adapted from *What Type Am I? Discover Who You Really Are* by Renee Baron (New York: Penguin Books, 1998))

When it comes to success in retail, not all of the four factors are of equal importance, but two are critical to retailing success: Extroverting Feeling (EF) types are without a doubt the best for retail. You want extroverts working in retail because these are people who derive their energy, excitement, and stimulation from dealing with other people. Along with strong extroverts, you want feeling types who are very personal in their decision-making and want to please others and make them feel good. An EF type of person is a real people person who is highly compassionate and empathetic and who gets their greatest fulfillment in being and working with other people. The other two Myers-Briggs variables are far less important in the retail environment, so an employment candidate could go either way in information gathering or lifestyle orientation, but the EF factors are critical when hiring. I wouldn't play amateur psychologist in trying to figure out what type of people are what. For example, I am a true introvert, needing time alone to energize and find direction, but I am not shy in a social setting so I can pass easily as an extrovert. Rather than do-it-yourself personality profiling, a quick check in the local Yellow Pages can guide you to trained psychologists and practitioners who can conduct the tests for you. That is one way to be sure that a candidate's personality type, at least, fits the bill, even though getting the absolutely right personality type is no guarantee that the person you hire will be a success.

In discussions with the retailers profiled here, many mention the critically important role hiring the right people for their store plays. Marla Malcolm Beck, CEO and founder of the rapidly growing Bluemercury apothecary and spa chain of 13 stores (soon to grow to 18), which currently employs some 200 people, says that she makes a priority of personally interviewing every new employee, a practice that she isn't about to give up even as the chain grows. Marla looks for caring people who want to share their passion for beauty products with others.

"One of the biggest problems is getting the right people. I look at people's résumés, but as a rule, I don't put a lot of weight on them. We definitely hire now on attitude, much more than aptitude," says Dan Bellman of Boxwoods Gardens & Gifts.

Dan Bellman of Boxwoods Gardens & Gifts says, "One of the biggest problems is getting the right people. I look at people's résumés, but as a rule, I don't put a lot of weight on them. We definitely hire now on attitude, much more than aptitude. A lot of it is gut feel, but I also ask a few silly questions, like did they ever achieve success in their mother or father's eyes? I have found that people that are striving to please mom and dad have a very good work ethic." This is an interesting observation and one that you might put to work immediately in identifying job candidates who are responsible and willing to make the extra effort it takes to create a truly outstanding shopping experience in a retail store.

Kate Collier at Feast! follows a similar guide to finding the right staff people by looking at personality first. She says, "A lot of it [success] has to do with finding the right person. We've had people that we've tried to train, and sometimes when people aren't just naturally friendly, it's tough to be friendly. We also want people who are really food lovers, but the most important thing in the interviewing process is finding out if they are friendly and do they actually cook."

In other words, you have to find people with the right passion; in the case of Feast! it is people who are passionate about other people and food; in the case of Bluemercury, people who are passionate about other people and cosmetics. If they have that passion, you can train them about the specifics of everything else. You can't train someone to be truly friendly and caring. That is something you simply can't fake; either you have it or you don't.

People Principle #3: Pay a Reasonable Wage

If you want to hire minimum people to work in your store, then pay them minimum wage. If you want to hire the best people to work with your truly precious customers, you better pay them a wage commensurate with their duties and responsibilities. In hiring, just like in every other aspect of commercial life, you get what you pay for and if you want to pay minimum wage, then you have got to expect minimum performance. While many national retailers offer generous employment packages including benefits and commissions that give the staff member a real incentive for serving the customer, few small retailers feel they can offer similar programs.

The simple fact is that people work for wages and retailers large and small need to compete for the best people by offering a competitive wage. Sherry Keefe of Damsels in This Dress shares the challenges of running a small business: "Of course in any small business—no matter how cool your shop is—it's a struggle. You don't get the tax breaks that big businesses do, but they can afford to pay the taxes that you re-

---

TYPICAL RETAIL WAGES

In 2004, retail salespersons held about 4.3 million wage and salary jobs. Median hourly earnings of retail salespersons, including commissions, were $8.98 in May 2004. Half of all retail salespeople earned between $7.46 and $12.22 an hour.

Source: U.S. Department of Labor, Bureau of Labor and Statistics

---

ally can't. You struggle against continually raising overhead, rent, benefits, and all the other things you have to have to run a business. And you have nobody to fall back on but yourself." Her answer is to keep her staff lean and pay those she employs well. Also, Sherry Keefe and her business partner carry a lot of the burden of day-to-day operations themselves.

In hiring, just like in every other aspect of commercial life, you get what you pay for and if you want to pay minimum wage, then you have got to expect minimum performance.

The successful business owners here look at their retail staff as integral to their overall success. They give back to the employees and take responsibility for providing their staff members with a living wage. Dan Tibby, of Prairie Edge, extends their company's fair-trade approach to paying their artists a fair price for their creativity to their sales employees too. "We take employee involvement more seriously than a lot of other companies do. We really have the feeling that our employees are the driving force in the company," Tibby says. He describes the company, its staff, its extended network of Native American artists, and its customers as part of the "family" in a way that isn't phony or condescending, but real and sincere. Boxwoods' Dan Bellman uses the exact same phrase: "We keep our employees a long time, and we try to promote a family feel in the business . . . This feeling we refer to as being part of the Boxwoods' family is hopefully conveyed to our customers, who then feel like friends of the family." They express the employer-employee relationship as so much more intimate and personal than a strictly business relationship. Just like family, part of being a member of a family is that you are taken care of.

As a small business owner myself, I know the huge chunk of working capital that employee wages, benefits, and payroll taxes command, but I also know that in a people-intensive business like retail you can't afford to scrimp on this critical line item. Hopefully, as you put more of the principles in this book to work in your retail store, you will achieve more business success, a portion of which you can reinvest back into the business in order to pay higher salaries and commissions to the staff members who give the extra effort to serving the customers, which makes the business even more successful. What goes around really does come around.

People Principle #4: Retailer's Job Is to Be the 'Host or Hostess with the Most-est'

Target was onto something when they abandoned the use of the term "customers" or "shoppers" and replaced it with "guests" in their corporate vocabulary. Words have tremendous power because they are one of the primary ways we communicate person-to-person. Simply by using the word "guest" to describe the people who come into the store, you create an entirely new way of relating to these people. They become more than just shoppers or customers; they become guests.

In keeping with the guest metaphor, the ultimate role the retail owner can play in his or her store is as the host or hostess with the most-est who welcomes the guests into their retail "home." The host/hostess is responsible for making the guests feel comfortable, for entertaining them and seeing that everybody has a wonderful time. That is the role the retail business owner or manager must play. You want the people who come into your store to visit to feel like they have happened upon a wonderful exciting party that they can become a part of. The Apple Stores have done this superbly through their Genius Bar, which simply draws the growing group of Apple enthusiasts to it like flies to honey. Mary Carol Garrity has mastered this in her Nell Hill's store where she invites customers to talk to other customers and people feel like the store is an "eight-hour cocktail party without the alcohol." Garrity, of course, assumes the vital role of party hostess in her store. She never leaves the floor, but spends virtually all her time with the customers, encouraging conversation, bringing people together, entertaining them, and making them feel welcome. Every day she is hosting a virtual party in her store, and that is one of the secrets to how she has built a thriving destination retail business based upon a customer base most of whom drive over an hour to shop in her store.

> *The retailer needs to think about his or her job as being host or hostess for a new and wonderfully fun party every day and plan accordingly.*

The best host spends all of his time with the guests and makes the guest the ultimate priority. The best hostess plans for the party up front and has everything ready before the first guest arrives. If the unexpected happens, which it often does, she is ready for it and can work seamlessly around any problem. She spends minimal time attending to the food, but gives most of her attention to the people. That, in a nutshell, is how the retail business owner should work in the store each and every day. The retailer needs to think about his job as being the host for a new and wonderfully fun party every day and plan accordingly.

People Principle #5: Party with the People

The best hosts and hostesses focus on their guests' enjoyment; at the same time they also make a point of enjoying the party too. In hosting a retail party, therefore, you need to enjoy the party too and one of the best ways to do that is to actually participate in the joy of shopping with the customers. Shopping is more fun when you are accompanied by someone who is equally committed to the experience. The very best retail salespeople that I have ever encountered have fun in showing me new things, giving me new ideas, opening up the wonders of the store to me. They don't sell me and they don't have to, because they have just as much fun shopping with me as I have with them.

Shopping with the guest, rather than trying to sell to the customer, is what a retail host or hostess with the most-est does.

The retail salesperson's job is to know the merchandise inside and out and be able to share his or her intimate knowledge with the customer, who can't possibly have the same depth of product knowledge as the salesperson. He or she makes shopping fun by acting as a guide to help the customer explore all the nooks and crannies of the store where wonderful things can be found. Shopping with the guest, rather than trying to sell to the customer, is what a retail host or hostess with the most-est does.

People Principle #6: Care for the Beast: Lessons in Jurassic Park Retailing

Now that my children are older my most frequent shopping companion is my husband. He has a habit when we go shopping that was totally unnerving to me until I started to plan for it. Whenever we go shopping, the first thing he has to do is get a bite to eat. Like Pavlov's dog that salivated when it heard the bell that signaled food was on the way, when my husband crosses the threshold of a store or mall, that means time for a treat. Savvy retailers, like Barnes & Noble, capitalize on that response by offering in-store cafés where you can get an extra charge from an espresso coffee drink and a sugar rush from a luscious piece of cake—and wouldn't you know that Barnes & Noble is my husband's absolutely favorite store for shopping. What goes in inevitably must come out and Barnes & Noble provides for that too with clean, accessible restrooms.

An essential part of serving people is providing for their baser animal needs. Deep inside every person there is a remnant of the reptile, thus the need to think about Jurassic Park retailing, which is about satisfying the beast in all of us. Far too few stores offer comfort services to their guests, yet none of us would invite people over to our house and not let them use the bathroom. Malls need to offer superior bathroom facilities to their guests that are spotlessly clean, comfortable, and safe. In my experience, many malls, even the most luxurious, don't attend to these facilities as they should.

Food service in retailing environments, too, could often use an improvement. Lifestyle centers like Easton Town Center have made providing fine dining for their guests an important competitive strategy. The result of offering a selection of different fine dining choices to their guests is that the center is more than just a place to shop, but a recreational destination for Columbus area residents. Most malls, on the other hand, offer mostly subsistence level food in food courts featuring fast food or midlevel sit-down restaurant chains. They serve only the people that are there, rather than drawing people all on their own.

Paying more attention to the shoppers' physical comfort also means more places to sit, not just in the mall but in the stores too, and central places to check packages and coats so you don't have to schlep around overburdened with stuff.

The Mall of America is on the forefront of Jurassic Park retailing with their new Nap Store where guests can escape for a few minutes of shuteye. Offered by PowerNap Sleep Centers Inc. of Boca Raton, Florida, this is the first mall-based napping center, though they also offer this service at the Boca Raton airport. It is an intriguing concept, even if at 70 cents per minute taking an instore nap can get a bit pricey.

People Principle #7: Imprint Yourself and Your Store in Shoppers' Memories

"Success is not so much what you are, but rather what you appear to be."
ANONYMOUS

Perhaps because I started my professional career right at the zenith of the Dress for Success trend, I have always subscribed to the belief that most people you come into contact with both in business and personally judge you by how you are dressed. Psychological research shows that first impressions are powerful and influence others' expectations of you. The way you are dressed, your clothes, style, and grooming, all make up a major component of your first impression, and because people are the first principle of retail, retailers need to attend to the first impression they make and be sure to make a positive and memorable one.

I personally am a big believer in wearing uniforms to distinguish one's profession and position. There is a reason why doctors wear lab coats and carry stethoscopes prominently around their necks. Their uniform sends an important message that they are in charge and your health is safe in their hands. Likewise in many retailing environments an appropriate uniform can eliminate confusion for the customer, so that they know who to approach for help. And in some settings that demand specialize expertise, uniforms send reinforcing messages about one's professional status. Appropriate uniforms, whether they are aprons, smocks, caps, lab coats, or slacks and a T-shirt, should be well designed, clean, and crisp so that they give off a positive impression. In other types of stores where a uniform is not appropriate, they might adopt a dress code, for example, everyone dresses in black and white, to create some level of conformity in the staff.

For store owners who greet the customers and spend time with them, they need to dress more like the customers they want to attract. People feel most comfortable with people who are like themselves, so you want to dress similarly to the customers who shop in your store. You want to be neither too casual nor too formal, but set the right tone for your store and your customers. I find that women generally are more attuned to dressing right for different occasions than men are. However, for you male retailers, especially if women make up an important segment of your shopper base, people notice if you are not well put together. That doesn't mean you have to dress in Italian suits, but well-fitting slacks, a cashmere or silk sweater, and a nice, well-fitted sport coat are never out of style and appropriate almost anywhere. As a shopper, I know I get better service when I dress up to go to the store than when I dress down. Likewise, retailers need to be attentive to their professional appearance.

One final thought in the style department: adopting some kind of distinctive style statement can be a powerful way to imprint yourself and your store in peoples' memories. It becomes your personal trademark. Maybe your style could be to wear distinctive hats, dramatic costume jewelry, designer scarves, or fun and funky eyeglasses. For me, I like to be thought of as the marketing consultant with the fantastic shoes (remember the red velvet heels?). It is all about finding something that sets you apart; something that people will notice and remember you by, that won't turn people off, but draw people in. I think many people are conservative with their personal appearance and individual style. Surely you can go overboard, but most people don't like to call attention to themselves through their fashion. Nevertheless, when you are trying to make an impression and be memorable, a personal trademark can be a valuable asset.

People Principle #8: Every Customer Interaction Is Market Research

One of my mottos is "you can never know enough about your customer." I've made that the cornerstone of my business: providing businesses with critical information and insight about their customer. How I do that is through research. Retailers have a distinct advantage in the research department, because unlike my business where I have to go out and find the types of people I need to research, retailers get to rub shoulders with their research subjects (i.e., customers) every day. Mary Carol Garrity of Nell Hill's makes ongoing customer research part of her job: "I love being out on the floor. I love working with my customer. I love listening to what they are asking for and what they are saying. I learn from my customer."

Every chance you get to talk to a customer is an opportunity to do your own market research to find out what they like, what they want, what turns them on, what turns them off. You engage them by asking questions about themselves in order to gather valuable business insights that you can use to continue to refine the shopping experience in your store.

In conducting your personal market research, it is important to make notes and record the things you learn. Too frequently, valuable insights get forgotten or lost in the day-to-day hubbub. Making a discipline out of recording your research findings, getting your staff members to do the same and then having the entire store staff share their findings on a regular basis can provide valuable learning. Monthly, maybe even weekly or biweekly staff meetings to discuss what customers are saying and feeling and experiencing in the store can help identify new opportunities and find new directions for the business. If you find that the meetings become repetitive and nothing new is coming out of them, then you better do more market research because you aren't asking the right questions or doing enough research. As a researcher, I find people endlessly fascinating and always changing. There is something valuable and new to learn every single day if you engage your customers in the right way. That starts with asking them questions, and probing for how they feel and what they think.

Every chance you get to talk to a customer is an opportunity to do your own market research to find out what they like, what they want, what turns them on, what turns them off.

In your market research, if you uncover any little criticism or negative comment, you'd better perk up and fast. I have found in my research with consumers that most of them want to be positive and give only good comments. They generally don't want to be critical or say something negative, so when I get even a hint of a negative comment, I jump on it with both feet to find out what is really going on. If you aren't attuned to those passing criticisms, they may well pass you by, but believe me, underneath those minor negative comments are serious issues that you can't afford to be ignorant of. Any time you get any passing mention at all critical, pay serious attention to it, and whenever possible make amends to the customer and fix the problem in your store immediately.

In the realm of market research in your store, I believe in building customer databases with names, addresses, phone numbers, e-mail addresses, and, if possible, product, style, or brand preferences. For example, in my business we ask everybody who calls the office if they want to be added to our mailing list, so they have the choice to opt in or out; virtually everyone opts in. For those who contact us by e-mail, we automatically enter them into the e-mail list. Then on a fairly regular basis, usually once a week, we send out e-mail blasts with important new research information that they can use in their business. Retailers can do the exact same thing by asking every customer if they want to get on an insiders' list to learn about new products that come into the store. Most people who enjoy the shopping experience are likely to sign right up, which can become a powerful resource for targeted promotions and building customer loyalty. Outbound communication can take the form of e-mail, the most cost effective way to communicate today and increasingly viable for consumer marketing, or mail, postcards being the most cost-effective and easiest snail-mail method for routine communications.

Many of the retailers I talk to don't make a priority of building their customer database, but that is just letting opportunity walk out your door. We are living in the information age and customer information is one of the most valuable business resources you can use. Just knowing the names of your best customers, the ones who spend the most money, can give you an opportunity to reach out to them to tell them when new shipments arrive or things they are bound to like come into the store. People are busy today and don't have time to regularly browse even their favorite places to shop. Store owners should bridge the gap by reaching out in a targeted fashion to those shoppers they know are most likely to be responsive to their offerings. And that is their existing customer base.

People Principle #9: Find Excitement Every Day

As we have seen, shoppers find excitement contagious. They are drawn to stores and shopping experiences that are exciting and stimulating, as Mary Carol Garrity of Nell Hill's describes: "I don't do it for the money. I do it because I love it. For my staff and myself, we are very high energy and very passionate about it. That passion is contagious to my staff and it's contagious to my customers."

The ultimate source of excitement in any store is the people: the interaction of the customers with staff and the customers with other customers. Excitement doesn't exist in the material things or the physical space, though they contribute to a positive feeling for shoppers and staff. Excitement is something that springs from the individual.

The ultimate source of excitement in any store is the people: the interaction of the customers with staff and the customers with other customers.

The retail store owner has to find that well of excitement in him or her self and be prime cheerleader to bring excitement and passion to the staff and the customers. This isn't an easy undertaking, because we all are human. We wake up on the wrong side of the bed, we get depressed, we face daunting personal challenges and defeats, but we can't let our troubles intrude upon our business. You have to put on a happy face on the shop floor and leave your blues in the back room. Like the retailer in the focus group who calls his store to make sure his staff members answer the phone with their "happy voice," the business of retail being a people business must focus on the pleasure, joy, and happiness of the customer. Everything else is secondary—and people respond to happy, enthusiastic, and excited people. Each of us is ultimately in control of our emotional responses, so we have no excuse for being less than happy and enthusiastic every day and every way. As Dale Carnegie said, "Happiness doesn't depend on any external conditions; it is governed by our mental attitude."

Putting the People Principles to Work

Here are some questions and activities you can do to put these people principles to work in your store.

1. Define the three primary objectives of your store. What are your primary goals in having a store where people shop? Make your shoppers the object of each store objective; i.e., my store objective is to deliver to my customers the most extraordinary fashions at good prices.
2. Among your staff, who is the best working with the customers? What makes them so good at working with people? (List five specific qualities.) Who doesn't have an easy time developing rapport with the customer? Thinking of this person or persons,

what skills, talents, special qualities do they bring to the store? (List five other qualities.) Ask yourself honestly, would they be better off working somewhere else? Would your store be better off without them?

3. How can you attract more people to work in your store who are like the person who works best with the customers? List four specific strategies to find more people like them, e.g., ask some of your friendliest customers if they would like a job.

4. Think about the last party you gave or attended. Name nine things the host or hostess did that made the party successful and the guests feel comfortable and welcome. How can you adapt one or more of these ideas into the operation of your retail store?

5. Stand in front of a mirror in a typical outfit that you would wear to work in your store. What do you like? What do you think? How do people see you? What could you add, subtract, change to look better? Is there anything distinctive that stands out about your outfit? Is there any style or fashion that you really like that you might not be wearing? Can you find one thing to wear that could become a personal trademark?

CHAPTER SEVENTEEN

Product Principles that Transform the Retail Store into a Shopping Experience

"In the factory we make cosmetics, but in my stores we sell hope."
CHARLES REVSON

Let's first abandon the notion that product can ever be the primary competitive strategy for any retailer in the new experiential shopping landscape. As the quantum theory of shopping shows, product-specific features play only a supporting role in the purchase equation— Propensity to buy = (Need + Features + Affordability) $\times$ Emotion^2— while emotion trumps features every time. Product features can stimulate emotion, though, and make one particular item so much more compelling to buy than another one. Clearly, looking and shopping for product, finding an item that one needs, or browsing the shelves looking for a specific product is an experience that shoppers desire.

Therefore, we shouldn't denigrate the overall role of product in the shopping equation, but for a particular retailer to rest their whole marketing strategy on stocking unique and different products that cannot be found anywhere else is to set themselves up for disaster. As Doug Rose of QVC says, "Customers more and more are realizing that the items often are not the point of differentiation between one store and another. It is the experience of that store, the environment." Today there are so many retail options for shoppers to choose from, so many stores that stock either the exact same product or a perfectly acceptable substitute, that unique products are not good enough anymore. Unfortunately, too many retailers believe they need exclusive products, items that nobody in their immediate neighborhood carries, and hold out for that something extra special. All the while, they are losing sales big time by not stocking the products that people want, in favor of a search for some illusory unique product.

You need to buy and stock new products, not because other competitive stores don't have them, but in order to present that product as part of a unified vision that expresses a unique point of view.

Today, uniqueness at a product level doesn't get you very far. However, uniqueness of selection, bringing in an assortment of different products to put them together with a unique and personal vision that connects to the customers, is a winning strategy that every retailer should strive for. You need to buy and stock new products, not because other competitive stores don't have them, but in order to present that product as part of a unified vision that expresses a unique point of view. In other words, retailers need to shift their search for uniqueness from the individual product level to the overall store or department level. That then delivers the kind of product experiences that shoppers crave.

Product Principle #1: Merchandise Won't Set Your Store Apart; Rather, the Way You Sell it Does

In the new experiential shopping landscape, shoppers are searching for product experiences, more so than product as simply product. They want products that deliver a punch, give a boost, and provide an emotional feeling, and they want to shop in stores that do the same. Specialty retailers in particular cling to the notion that product is their point of difference, but that is an illusion. As we have discussed, product alone can no longer be the differentiator. Rather, how you sell the product is truly the point of difference. A big part of how a retailer sells their product is based upon the people principles described in the previous chapter, but there are other aspects that are product specific.

For example, the way you select product to bring into your store is an important part of the way you sell the product. It is a vision of how one item links or connects to the whole. Merchants who do the buying for shops that pop tend to be guided by clearly defined objectives when they look for merchandise to carry. It is a matter of understanding your customer and why they shop in your store in the first place.

For Kate Collier at Feast! her customers come for the superior quality of food, in particular, cheese. So while she has dabbled in other product categories, she has found the secret of success is to stay true to her unique value proposition: "Our main focus is artisanal cheese, so we try to have many products that are made by hand. So that is our focus on product; it is a combination of small batches, great flavor, and consistent quality," she says. She doesn't just show or display great cheese for her customers; she proves it to them by making tasting a central part of the Feast! experience: "The tastings definitely hook them. That makes them a lot more comfortable to go to the cheese counter. And then that gets them to have a comfortable interaction with the person at the cheese counter. Then as the cheese is being wrapped and labeled, they may see baguettes or slide over to the meat counter. It relaxes them." The Feast! product experience then extends beyond the simple products she sells to the tasting experience that gives the shopper confidence and comfort in buying.

At Bluemercury, making sure the products she sells deliver results to the customer is priority number one for Marla Malcolm Beck. Magnolia Audio Video has designed their showrooms with their customers' homes in mind so that the product demonstration in the store is what they can expect once they get the item home.

All the shops that pop profiled here share this bigger picture view of their products, not just as things to buy, but wonderful product experiences to be delivered to the customer. Colonial Williamsburg Marketplace invites deeper participation of shoppers in the Williamsburg experience by touching and feeling the reproduction items (something they can't do in the museum setting), trying them on, and bringing a personal piece of Williamsburg back home. Prairie Edge shares the experience of Native American culture, past and present, through the products they stock in the store. Each item stands on its own as a work of art, but works together to deliver a truly unique, 360-degree cultural experience for the shopper.

Saks Fifth Avenue was founded with the idea of searching the world to bring back distinctive, luxury products and create a luxury emporium that truly reflects the best of the best. As Kimberly Grabel of Saks describes it, their product merchandising reflects "the idea of retail as inspiration, as well as aspiration." The store becomes a showplace where the shopper can "experience all of these wonderful products in a wonderful setting." And guess what . . . most of the brands of products that the New York Saks Fifth Avenue flagship store stocks can be readily found in boutiques, department stores, and brand stores within a couple of blocks. Saks understands their merchandise is special not because you can't find it anywhere else, which clearly is not true, but because of the way they sell it, present it, bring it together, and tell a story for the customer.

Product Principle #2: Create Story-Based Displays Throughout the Store

Stories are powerful communicators of meaning and in product selection, it is all about the meaning for the customer. A story-based display is one that uses cross merchandising and bringing different products together into a vignette that communicates a message, a concept, or an idea to the consumer. Most retailers do this selectively, in their windows, on end caps, and various other places in the store, but the shops that pop tell stories with their displays throughout the store, not just in a couple of select places. Through story-based displays, not just lining products up on a shelf, retailers can communicate their product vision to the consumer, so the experience of the store is not product-focused, but story-based. If you get a chance to visit Boxwoods Gardens & Gifts in Buckhead, Georgia, right outside Atlanta, you would get a hands-on lesson in telling stories through product displays. The store itself is located in a quaint cottage-style home filled with cozy rooms and all kinds of nooks and crannies to fill. While the rooms tend to have a theme—one room is devoted to garden and plant materials, another to fashion accessories, which they call the "girlie" stuff, another to gifts and home furnishings— each room has an amazing mixture of different things that are idiosyncratic and wonderfully creative. They don't have any store fixtures per se, but use antiques and furniture they sell for product displays. A shopper can come in, see a lovely hutch with a centerpiece and candlesticks with linens peeking out of the drawers, and buy the entire display for their home. Dan Bellman describes their product strategy simply: "We want a fun and friendly shopping experience that showcases unusual one-of-a-kind items and also highlights our creative floral abilities. We use old and antique pieces as our display fixtures, as well as old chandeliers and sconces, all of which are available for purchase. We try to constantly change our merchandise and change our displays based on what new items and plants have arrived, what season it is, and how we can express our creativity."

Nell Hill's is another store where the displays are carefully crafted to tell stories. This demands consistent effort on the part of the store's staff, but it pays off in attracting customers and getting them to buy. Talking about the effectiveness of her store displays, Mary Carol Garrity describes them as her "silent salespeople."

Compelling product displays are not exclusive to home furnishings or fashion retail. Marla Malcolm Beck's Bluemercury stores are designed to provide a monochromatic backdrop to display the drop-dead gorgeous product packages. "You don't see much color in our stores because we feel our brands pick up the color. We have white walls, maple counters and cabinets and floors, and glass shelves. It looks like nothing before the product is there. Our stores are designed to display products effectively, whether it is a skincare line that comes in clinical white and brown packaging or a bath and body line in beautiful colors. It really shows up," Beck says.

Product Principle #3: Find Daily or Weekly Specials to Showcase Something New

Most shops that pop tend to look for staff members who are both highly personable and highly engaged in the product category. Marla Malcolm Beck of Bluemercury says her staff loving the products spreads a contagious quality throughout the store: "It's all about loving the products. I love the products. The staff loves the products. Everyone's excited about what comes in new." Manny Gonzales of Tiger Lily says the same thing about flowers: "We'll talk about flowers with them [customers]. And they're very receptive generally to talk about it and get very excited."

Developing a program of daily or weekly specials where staff members are fully versed about just one specific product and encouraged to talk up that exciting new product with customers can be a spark of contagious excitement throughout the store and out into the community.

A winning combination for any retailer is to transmit the enthusiasm staff members have for particular products to the customers in a structured, organized way. Developing a program of daily or weekly specials where staff members are fully versed about just one specific product and encouraged to talk up that exciting new product with customers can be a spark of contagious excitement throughout the store and into the community. Feast! showcases two different cheeses daily which generates sales and stimulates discussion by giving staff members something that they are excited by [cheese] to talk to the customer about. Tiger Lily makes a regular practice of marking down individual flowers by 50 percent and, because of the seasonal nature of flowers in the store, Manny Gonzales and his staff always have something new to talk up every single day.

Retailers know that shoppers are always looking for what's new, so a structured, organized program of showcasing something, anything, new, can be powerful source of excitement and more sales.

Product Principle #4: Make it Personal Every Day

There is lots of talk in retailing and marketing circles about the growing trend toward personalization of products. In this day of mass-manufactured products, it is hard to envision an approach to create a one-of-a-kind product to sell. The real opportunity exists at the retail level where the individual sale to one customer is performed. Some linen stores offer customized monogramming. Jewelers engrave. Things Remembered, the specialty gift store chain with 600 stores, bases their whole product strategy on personalizing a wide range of gift items. There are other ways, besides engraving or monogramming one's initials, to personalize a product.

The new Italian-style charm bracelets of interlocking links let people create their own jewelry statements. Damsels in This Dress hosts special events where a handbag designer comes to the store and designs custom bags to the customers' specifications. Virtually everything that Tiger Lily sells is a customize product and his store is really a factory where customized floral creations are made. The same goes for Boxwoods Gardens & Gifts, which sells customized plants and plant arrangements. And Feast! offers gift baskets where the customer picks their own gift assortment off the shelves.

Creativity is the guide for the retailer to find ways to remanufacture the products they sell in their store into customized, personalized packages.

Virtually every store has some way they can customize, or make more personal the products they sell, even if it is just putting individual products together into a customized package designed specifically for a customer's needs. Like most cosmetics and personal care retailers, Bluemercury sells many of the leading brands, but unlike most other retailers, they pick and choose products from one line and another to create a customized skincare or hair-care regime for the client. So they personalize their products by putting different brands together in individualized, unique ways.

Creativity is the guide for the retailer to find ways to remanufacture the products they sell in their store into customized, personalized packages. Customers are craving this kind of special treatment and will enthusiastically patronize stores that offer such services. That will also give customers something remarkable to talk up your store with their friends for viral word-of-mouth marketing.

Product Principle #5: Keep Trying Something New

One of the things I have noticed as retailers face increasing competitive pressure is that they retreat from exploring and taking chances on product lines that are new or different. They get hesitant to try out new lines and tend to opt for products that are safe or have a track record of success. Nobody gets anywhere by playing it safe, though. You have to take chances with something new, different, outside the box. Characteristic of the "shops that pop" retailers profiled here is a willingness—even a passion—to stretch beyond their established limits and go out on a limb.

Mary Carol Garrity of Nell Hill's gives a guide to other retailers about how to move beyond their safety zone. She originally founded her store as a gourmet food shop selling coffee and cheese, but every time she went to market she found one new category of goods to give a try back in the store. Every new market meant a new product category until she figured out she could do better selling the new stuff, so she abandoned the food business altogether in favor of gifts and home furnishings. Kate Collier of Feast! tried a similar strategy and moved into gifts, but unlike Garrity this was not the best strategy for her local market and her business and she abandoned that expansion model to return to what she does best: cheese.

You will never know until you try something new and you can't judge the success of an expansion effort in your store based upon other people's success. You simply have got to put your foot in the water and take the plunge. Doug Rose of QVC is always on the lookout for new brands and new products to test on-air. In fact, finding something new for their viewing shoppers' delight is an ongoing core strategy for the business. He explains, "Our customers are looking at us as a way to come up with a new idea." Dan Bellman of Boxwoods Gardens & Gifts found an entirely new and extremely profitable category in fashion accessories that were way outside his and his partner's comfort zone; therefore, they turned over the buying of the "girlie" stuff to one of their staff with plenty of success to go around.

Product Principle #6: Private Label Is Becoming More Available to Smaller Retailers and a Good Branding Strategy

For years, private label goods seemed to be out of the reach of smaller retailers who couldn't go over to the factories in the Orient and buy massive quantities of goods, but today many smaller, largely American-based manufacturers are looking to expand their product lines by private labeling for their clients. Here in this totally unrepresentative sample of extraordinary retailers, we found two companies that are offering their customers their own store-branded goods. Nell Hill's Mary Carol Garrity is following in the footsteps of Martha Stewart to create a line of her own paints. She is working with a privately owned, U.S.-based paint factory to mix up 20 customized colors. "We have our own line of paint that we just came out with this year. It's real simple, just 20 colors. We worked on it and feel we have the best robin's egg blue, the best red, so we only do that one perfect shade in each color. So we have only one shade of sage green. We keep it simple. And I just keep thinking up new product and new ways to do it."

Feast! too is expanding its branded line of food goods. Their goal is to build the Feast! brand, and private label product is a foundation of that expansion. Kate Collier says, "For the future our goal is to increase the awareness and value of the Feast! brand. We are launching a print catalog and support Internet sales where you can order online. We also are creating new food products. One of our biggest hits is our pimento cheese. We also do a selection of dips, spreads, and salad dressings. So we're going to really try and make it a national brand."

In the future more manufacturing companies are going to offer private label services for retailers that sell on a smaller scale than has traditionally been associated with private label. Key for retailers is to look out for these opportunities and think creatively about what product direction your store's brand can take you into.

Product Principle #7: Be Cutting Edge, Be First on the Block with Something New

Taking a stance to be cutting edge and out there first with new product trends can be a powerful competitive position for any retailer. As we have seen, shoppers are naturally excited about what is new and what is different. This is an especially strong position for anyone in the fashion or electronics business, which are so strongly influenced by trends. Magnolia Audio Video, for instance, is always looking out for the next new thing to attract their early-adopter clientele into the store. This strategy also has the advantage of giving Magnolia greater pricing flexibility, because the cutting edge electronics products are also the priciest. Jim Tweten explains, "What we are known for among all of our vendors is we sell the best. We sell the best TVs, we sell the best audio components. We provide for a premium experience because that is how we differentiate ourselves from other retailers that just sell consumer electronics. Our focus is on the premium customer."

Being first with the best is a powerful retailing position for Magnolia in their niche. Damsels in This Dress takes a similar tack for fashion, looking for items that are truly distinctive and give a woman an opportunity to create her own style. Retailers out on the cutting edge cannot be afraid of the higher prices they must charge for their trendsetting goods, but if you can develop a reputation of being right about the new trends, that can lead to a loyal following of customers who value having that cutting edge.

Product Principle #8: Have a Distinctive Point of View and Attitude Reflected in Your Product

"I cannot give you the formula for success, but I can give you the formula for failure, which is—try to please everybody."
HERBERT BAYARD SWOPE

Ultimately the successful retailers profiled in this book all present a unique and distinctive point of view in the products that they sell. Saks Fifth Avenue presents luxury with attitude. Aerosoles presents fashion footwear that's comfortable too. Bluemercury offers skincare and cosmetics that really work. Colonial Williamsburg Marketplace presents authentic Williamsburg reproductions. These retailers and every other one profiled here knows what they are all about, what their customers value, and what they need to keep doing to continue to be successful. As we have said repeatedly in this section, product is largely secondary to the people in making a store pop, yet shoppers want a product experience. Extraordinary retailers deliver that product experience by offering a total vision that is truly distinctive and reflects a personality and vision, often that of the founder.

Extraordinary retailers deliver that product experience by offering a total vision that is truly distinctive and reflects a personality and vision, often that of the founder.

Manny Gonzales of Tiger Lily provides an excellent lesson for retailers in how to create that unique point of view: follow your own vision. Starting his flower shop with no floral background, he and his business partner-wife went out and learned all they could about how to run a flower shop. What they learned was simple: how to be an ordinary florist. It wasn't until they had their back up against the wall with the business on the edge that they decided the only answer was to become an extraordinary florist. "We try to be different. We try to be awesome. How can you do that when you're following a book? Yet so many florists feel that the wire service is their lifeline, their major source of sales. To me it was our major source of mediocrity, and mediocrity is a four-letter word around here," Gonzales says.

Retailing entrepreneurs start their stores with a vision, but often in the challenges of day-to-day operations, they lose some of that vision. That is the true secret of retailing success, though: the passion to create a wonderful, unique experience designed for the pleasure and delight of the customer. Products are only a part of that experience, yet they are ultimately critical to your overall success.

Putting the Product Principles to Work

1. Go outside your store and look at the product displayed in your store's windows. How long has this selection of product been on display? What does the combination of product say about your store? What story do the products displayed tell to your customers? Be specific in describing the product story on display in terms of what it says about your store and what it says about your customer.

2. Step inside your store's front door. Describe what you see first. What story does that first thing you see tell your customer about your store? Be specific. Does it match the story told in the window displays? Does it tell another story? Do they work together or separately? What three things could you do to the first thing you see to make the inside of your store more inviting, more compelling, and more interesting?

3. Think about the last totally new product or product line you brought into your store. (Think about a product or product line that was totally outside your store's typical product range, such as Boxwoods, which added fashion accessories into an otherwise home furnishings-type store.) Where did you display it? How did you decide where to display it? Was this new product introduction successful or a failure? Why? List five things you learned about your customers and what they want or don't want based upon this addition to your store.

4. Walk around your store and pull together three to five totally different items that in some way or another seem to go together; either they all work together or could be used by a customer together. How can you take these items and make an interesting display near your store's checkout counter? What story do they tell? How can you take these items and make them into a personalized packet or gift package that can be sold separately?

CHAPTER EIGHTEEN

Pricing Principles that Transform the Retail Store into a Shopping Experience

"Goodwill is the one and only asset that competition cannot undersell or destroy."
MARSHALL FIELD

When marketers and retailers think about pricing and pricing strategy, they must relate to the affordability factor in the consumer's terms, with affordability being one of the important factors in the quantum theory of shopping. However, the concept of affordability is not necessarily clear-cut. There is absolute affordability: for instance, either you can afford to spend $18,000 for an Hermes handbag or you cannot. There is also variable affordability, which is how much one is willing to stretch their budget to make a purchase. While an $18,000 Hermes bag is something I cannot afford, I can afford to spend $1,800 on a Chanel handbag, but I would much rather pay $180 for last season's Coach bag at the local outlet. There are others for whom the $180 Coach bag is a stretch and so they cruise TJ Maxx or Marshall's for a look-alike bag marked down to $18. Every day in stores everywhere shoppers are making decisions about how much a particular purchase is worth to them personally.

Most people have a price range within which they are willing to spend, with the most affluent consumers having a much wider range than others. It is in the realm of variable affordability—how much is that particular item worth to me—where emotion plays out for consumers, because emotion can drive someone to spend more than they would prefer to spend to buy something wonderful. Even more prevalent, emotion can drive people to make purchases they otherwise don't need simply because the price is so outrageously low. Three of the five personality types described in Chapter 6—Theresa the Therapeutic shopper, Ursula the Uber-Shopper, and Diana the Bargain Hunter—are distinguished by their passion for finding a bargain or getting something at a great price. The emotional thrill in their shopping equation is how much money they save.

Because markdowns and discounts work so well in motivating shoppers to purchase, that is the emotional hot button that retailers push most often, but because it is so frequently and indiscriminately used, it has virtually trained shoppers not to buy anything at full price, but instead to wait until it goes on sale.

For retailers, if they can make a discount strategy work, like Target and Wal-Mart and many others in the discount or off-price shopping realm, that is a powerful position, but it is also an incredibly risky strategy. The fact is, no matter how low you can go in price, some other retailer somewhere can go lower.

The "how low can you go" strategy also is one where most small specialty retailers without the ability to buy huge volumes of product and thus gain pricing advantage simply cannot participate. Rather, for the small specialty retailers they are often left in the unenviable position of having to explain or apologize for having to charge their customers more. Sherry Keefe of Damsels in This Dress expressed her frustration in having to explain to her customers why a handcrafted sweater in her store costs $299 while a look-alike mass-produced number costs $99 in Macy's. Yet it is by telling the story of why her special things cost more than what everybody else sells that she enhances the overall value to the customer of what she sells. Her store's success speaks for itself: "I didn't realize there were so many people out there that really had the need and wanted to have an individual art look."

The fact is, we will always have discounters operating in the retail market. Their core target market is people who have to shop at discount, which ultimately is a very risky place to be. People who have to vigilantly watch their wallets are the first ones to suffer when the price of gasoline or heating oil goes up and so have to sacrifice retail spending for other essential purchases. Rather, there is much more power and profitability playing to the more affluent consumers who don't have to shop down-market, but who may choose to shop there in certain situations. The pricing principles that follow are specifically for retailers like Keefe who chose to compete on price by adding more value, rather than cutting more off the price.

Pricing Principle #1: Play to Consumers' Passion and Their Desire for Luxury

Shopping provides pleasure before, during, and after the experience when the shopper takes his or her purchases home. For some—Theresa the Therapeutic Shopper, for example—they don't even need to buy to achieve pleasure in shopping. Luxury, at its root, is also all about pleasure. When we talk to affluent consumers about what luxury is, they inevitably define it in terms of creature comforts, those things in life that make it more pleasurable, more enjoyable, more fulfilling.

For retailers, playing to consumers' passion is all about adding luxury value into the shopping experience.

For retailers, playing to consumers' passion is all about adding luxury value into the shopping experience. It is about positioning your store and the merchandise you carry as being more luxurious, more special. It is about promising to deliver a more luxurious experience to the shopper, both in the things that you sell and the way that you sell them.

However, in today's new luxury world, which focuses on how the consumer experiences luxury, not the thing itself, you don't have to pursue a luxury pricing strategy by selling only the most expensive products. Rather, you want to sell things that are distinctive and special in a way that is special and distinctive, but you don't necessarily want to price them the highest or sell only the most exclusive brands. It is about playing to consumers' passion for luxury at a fair and reasonable price.

The question of pricing ultimately boils down to: Is an $18,000 Hermes handbag really ten times better than a $1,800 Chanel bag? Is a $1,800 Chanel handbag really ten times better than a $180 Coach bag? Is a $180 Coach bag really ten times better than an $18 TJ Maxx special? Every shopper will answer those questions differently, but no matter whom she is the majority of shoppers would rather pay less than $18,000 for Hermes or $1,800 for Chanel or $180 for Coach or even $18 for TJ Maxx if she can, rather than more. How much less is the variable factor that the savvy retailer has to figure out and price to for their target market.

When I visited Boxwoods Gardens & Gifts in Atlanta, I was impressed both by the fact that they had devoted a whole room in their store, which is largely a home furnishings and gift store, to fashion accessories and that the prices of the wonderful handbags, jewelry, and shawls that they stocked were really exceptional. Handbags that looked like they would retail for $200 to $300 in a department store were being sold for around $100. Offering that kind of luxury value at a reasonable price doesn't go unnoticed by luxury shoppers who are in the know about shopping, as Dan Bellman shared in his story of the woman who came into the store and bought 12 handbags as Christmas gifts for her nieces.

Nell Hill's in Atchison, Kansas, follows a similar luxury pricing strategy. She offers more luxury value for less money. Mary Carol Garrity says, "Our price is perfect. We have the best price. Our regular price is such a value. It is beautifully displayed, it's wonderful quality, and the value is there because people are always saying 'I can't believe these prices.'"

This is also the ticket for success at Rapid City, South Dakota's Prairie Edge in their marketing of one-of-a-kind Native American arts and crafts. At Prairie Edge they offer more true artistic value for less than the customer would expect to pay. Furthermore, this pricing strategy works to bring in customers from all over the world, Dan Tibby explains, who fly in to buy the artwork they sell for a third to less than half the price found in Native American art hotspots like Santa Fe, New Mexico.

Pricing Principle #2: Focus on the Meaning, Not the Money

If you set out to target the luxury leanings of your customer then you are playing to shoppers' emotions, delivering to them the feelings of luxury through the products you sell as well as the environment in which you sell them. As the research has shown, for shoppers getting more for less, finding a bargain is one of the most powerful emotional motivators of all. In the discounting realm of shopping, the focus of retailers giving their shoppers more for less is the less-than part of the equation. They look primarily at marking down, cutting prices as low as possible.

Pricing becomes a question of finding out what your shoppers would expect to pay for specific products with specific features and then charging them somewhat less than they would expect to pay, but not necessarily a whole lot less.

If you are playing to the luxury side of retail, however, your focus needs to be on the side of giving more to the shopper. In other words, adding more value, rather than simply cutting price. Luxury retailing is about offering products that have added value, more meaning, more wonderfulness while charging a fair and reasonable price, not necessarily cheap, but also not necessarily an exorbitant price either.

I advise my luxury goods clients to think about luxury pricing as a three-to-two ratio: Three times the value over the ordinary product for two times the price of the ordinary one. That means you give the shopper significantly more added value in the products that you sell, but charge them less than they would expect to pay. The focus in this three-to-two pricing strategy is on adding value, not discounting price. You want to give more for less, but not too much less. That is what Boxwoods, Nell Hill's, Damsels in This Dress, and Prairie Edge do. They focus on adding value to the products they sell and pricing them less than the customer would expect to pay, so they feel good about the price they are asked to pay.

In this luxury approach to pricing, which is giving more for less, the retailer needs to understand the price ranges that exist in the marketplace for comparable types of goods: What are the low, medium, and high price ranges that are typical for your customers to see in the stores they shop? In the cosmetic market, for example, the low range of price for lipstick might be under $7; the medium range from $7 to about $15; the high range for the most exclusive brands might be upwards of $15. If that is the popular range of prices, I would look to offer products that have all the features and benefits of the high priced brands, priced around $20–$25, but offer these added-value products in the $15–$17 price range, slightly less than the shopper would expect to pay for comparable value.

Pricing becomes a question of finding out what your shoppers would expect to pay for specific products with specific features and then charging them somewhat less than they would expect to pay, but not necessarily a whole lot less. This requires retailers to be very aware of the pricing dynamics in their local markets where their shoppers are most likely to be perusing. New York City shoppers have a totally different perception of prices than St. Louis shoppers, for example. The key is to know your local markets and what shoppers expect to pay for quality, then charge them somewhat less using the three-times the value for two times the price rule.

Pricing Principle #3: Pay Attention to Educating the Customer About the Value You Offer

For the discounters, cheap price is all they need to talk about because that is the main driver in their selling proposition, so they use shelf tags to display their discounted price and comparable or list price. If you are selling to shoppers' luxury feeling and emotions, you need to play up the value side of the equation and explain how much more value your products offer. Sherry Keefe of Worthington, Ohio's Damsels in This Dress says, "I try to give my customer quality, and I use the word quality instead of value because you value quality. And I try to teach them what quality means." In selling fashion she is in a constant competitive battle with department stores where sales are rampant. She has to explain why her store's sweaters sell for two or three times more than the department store version. When she tells the story of her sweater's added value, her explanation is compelling to a certain type of shopper, but clearly not all shoppers. For the type of shoppers she wants in her store—women who value fashion and style and who can afford to pay her prices—her value story is compelling. It's about quality of fabric, quality of design, and quality of fit and sizing.

Keefe also follows the three times the value for two times the price guideline. She says, "I try to keep my prices keystone [double the wholesale price] or a little bit below so you can have the opportunity to be able to afford it . . . I had a lady come in yesterday, and she bought a handbag. She said, 'I just saw a handbag like this in *Town & Country* but it was $1,000 and yours is only $70.' I told her it is not exactly the same handbag, but it's the look. So you can try to offer your customer the same sort of look for affordable money."

You need to communicate all the many aspects of the value proposition to the customer so that she can fairly and effectively judge the value of the product in her own terms.

The simple fact is your typical shopper is not as well educated in the value proposition of various product categories as you, the retailer, are. She may be informed and have done her research, but usually you know more. So you need to communicate all the many aspects of the value proposition to the customer so that she can fairly and effectively judge the value of the product in her own terms. That, of course, gets back to the people principles we talked about first. Retailing is a people business and the more you know about the people who shop in your store, what they value, and what they want, the better able you are to find the products they want at the prices they are willing to spend.

Pricing Principle #4: Shop the Markets Very Carefully to Find the Maximum Value for the Minimum Price

I was talking with the CEO of a rapidly growing company in the gifts and home business recently about the falloff in attendance at the various wholesale gift and home markets over the last few years. She said that lots of specialty retailers are cutting back on the shows they attend and the time they spend at the shows. She also said they are delaying writing orders at the shows, which doesn't make sense because that is when things are fresh in their minds.

Good shopping on your part will mean good shopping for your customers.

There is no question that attending a buyers' show with thousands and thousands of vendors' products on display is a daunting prospect, but the good show shoppers who really work aggressively to see it all and make careful selections have a distinct advantage. They find the treasures among the trash, and can hone in on super value products that they can retail in their store at excellent prices. In other words, good shopping on your part means good shopping for your customers. Dan Bellman of Boxwoods Gardens & Gifts explains that one of the secrets of the success of his store is his absolute devotion to careful shopping of the big Atlanta wholesale gift show: "We're there the whole time. We're there from early in the morning until they turn the lights off—ten days straight. We go to every showroom we can. We look at everything. We try to find unique stuff."

Putting the Pricing Principles to Work

1. Browse your store and find seven regularly priced products (nothing on sale) that offer your customer a great value at a good price. Take each product and review. Write down what you think the product would retail for in a department store.

What is the price difference? How did you find this high value/less costly product? What are you doing to bring each product's high value/reasonable cost to the attention of the customer?

2. Browse your store and find three products that you consider high priced luxuries in your store. What makes these products more expensive than other things that you carry? What special features add value to the product and make them cost more? How do you tell the customer about these added-value features? Take each product and tell the story of why it costs more and why it is worth it.

3. Think about the next trade show coming up. How can you find really great products that you can sell for less money than they appear to be worth? What vendors offer great products at reasonable prices? How can you find new vendors that have great price/value products? Plan on spending half a day more at the show than you usually would to hunt new vendors with great products at good prices.

CHAPTER NINETEEN

Promotion Principles that Transform the Retail Store into a Shopping Experience

"Half the money I spend on advertising is wasted; the trouble is I don't know which half."

JOHN WANAMAKER

In the focus group among retailers discussed in more depth in Chapter 7: Retailers' View from the Trenches, the number one business challenge these retailers face is attracting more customers to their shop and keeping the ones they already have. The problem is that many retailers believe—incorrectly—that the solution to attracting more customers is advertising. I am of the opinion that the whole business of advertising is misunderstood, misapplied, and often misused. Advertising is a far better tool for brand building than building sales. It builds consumer awareness among those people who see and internalize the ad, but it doesn't do much to push the revenue needle. It is something that businesses must invest in at some level, but there are other, better ways by which retailers can reach out and grab new customers that don't cost half as much. The statement above from retailing pioneer John Wanamaker remains as true today as it did in the early part of the last century.

We've seen that the ultimate solution to attracting more customers and keeping the ones you already have is to align the store, its offerings, its environment, and its service with the expectations of the shoppers so that shopping there is fun, not a chore. If the retailing experience in your store is remarkable, as defined by Seth Godin as so special it is worth remarking about to others, then you can build your customer base virally customer-to-customer. Many of the retailers profiled here have talked about how their businesses have grown through word-of-mouth where one friend tells another one about the wonderful experience shopping in that store. How else can you explain Nell Hill's building such a dynamic business in Atchison, Kansas, in a town with only 10,000 people? Nell Hill's reached out virally and through word-of-mouth jumped communities to attract a steady customer base of people who typically drive over an hour to shop in her store. No amount of advertising could have achieved this kind of success. It takes a lot more than just giving away money to advertising agencies for creative and media placements. You have got to put your money where your mouth is, and that is to invest in making your store a wonderful shopping experience for your customers and the rest will follow.

Clearly, you need to build awareness and start with some outreach through advertising and promotion to get the ball rolling.

Promotion Principle #1: Expand How You Look at Your Store, Not as a Shop that Sells Certain Types of Things, but as a Shop that Delivers an Experience to the Consumer

One common mistake retailers make that holds them back from reaching their full potential is to define their store in terms of what they sell, which in turn keeps the retailer focused necessarily on the product, and not on the shoppers' experience. In a recent discussion with a fledgling retailer opening her first store, she described her business concept as "a store that sells kitchen cabinets and countertops." My advice was to change the entire way she was thinking about her store from a focus on the thing she will sell, kitchen cabinets and countertops, to the experience she delivers to her customers, customized kitchen transformation through fine cabinetry and long-lasting, high-quality countertops. What's the difference? Everything. By putting the consumer and the experience they can expect from shopping in the store at the center, you immediately make your store relevant to people's lives. I look at my kitchen and I don't need new cabinets, so I don't need her store. Yet every day when I cook, the elements in my kitchen and their location remind me of how badly I need a kitchen transformation; they simply do not work for me, but the cabinets in and of themselves are just fine. Therefore, a store that offers me kitchen transformation would draw me in, but I'm not necessarily in need of new cabinets. The lesson for retailers in this new experiential shopping world is simple: Make sure you define the store in terms of the experiences you deliver to the consumer, *not* the thing that you sell.

The lesson for retailers in this new experiential shopping world is simple: Make sure you define the store in terms of the experiences you deliver to the consumer, not the thing that you sell.

Those of you who have done considerable business writing know that passive voice is where the subject of the sentence receives the action, for example, "The boy was bitten by the dog." By contrast, active voice is where the subject performs the action, "The dog bit the boy." Passive voice simply makes your writing flat and uninteresting. Active voice, on the other hand, gives vibrancy to the ideas you express and makes your writing come to life.

Describing your store by focusing on what you sell is like using passive voice in your store's description: a store that sells clothes; a store that sells home entertainment equipment; a store that sells skincare and cosmetics. Each of these is dull and doesn't connect with the consumer unless they have a specific point of need for what you have to sell. On the other hand, an active voice description connects with the consumer's passion and makes the store relevant far beyond selling stuff: a shop where you can discover and express your personal style (Damsels in This Dress); a store within a store where you can create customized home entertainment experiences (Magnolia Audio Video); or a store where trained skincare and cosmetics consultants create a skincare regime that is best for your unique type of skin and a look that brings out your best features (Bluemercury).

It all comes down to expanding the way you think about your store, what you sell, and what you ultimately do for the customer. Rather than putting the emphasis on the thing that you sell, put the emphasis on the experience that you deliver to the customer. This is something simple and easy to do, but it will be absolutely revolutionary as you shift your attention from the products you sell to the experience you deliver to your customer.

Promotion Principle #2: Define a Concept for Your Store that Is Your Brand

In my company's research with luxury consumers, we have found three factors that most strongly influence luxury consumers in their purchases: brand of the product, brand of the store, and price/value relationship. These factors are all so closely intertwined that you cannot separate them to say that one is more important than another. Each is equally important in influencing the luxury consumer as they shop. That is why I call these three factors together the luxury branding "triple play." Many retailers tend to emphasize product brands, while they don't really grasp how important their store brand is to the whole shopping experience.

The store brand is the defining concept of what kind of experiences the store ultimately sets out to deliver to the consumer. Each of the retailers profiled here expresses that branding concept clearly and succinctly. It is the founding principle of the store and the roadmap to the future. It is expressed in terms of what the store promises to deliver to the consumer. For Barnes & Noble the defining branding concept was to create a nonintimidating bookstore environment for everyone. For Tiger Lily florist it was to be "the best place to buy awesome flowers," as Manny Gonzales said. For Saks Fifth Avenue it was to be an emporium of the finest luxury goods found in the world. For Magnolia Audio and Video it was to deliver the ultimate home entertainment experience. For Aerosoles, it is to deliver stylish shoes that are super-comfortable at a great price. These defining concepts become the start of the business, its founding principle, and the guiding light for all future growth of the business.

The defining branding concept for a store must be expansive enough to provide room to grow, but concise enough so that the store and its objectives easily and clearly communicate with the shopper. All marketing and promotion materials must clearly communicate the branding concept, as well as all in-store cues and clues that define the store and structure the store experience.

There are whole libraries of great books about branding available through your local bookstore or favorite Internet bookseller. Retailers who want to learn more about branding their store should review what is available. Many of you already have a pretty clear vision of what your store's concept is. All you have to do is write it down, wordsmith it a little bit to refine and hone it, and then make sure it becomes the focus of all marketing and advertising, in-store signage, printed materials, and sales communications with customers.

Promotion Principle #3: Communicate Information that the Customer Needs to Know

One of the biggest failures in advertising is that it focuses the message on what you want the customer to know or what you want the customer to do. Rather, your advertising messages will be much more successful if you communicate information that the customer needs to know or that is most relevant to his or her interests. For example, Manny Gonzales of Tiger Lily, whose branding concept is to deliver the best, most awesome flowers ever, doesn't use his advertising to tell the target customer about how good Tiger Lily is or how beautiful their flowers are. Rather, the focus of Tiger Lily's advertising is the awards they have won in pursuing their vision. Every company's own advertising says they are great, but only one store can claim they won the readers' award for best Charleston florist year after year. That lends the note of authenticity to the advertising and for potential customers who want the very best floral arrangements; that is the information they need to know.

Advertising messages should be relevant to the intended reader. What do your customers value in your shop? In what ways do they connect with your shop? What do other people who are similar to your customers need to know about you to make them aware of your store as an alternative? Manny is onto something when he struts his stuff in his advertising, on the side of his delivery vans, through signage outside and inside the store. He proclaims that people who want the best flowers can feel confident that Tiger Lily will deliver the best, because they win all the awards for best flowers.

Promotion Principle #4: Use Technology

In the people principles we talked about the need to record customers' names, addresses, phone numbers, and e-mail addresses. To know who their customer is and to reach out on a regular basis to him or her is critically important. Every couple of months I receive special invitations to shop in some of my favorite stores. Often these invitations include a discount offer of some kind, access to special sale prices before the general public, or double points for purchases on my loyalty card. These invitations all come from national retailers and I don't recall ever getting such an invitation from any of the small specialty shops where I have been known to drop significant amounts of cash. This oversight by these small retailers is unfortunate, because the best potential customers for your store are your existing customers and you must pay attention to drawing them back in on a regular basis for more pleasurable shopping. It goes without saying then that retailers need to record critical contact information about their customers, maybe not each and every one that comes into your store, but clearly for any customer who spends more than the average ticket on a single day. Their high level of spending says you have connected with a happy customer who likes what you have to offer, so record that name and use it at least several times a year sending out invitations, post cards, or e-mail inviting them back for some special event or special sale.

Another serious oversight among many specialty retailers I talk to is that they have failed to make the leap into the information age and so have not created a store Web site. I admit, building and maintaining a Web site is an intimidating task, but lots of Internet host companies offer quick turnaround Web site creation through templates that almost anyone can use. For small specialty retailers I don't think going the full route to creating an e-commerce capability where shoppers can actually make purchases online is necessary. Nevertheless, today where the Internet is replacing the old-fashioned Yellow Pages as shoppers' primary store-locating tool, specialty retailers absolutely need to have a basic brochure-type Web site that describes the store, the branding concept, the scope of the products carried, any brand name products carried, the hours of operation, location, and any other relevant information that will help the shopper decide to visit your store.

Once the Web site is up and running, you can begin to implement e-mail blasts to your customers, telling them about new arrivals or other things they would find interesting. You don't want to overload your customers and fill up their in-box with too much information, but used on an infrequent basis with an eye toward communicating valuable information to them, e-mail can be a powerful way to build customer loyalty.

Promotion Principle #5: Exploit the Power of Gifting

Retailers are well aware of the wonderful fourth quarter revenue boost that gift spending gives them, but many don't maximize their gifting sales throughout the rest of the year. They also overlook the marketing power of reaching out to the gift recipient as well. My company, Unity Marketing, conducts a quarterly gift tracking study that measures gift purchases and spending throughout the year. While Christmas gifting accounts for roughly half of the typical gifters' annual budget—$870 spent on Christmas gifts, or 45 percent of the total annual gift spending of $1,934 in 2005—the majority of gifters' spending occurs throughout the rest of the gift holidays with Mother's Day, Valentine's Day, and Father's Day being the most important, and occasions such as birthdays, anniversaries, weddings, and new babies. However, most retailers don't even think about gifting except for the vital fourth quarter period. This is a big oversight because shoppers' needs for good gift ideas and services that support gifting, such as gift wrapping, continue throughout the year.

In addition to stocking popular gift items in the store, gifting is a unique marketing opportunity for any retailer because it enables the retailer to touch and potentially influence two target markets at one time—both the gift giver and the gift recipient. Unlike other consumer marketing efforts which target the individual consumer or a marketplace of one, the gifting market is a unique opportunity for retailers to achieve exponential marketing. For marketers, gifting has all the

---

SHOPPING FACTOID
Most Popular Gifting Categories, 2005

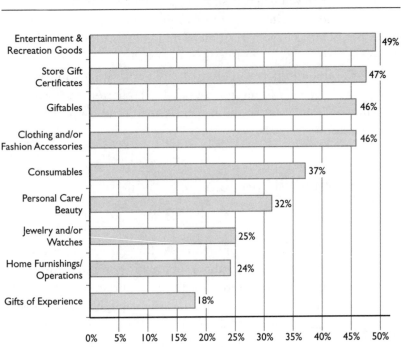

Entertainment & Recreation Goods — 49%
Store Gift Certificates — 47%
Giftables — 46%
Clothing and/or Fashion Accessories — 46%
Consumables — 37%
Personal Care/ Beauty — 32%
Jewelry and/or Watches — 25%
Home Furnishings/ Operations — 24%
Gifts of Experience — 18%

(0% 5% 10% 15% 20% 25% 30% 35% 40% 45% 50%)

Throughout 2005, entertainment and recreation gifts, which include gifts such as toys, books, CDs, DVDs and entertainment equipment, sporting goods, photographic equipment, and electronics, were the top choice to give as gifts, bought by 49 percent of all people as a gift. Store gift certifitcates (bought by 47 percent of gifters), giftables, which includes products such as candles and candle accessories, flowers and plants, figurines, stationery, collectibles, seasonal decorations, and other popular gift items (46 percent) , and clothing and fashion accessories (46 percent) were the next most popular gift items.

No matter what category, except jewelry and watches where average spending tends to be higher, the most popular price point for a gift is between $25 and $50.

Source: Unity Marketing's Gifting Report 2006

advantages and the promotional marketing power of sampling and word-of-mouth, but gifting magnifies and intensifies that power through the unique emotional connection between the giver and the recipient. Because it is "two times two," gifting is exponential marketing.

Thinking about buying a gift is the ultimate in "emotional consumerism," because gift giving is all about emotionally connecting gift givers and gift recipients. Whenever emotion drives the consumer's shopping behavior, the goal of the shopping experience is not about the thing itself but the experience. The challenge for gift retailers, then, is how to enhance the "gifting" experience.

Offering year-round gift wrapping services, and not just a slap dash wrap job, but giving people a selection of expert gift wrapping options from basic at a minimal or no cost to luxury decorator wrap for a suitable fee, is called for. However you wrap the gift, it should be carefully packaged so that the recipient has a wonderful experience unwrapping the gift. Internet gift marketer Red Envelope (*www.redenvelope.com*) makes their overall gift presentation a core value in their branding strategy.

Further retailers must put some kind of response device into the package that identifies the place where the gift was bought and that invites the recipient back the next time they need to buy a gift or if they like the item. That could be in the form of a basic gift card, with identifying information on the back or a well-designed brochure. Take a tip from florists who always identify their shop as the source for the wonderful arrangement that is enclosed. The response device shouldn't be intrusive or overly promotional, but it absolutely needs to identify your store as the source for the wonderful gift they just received.

Finally, a really important aspect of the gift shopping experience is the return policy. Gifters value stores that offer generous and easy return policies for gift recipients who want to choose something else. Making your store a pleasant place in which to do returns goes far in building good customer relations.

Putting the Promotion Principles to Work

Here are some questions and activities you can do to put these promotion principles to work in your store.

1. Make a list of all places where you pay to advertise your business, such as local newspaper, telephone Yellow Pages, Internet Web site, coupon-clipper magazine. Which of these advertisements bring you the most customers? Write three reasons why that advertising medium works. What could you do to make the other less productive advertising media work better for your store?

2. What tag line/description do you use in your printed material/advertising that describes your store? Write the tag line on a piece of paper. Does the tag line describe what your store sells or the experience you store delivers to the customer (e.g., a store that sells kitchen cabinets or store that helps you transform your kitchen)? How can you change the tag line or description of your store to focus on the consumer and what your store delivers to the consumer? (Think about the difference between selling fashion apparel vs. helping customers discover their personal fashion style.) Rewrite your store's description to put the customer and what special experience you deliver to the customer first.

3. Do you have an Internet Web site? When was the last time it was updated? Do you have a customer database or mailing list? How often is it updated? If you don't have either or both, investigate local Web providers about setting up your own store Web site. Visit the local computer store and check out different software programs that can help retailers build customer databases. Get started today. If you have these services but they are not current, get to work updating the Web site and/or the customer database. No time like the present.

CHAPTER TWENTY

Place Principles that Transform the Retail Store into a Shopping Experience

"All the world's a stage, and all the men and women merely players."
WILLIAM SHAKESPEARE, *AS YOU LIKE IT*

The place principles refer to the location and design of the store. In this respect the principles you need to implement to transform your store into a shopping experience are very simple: design your store for the comfort, ease, and enjoyment of your customer. Make the shopper number one in all aspects of design and location and you cannot go wrong.

The importance of place in retail is not unlike the design of a stage setting as a backdrop for a play. The store itself is the stage on which the retailer performs their retail "magic" that excites the shopper, interests him or her to explore further, and inclines the shopper to buy. Both the tangible aspects of store design, such as how the aisles are arranged and merchandise displayed, and the intangibles, such as lighting and music, all play a central role in influencing how the shopper feels and ultimately how the shopper acts. These factors are generally described as "atmospherics" that emotionally impact the shopper, including how long the shopper spends in a store, which is directly related to how much shoppers spend. Careful attendance to store design and atmospherics can have a direct impact on the shop's retail performance.

Place Principle #1: Watch the Traffic
Outside Your Door

In this day of rapidly increasing retail competition and consumers' changing patterns of shopping, you must be vigilant to watch traffic trends right in front of your store: Is there more or less foot traffic passing by your door? Many shoppers are turning away from big centralized malls. The concept of anchor department stores attracting mall traffic is rapidly becoming antiquated and the shops located along the aisles between anchors are losing their traffic, as a result. In the focus groups with consumers we heard from people who drive up and park at one anchor store, then drive along and park at another anchor store, bypassing the mall corridors altogether. Thus the smaller retailers dependent upon that pedestrian traffic between the anchor stores lose out. Retailers often wait too long to address the very hard decision about moving their store. However, by delaying the inevitable, they end up closing doors altogether rather than moving across town to a more promising location. By waiting too long, their revenues dry up and leave the shop owner with little capital to invest in the costly and time-consuming task of a store move.

At least three to four times a year, on a given day, say the third Saturday in the last month of each quarter for a three-hour period, from noon to three, the retailer should do a traffic audit by simply counting the traffic passing by the door. This kind of traffic audit should be backed up with regular monthly shopper audits documenting the number of customers actually in the store during a certain set period of time. This data collected over the course of a year or two can provide valuable trend information to help determine the direction of change of traffic in and around the store. It may give an early warning of reduced traffic before the results start to be felt in the cash drawer.

Place Principle #2: A Change in Lighting Can Be a Low Cost Way to Build Sales

The lighting in a store can make a huge difference in how people feel when they shop. In a recent survey on atmospherics conducted by Leo J. Shapiro and Associates, they found that lighting was the most important element to shoppers in creating a unique store atmosphere, with signage, promotional events, fixtures, flooring, and music following in order of importance. The value of having the right lighting was brought home to me recently when a specialty retailer told me how a $50 investment in track lighting had doubled sales in the section of her store that she lit up. She was astounded at how strong an impact such a minimal investment in lighting represented.

One of my personal bugaboos with store lighting is the rampant use of fluorescent lights. These are chosen, no doubt, for the convenience of the store, but florescent lights are not complementary to colors or people's faces. This may not be a problem in the grocery store, but using fluorescent lighting in a store or a section of a store that sells cosmetics, fashion, home furnishings, and other color-sensitive categories is deadly. Display these products under the same kind of lights they will be used under at home. Today there are so many types of products available for area, accent, and spot lighting that retailers cannot make excuses about not creating the proper lighting effects in their store.

Place Principle #3: Pay Heed to the Flow of Traffic in Your Store; Make Shoppers Curious to Discover More

The most popular model today for regulating and directing traffic flow in retail stores is the racetrack model where shoppers are guided around the perimeter of the store so they can view all the merchandise and departments within the center of the store. While this model might work for large-scale retailers, it is hardly feasible for most small specialty retailers with minimal space or odd configurations.

In the Bluemercury store, Marla Malcolm Beck recognizes the challenges of designing a store of a certain size. Even a very modest-sized store, like their Philadelphia Walnut Street store, requires special attention to customer flow. "We work a lot on flow, just how a customer walks through the store, trying to make sure that the flow is effective. The Philly store is tricky because it is one of our tinier stores, but it's something we have really worked at over time to make sure there's a clear pathway through the store," she says.

Both Boxwoods Gardens & Gifts and Nell Hill's stores have idiosyncratic store layouts that are designed to the shopper's advantage. They are arranged largely in room-sized settings and each virtual display room presents a thematic, engaging merchandise arrangement. Each room then leads the shopper into the next room, using sight lines to give glimpses of other wonders that lie ahead in the next room and around the next corner. In setting up these stores, the retailers pay careful attention to drawing the customer's attention through the rest of the store, enticing the shopper to find out what is up ahead.

Retailers might seek out the help of a designer with some retail experience to help design intriguing store tableaus that encourage the shopper to explore the full breadth and length of the store. Many retailers will benefit from getting rid of their box or grid-like store arrangement and looking into creating discrete spaces that tell interesting stories for the shopper.

Place Principle #4: Appeal to All the Senses

We have already mentioned the important role of lighting in store atmospherics, but all other senses can be tapped to create distinctive and emotionally compelling store environments. Encouraging customers to touch and feel the merchandise is one way to do this. While some merchandise must be displayed behind glass, like jewelry and watches, retailers should minimize the use of locked glass cabinets for most merchandise displays. People like to touch and the more merchandise they pick up and touch, the more likely they are to make purchases, so the store environment itself should be designed to encourage shoppers to get up close and personal with the merchandise.

Scent, too, is a powerful emotional stimulant that many retailers can put to use. While burning candles in the store may not be feasible or even legal in your area, there are lots of nonigniting fragrance options, including essential oils, diffusers, and mists. The candle companies report vanilla, lavender, baking scents, and other floral fragrances as their most popular scents so they are the ones most likely to appeal to everybody.

Music is another mood enhancer, but people's taste in music is so varied and different that one music selection might be more of a turn-off than turn-on to certain shoppers. In the Leo J. Shapiro and Associates atmospheric study mentioned previously, they found that more people (40 percent) said they walked out of a store because of the music than said they spent more time in a store as a result of the music (22 percent). This is not news to me, because I am often bombarded with what I consider very unpleasant music in youth-skewing stores that sends me right out the door. The mistake they make is that when I leave the store, so does the likelihood that my teenage son will make a purchase.

In my travels to find truly outstanding shops to profile in this book, one of my contacts recommended I check out the new Ruehl No. 925 chain of stores. Ruehl is a more upscale and slightly more mature sister chain to Abercrombie and Fitch with fewer than ten stores nationwide as of this writing. All I can say is I was repelled by the store atmospherics. The music was so loud that I couldn't carry on a reasonable conversation with my shopping buddy and the lighting was so dark and moody that I felt claustrophobic, like I was trapped in a cave and all I wanted to do was get out of there. Then I couldn't even find the door to escape. What they did right is arrange their store into interesting rooms and storytelling vignettes. If only they turned the music down so that it was in the background, not dominating the experience, and if they turned up the lights so I could see everything, I would have been a much happier shopper and might just have made a purchase.

Place Principle #5: Get Out from Behind the Counter

Architect and retail-design guru Ken Nisch talked about the new way of selling from the sides of the counters rather than across the counters in order to maximize interaction with customers. This is a revolutionary way to set up the traditional cash wrap station in a specialty store, but one that virtually everyone can do that will enhance the shopping experience for the customer.

The Aerosoles stores have implemented this side-by-side approach to their cash wrap center, which helps build connection between the store staff and the customers. Kimberly Grayson explains that one of the innovations they implemented in each of their Aerosoles branded stores was to move the cash wrap to the center of the store. "One thing we have done in our stores which is unique is we took our cash racks and moved them out into the center of the store. So now the nonverbal message our sales associates give is how approachable they are. They aren't behind the counter at the back of the store waiting for a customer to come in and ask them for assistance, but constantly mingling and moving through the store. They are out there with the shoppers. And every customer, when she makes a purchase, the sales associate transacts the sale, and then she steps to the side of the cash rack, and hands the shopper her bag, thanks her, and she completes the experience. It's not just completing the sale. It's completing the experience and cultivating the relationship."

Putting the Place Principles to Work

1. Interview your store's neighbors about traffic patterns in your shopping area. Do they find traffic is growing, declining, or remaining the same? Are different types of customers shopping in your area? Are people spending more, less, or the same in their stores? How is parking in your area? Work with your store's neighbors to identify three action steps you jointly can take to build foot traffic in your shopping area.

2. Step outside your store, turn around, and then come back in. What is the logical foot path to take you from the front door to the back of the store? Is anything in your way as you move from the front door to the back of the store? What things do you see? What displays are you missing?

3. Diagram your store to scale, showing the walkways, product shelves, displays, and so on. (A craft store often has room-arranging diagram kits.) Take your scale diagram and figure out one way to improve traffic flow in your store, perhaps moving one shelf.

4. Visit five stores in your local area and ask the owner/manager if you can take pictures of their cash wrap station. Try to find types of retailers different than your store. Mount the pictures on a board and borrow one idea that you can implement in your store from each of the five different cash wrap stations. Make the changes to your store's cash wrap station.

Conclusion

Love Your Customers and They Will Love You Back

"It is not impossibilities which fill us with the deepest despair, but possibilities which we have failed to realize."

ROBERT MALLETT

In a recent retailer seminar I was conducting, one of the participants—a more mature man with a long-established business—cried out in absolute frustration, "But what if I don't want to do all these things you are telling me to do? What if I just want to stay like I am?" This man expressed the feelings that were running rampantly, but silently, throughout the entire seminar audience. Everybody felt uncomfortable, put upon, and challenged by the need to change his or her business. They knew in their hearts that a dramatic transformation had to occur to keep their retail business in business, not to mention to make it grow and thrive in the new challenging retailing environment, but the kind of transformation they needed to undertake was a very difficult thing to come to terms with.

Nothing is harder than stepping out into the unknown, moving beyond the way you have done business for years, the store that you have known, that you built, that reflects your dreams and ideals, and change it into something else. Well, you really don't have to do it. You can decide that your business is good right where it is, doing what it has always done in the same way it has always been done. The downside of that decision, however, may well be dissolution, closing your doors for good because the retailing world is changing and your customers are changing and if you don't change with them, you will be left behind.

273

Smaller Is Better When it Comes to Change

"Dinosaurs had their chance on earth and nature
selected them for extinction."
JEFF GOLDBLUM AS DR. IAN MALCOLM IN *JURASSIC PARK*

In the people principles in Chapter 16, I mentioned the concept of Jurassic Park retailing in reference to caring for the "beast" in your customers. There is another, darker side to Jurassic Park retailing: the inevitable extinction of retailers and retailing concepts that do not evolve as the environment changes. We learn from Jurassic Park that the dinosaurs, big behemoths that ravaged their landscape in a never-ending search for food, were selected for extinction while smaller, agile mammals that could adapt, even thrive in the changing environment survived.

Big retailing companies do a lot of things really well, but what they don't do at all well is innovate and that is what this research and analysis of the new customer and their passion for an extraordinary shopping experience requires.

In retailing, I see the brightest future and greatest opportunity for the small retailers where true innovation, passion, and drive for excellence reside. Their key advantage is flexibility. Small retailers can change on a dime, unlike a big behemoth retailer that organizes committees and holds meetings to make plans for the future, the results of which are to make plans for future meetings that may lead to more committees and more meetings and nothing ultimately gets done. This isn't to say that big retailers can't change, because they do; however, they are just very slow to make the kind of transformations in their business and their way of doing business that is called for today in retail.

Small, independent retailers, on the other hand, can manage transformation so much easier because every day they are up close and personal with their customers, learning about their desires and feeling their frustrations. Big retailing companies do a lot of things really well, but what they don't do at all well is innovate and that is what this research and analysis of the new customer and their passion for an extraordinary shopping experience requires.

> *"When a customer enters my store, forget me. He is king."*
> JOHN WANAMAKER

The future for retailers is to transform the retail experience to focus on the shopper, what they want and desire in the shopping experience. It is not about selling more stuff to the consumers, although that will be the end result of the transformation to a consumer-centered retailing environment. It is about expressing real care for the shopper, worrying about his or her comfort, attending to his or her needs and desires, and being personable and personal with the shopper. In a very real sense you have got to love your customer, and to do that you have to place them first in the design and operations of your retail store. The customer will then reward your efforts by loving you back, spending time in your shop, returning again and again, and telling friends about the wonderful shopping experience at your store.

This book has given you the tools you need to start that transformation process of changing your store from the ordinary into an extraordinary experience for your customer. We have grounded the principles for this transformation with in-depth research about the new experientially driven customer who shops because they love to shop, not because they need to shop. For this new shopper recreation and fun *is* the real need, and not the stuff retailers sell. We have explored shopping environments that pop for their shopper—that represent retailing environments that are truly extraordinary, from big retailing players, like Nordstrom and Target, to small, independent specialty stores that play their competitive advantages for all they are worth and beat the retailing "Goliaths" every day. We have defined principles to guide you as your transform your store into a retailing experience around the five key aspects of marketing—Product, Price, Promotion, Place and the missing and most important *P*, People.

Now my work is over and your hard work begins. I can get back to doing more research and analysis of consumers, and their psychology and behavior, and you can get busy transforming your store into a shop that pops! Good luck to all of you.

Appendix

The research results reported in here are published in full in a Unity Marketing consumer insights study called *Recreational Shopping Report 2006*. The research includes insights from a series of focus groups among high-income women who love to shop. Also included to gain insights into the challenges in the face of increased retail consolidation is a section devoted to a discussion group among owners of specialty retail stores, including a florist, gift shop owner, fashion boutique, toy store, hobby shop, t-shirt retailer, and home furnishings specialty store.

The heart of the research study, however, is a survey among 1,248 upper-income shoppers (aged 25 to 65 years; average household income $111,800; 64 percent female and 36 percent male). The survey examines two key segments in the shopper sample:

- The majority (70 percent) who view shopping as entertainment, called the recreational shopper segment
- Roughly 30 percent of nonrecreational shoppers who provide perspective on what makes the recreational shopper truly distinctive

Details about shopping gathered in the survey include:

Necessities shopping. (i.e., shopping for basic household necessities such as food, clothing, household cleaning, prescription drugs, and so on)

- Whether they are the family's primary shopper for necessities
- How often they shop for necessities

- What types of stores they frequent (12 types of stores are included; see survey for details) and which store they shop at most often for necessities
- Attributes that they find most important about choosing a shopping destination for necessities shopping (20 attributes are measured; see survey for details)
- How much they spend shopping for necessities

Recreational shopping.

- How often they shop recreationally
- What types of stores they frequent for recreational shopping (21 types of stores are included; see survey for details) and their favorite store for shopping fun
- Attributes that they find most important about choosing a store for recreational shopping, i.e., what features they value most in a store where they shop for fun (20 attributes are measured; see survey for details)
- How much they spend monthly shopping for recreation
- What categories of goods they buy for fun, including home furnishings, entertainment and recreational products, personal fashion and clothing, and other goods (31 product categories included; see survey for details)
- How frequently they recreationally shop for practical things for their home, decorative things for their home, things for recreation and entertainment, things for oneself, things for hobbies
- Whether they get the most fun out of browsing, buying, exploring, bargain shopping
- What types of shopping destinations they favor, such as enclosed malls, strip centers, downtown shopping areas, open air lifestyle centers, tourist/vacation shopping, historic shopping, freestanding stores, artistic/bohemian shopping, and luxury shopping districts
- How they define shopping, such as Shopping is . . . Fun; Exciting; a Mission; Something that has to be done; etc. (see survey for details)

■ Attitudes and motivations that drive the shopper when they shop, including 25 attitude statements (see survey for details)

Methodology. This report is based upon findings from both qualitative and quantitative research.

Focus Group Research

Shopper focus groups were conducted between August and October 2005, in Atlanta, Georgia (8-24); Chicago/Schaumburg, Illinois (9-13); and Columbus, Ohio (10-5). All 38 respondents who were recruited for the focus groups were women, with household incomes of $125,000 and above, and aged 25 to 59 years. The average age of respondents recruited was 44.8 years, which would be a member of the Baby Boomer generation. Each respondent had averaged two or more shopping trips for nonessential items (essentials defined as things like food, medicines, cleaning products) and spent in excess of $100 on their last shopping trip for nonessentials. They were also screened to have shopped for luxuries in the past three months. Their categories of luxury shopping included home luxuries, such as art and antiques, electronics, furniture, lamps and floor coverings, garden/outdoor, home decorating fabrics, window and wall coverings, kitchen appliances, kitchenware, cookware, housewares, linens, bedding and tabletop, and personal luxuries, such as clothing and apparel, fashion accessories, jewelry and/or watches, pet accessories, cosmetics and beauty products, and wine and spirits.

They also were required to agree or strongly agree with two out of the following five attitudinal statements:

■ I enjoy shopping and think of it as a form of entertainment. (35 agreed out of total 38 recruited)
■ I often spend time browsing in different shops to see what they have and what is "hot" right now. (38 agreed)
■ I rarely feel guilty about the luxuries I buy. Luxuries are the rewards I give myself. (26 agreed)
■ I shop at certain stores because of the special treatment and services that I receive. (34 agreed)

■ I have a couple of favorite stores that I regularly shop at to find the latest and most up-to-date things. (36 agreed)

Retailer Focus Group

One focus group among independent specialty retailers was also conducted. A total of 12 owners of independent stores were recruited. Most (ten respondents) operated a single store while two respondents operated stores in two retail locations. Four of the respondents reported store revenues of $25,000–$499,900); three had revenues of $500,000–$1 million) and five had retail revenues of $1 million or more. Their age ranged from 35 to over 55 and eight men and four women took part in the focus group. The types of stores represented in the groups were electronics, jewelry, gifts and home decor, jewelry, t-shirts, women's apparel, furniture, toys, hobby store, video games, and florist. They were all very or somewhat concerned about the encroachment of national retailers, big boxes, and discounters in their local market areas.

Quantitative Consumer Survey

A consumer survey of 1,248 upper-income consumers (household income of $50,000 or more) who like to shop was conducted with questions focused on their shopping preferences for necessities, defined as basic personal, family and household necessities such as food, drugs and prescriptions, basic clothing and accessories, home cleaning and care, home equipment, and so on; and recreational shopping for fun. Upper-income households were selected as the survey sample because they are most likely to have ample levels of discretionary income that can be spent for recreational shopping.

A series of four attitude questions were used to classify survey respondents into segments called "recreational shoppers" and regular shoppers. It is important to note that all respondents at some level like to shop but only the recreational shoppers agreed with the following statement:

■ I enjoy shopping and think of it as a form of entertainment.

Those who disagreed with this statement, but who agreed with two or more of the following statements, were classified as "regular shoppers":

- I like to shop at certain stores because of the special treatment and services that I receive.
- I enjoy spending time browsing in different shops to see what they have and what is "hot" right now.
- I often buy things on sale that I don't strictly need but are at such a good price that I can't pass them up.

Those respondents who were neutral on the first attitudinal question (I enjoy shopping and think of it as a form of entertainment) also had to agree with two or more of the other statements in order to be classified as a recreational shopper. Otherwise they fell into the regular shopper category. It is important to point out that all survey respondents at some level like to shop, but those classified as the recreational shoppers are very active and highly motivated to shop for fun. A total of 70 percent of those surveyed were recreational shoppers while 30 percent were regular shoppers and included in this report for comparative purposes.

The survey was conducted in November 2005, using an electronic online survey panel. Not unexpectedly, the survey sample skewed female with 64 percent being women and 36 percent men. Of the recreational shoppers there is a more pronounced female-skew with 70 percent of recreational shoppers being women and 30 percent men. Nearly 80 percent of the sample (77 percent) was married. High education levels characterized the sample with the majority (63 percent) being a college graduate or having some postgraduate educational experience. Some 89 percent were white/Caucasian.

The average age of survey respondents was 43.6 years. Recreational shoppers are slightly younger (average age 42.9 years) and regular shoppers are older (45.4 years). Some 24 percent of the sample was aged 25–34 years, 45–54 years, and 55–64 years and 28 percent were 35–44 years. Members of the baby boomer generation comprised half of the sample, while 36 percent were GenXers; 10 percent swing generation and 7 percent millennials.

The average income of the sample was $111,800, due to our sampling strategy designed to attract the more affluent shopping households with plenty of discretionary funds. The recreational shopper sample was only 4.5 percent more affluent than the regular shoppers, or $113,000 average income for recreational and $108,700 for regular. The sample reflects fairly even distribution of incomes across these ranges: $50,000–$74,900, 23 percent of total sample; $75,000–$99,900, 25 percent; $100,000–$149,900, 30 percent; and $150,000 and above, 22 percent.

Index